D0364487

C333707059

WITH ALL
FOR ALL

WITH ALL
FOR ALL

The Life of
SIMON DE MONTFORT

DARREN BAKER

AMBERLEY

For Eva, Dagmar and Michal

First published 2015

Amberley Publishing
The Hill, Stroud
Gloucestershire, GL5 4EP

www.amberley-books.com

Copyright © Darren Baker, 2015

The right of Darren Baker to be identified as the Author of this work has been asserted in accordance with the Copyrights, Designs and Patents Act 1988.

British Library Cataloguing in Publication Data.
A catalogue record for this book is available from the British Library.

ISBN 978 1 4456 4574 2 (hardback)
ISBN 978 1 4456 4578 0 (ebook)

Map design by Thomas Bohm, User design.

Typesetting and Origination by Amberley Publishing.
Printed in the UK.

Contents

Preface

When Brutus saw that all was lost, that Rome would never again be free of the rule of one man, he fell on his sword. Shakespeare famously has Octavian, who would be that one man, eulogise him as the noblest Roman of them all. Unlike Brutus, Simon de Montfort chose to fight it out to the end, with the same defiance that had always marked his difficulties with the Crown. In 1265 at Evesham, where it all came to an end, the man who would someday wear that crown was a warrior at heart, not an orator, and what, if anything, the future Edward I of England had to say about his fallen adversary has been lost to history.

We can be sure it was nothing about Montfort being the noblest Englishman of them all. His birth and upbringing in France had always been a source of resentment, from his first years as a foreign favourite to his leadership of the movement that sought to oust all foreigners and favourites from the realm. Edward had once admired him, but that was during the heyday of reform, before a palace revolution against his father Henry III led to both the king and his son being held captive as Montfort took over the government. After making his escape and raising an army, the young prince knew that final victory depended on more than just eliminating this one man, his uncle and godfather by the way. There would have to be more, a reminder to all and sundry about what happens to those who challenge the whole notion of kingship. And so, if at some point he had been present around the lifeless form of his former ally, he might have preferred to keep it short and simple.

'Have at it, boys.'

What followed was the fiendish dismemberment of Montfort's body that left even his most inveterate enemy among the chroniclers aghast. Such were the passions aroused by the founder of the first political party in English history. No amount of physical obliteration, however, could suppress the veneration subsequently felt for him across all sections of society. His legacy would grow over the centuries until he was even being hailed as the founder of Parliament itself.

It's a controversial claim to say the least. He was hardly the only one with a hand in developing that institution, and some historians are apt to see his contribution as the unintended consequence of his success. The paper trail also shows that he combined personal grievances with revolution. This makes his idealism suspect, and so it has been natural to speculate whether Montfort used rebellion for his own ends.

His supporters didn't have a problem with that. They were engaged in a power struggle with the king over matters of principle and conscience far ahead of their time. No ordinary warrior or statesman would do, rather a leader with the matchless ability to impose his will on whatever situation he took in hand. Like his crusading father before him, Simon de Montfort's combination of charisma, determination and fearlessness, bolstered by a wife with similar qualities, made him a force to be reckoned with, made the men and women of his era stop and take notice. Those inclined today to question the purity of his motives will have to admit that anyone taking up his story for the first time is in for quite a ride.

Much of the appeal is thanks to the king himself. Henry III was the most likeable of the Plantagenets, a generous family man who appreciated the arts and was full of good intentions. Far from being simple and dull-witted, as he is often portrayed, Henry was quite clever and sharp, easily Montfort's equal in a public forum, and that's saying a lot. His people enjoyed peace and prosperity through most of his long reign, and if it did almost end catastrophically, much of that had to do with the different natures of these two individuals, one made of wax, the other steel.

A second departure in this biography will be the absence of any traditional reference to the 'Second Barons' War'. The only

Barons' War of that period saw Henry's father John pitted against the majority of his barons over the enactment of Magna Carta. In Henry's case, most of the nobility had deserted the reforming Provisions of Oxford long before hostilities broke out. While the term 'barons' was used in the official documents of the time, 'Montfortians' will be used here because of the near-total identification of the Provisions with the man determined to force the king to abide by them.

The last major theme follows the preceding one in deciding what we should remember Simon de Montfort for. There is too much mythology in presenting him, or anyone, as the founder of Parliament, but he did recognise and cultivate a new awakening in national identity and political awareness. After two centuries, it seemed the English finally had the Norman Conquest behind them. It may be a peculiar irony, a Frenchman rallying the English nation, but it was the logical conclusion of what Montfort, from the outset, called 'the common enterprise'. They were all in it together.

Strange as it may seem, I remember reading about Simon de Montfort for the first time as a young boy. My mother read lots of books on English history and one of them briefly described how this Frenchman captured his brother-in-law the king and ruled in his name. Something exceptional, if confusing, was going on there.

More confusion followed decades later when I visited England and found only modest observances of the events that took place at Lewes and Evesham. Anybody looking for a memorial to Montfort today would do better to go to Washington than Westminster. As the Plantagenets were superseded by the Tudors in the historical consciousness of the nation, so too it seems were the Montfortians by the Cromwellians.

Not that Simon or Henry have been completely forgotten, and this work was made possible by the historians and scholars dedicated to keeping their famous political duel in the public eye. Lately they include David Carpenter, Margaret Howell, Michael Prestwich, Huw Ridgeway, David Crouch, Michael Clanchy, Louise Wilkinson, Katherine Ashe, Marc Morris and John Paul Davis. Sue Campbell and the Simon de Montfort Society continue to do much to preserve the memory of those fateful events. A special mark of credit goes to John Maddicott, the author of the last biography on

Montfort to appear, who kindly vetted this manuscript and made many helpful suggestions.

Others who deserve my thanks in the preparation of this book are Jana and Chris Veyres, Milan Hrabec, Paul Heley, and Ondřej Urban. My editor Alex Bennett provided a professional and insightful approach in shaping the final story. I also mustn't forget to mention those who inspired me to take up history as a lifelong pursuit. In addition to my mother Jacqueline Baker, they include Marty Davis, John Pridgeon, Forrest McDonald and Magdalena Sanchez. The biggest mark of my appreciation of course goes to my wife and children, who have been there all along, fully supportive of our own peculiar irony, that of an American living in the Czech Republic, seemingly obsessed with a Frenchman at the centre of English history.

Cast of Characters

De Montforts
They trace their ancestry back to the eleventh century to a family seat situated halfway between Normandy and Paris.

Simon III (1165–1218)
The nephew and heir of the Earl of Leicester, appointed military commander of the papal crusade against the Cathars.

Alice de Montmorency (1175–1221)
Married to Simon III, she championed his cause while raising a family.

Amaury (1192–1241)
Simon and Alice's oldest son, he was an established member of the French nobility and so unable to receive the earldom of Leicester.

Simon IV (1208–1265)
Their third son, he received the earldom and went on to rule England for fifteen months as caretaker.

Eleanor Plantagenet (1215–1275)
The able and ambitious sister of Henry III and later wife of Simon de Montfort.

Henry (1238–1265)
The eldest son of Simon and Eleanor, he fell with his father at Evesham.

Simon (1240–1271)
Their second son, he failed to come to his father's rescue at Evesham.

Amaury (1242–1300)
The Montfort son who was just about everything, from priest and lawyer to doctor and knight.

Guy (1244–1291)
A survivor of Evesham, he rose up high in Italian politics after his family's demise in England and sacrificed everything to avenge them.

Eleanor (after 1250–1282)
Their only surviving daughter, she married Llywelyn, the last Prince of Wales, and died in childbirth.

Plantagenets
Their dynasty in England begins with Henry II in 1154. Henry's father was the Count of Anjou, whose emblem was a flower known in Latin as *planta genista.*

King John (1166–1216)
The youngest son of Henry II and Eleanor of Aquitaine, his diabolical rule resulted in the creation of Magna Carta.

Isabella of Angoulême (1188–1246)
John's second wife and mother of his children, she went back to her native France after his death in the hope of playing a larger role in political affairs.

Henry III (1207–1272)
The first child king of post-Saxon England, he had been on the throne for more than forty years when his nobles set out to impose a power-sharing relationship on him.

Eleanor of Provence (1223–1291)
Henry's wife and queen, her great desire was to establish her

relatives from Savoy in England and put the control of her children into their hands.

Richard of Cornwall (1209–1272)
Henry's brother, better endowed to handle people and money, but greedy and vain at heart. In 1257 he set out to buy the crown of Germany.

Edward (1239–1307)
Henry's heir, his defection back to his father's side was key in the eventual defeat of the reform movement.

Eleanor of Castile (1241–1290)
Her marriage to Edward was arranged as a means of ending Henry's troubles in Gascony.

Henry of Almain (1235–1271)
Richard of Cornwall's eldest son, his desertion of Simon de Montfort would cost him his life long after the conflict was over.

Lusignans
They take their name from a village near Poitiers and are more famous in history as crusaders and rulers in the holy land.

Hugh (1183–1249)
The Count of La Marche and second husband of Isabella of Angoulême. Hugh and Isabella's revolt against the French monarchy cost them everything and made a fool out of her son Henry III.

Hugh and Isabella had nine children, including five who went to England at the invitation of their half-brother Henry. **Guy** (1225–1281) and **Geoffrey** (1226–1274) fluctuated between England and France, but **William de Valence** (1228–1296) acquired an heiress through marriage, and **Aymer** (1222–1260) was elected the Bishop of Winchester at Henry's insistence. **Alice** (1224–1257) was married to the Earl of Surrey, and this practice of marrying family members from abroad to underage English nobles provoked widespread discontent.

Savoyards
The position of medieval Savoy, around present-day Geneva, made it a strategic player as relations worsened between the Holy Roman Empire and the papacy in the mid-thirteenth century.

Beatrice (1205–1265)
Queen Eleanor's mother and a fixer in her own right. Lauded in history as the mother of four queens, her other daughters were **Margaret** (1221–1295), married to Louis IX of France, **Sanchia** (1228–1261), the second wife of Richard of Cornwall, and **Beatrice** (1231–1267), married to Louis' brother Charles of Anjou, the future King of Sicily.

Of Beatrice's several older brothers, four received enormous favours from Henry in his belief they could help him become a force in European affairs. **William** (d. 1239) became the head of his council, **Thomas** (1199–1259) received money for various plots on the Continent, **Peter** (1203–1268) was set up in England as a major landowner and **Boniface** (1217–1270) was made the Archbishop of Canterbury.

Other Monarchies
The intermarriage of royal houses subjected most of medieval Europe to a giant turf war.

Frederick II (1194–1250)
The Holy Roman Emperor and leading personality of his age. His quarrel with the papacy over control of Italy long outlived him, his heirs and a succession of popes.

Louis VIII (1187–1226)
The heir of Philip II of France, he was invited by the baronage of England to become king in place of John but was forced out after John unexpectedly died.

Blanche of Castile (1188–1252)
As the wife of Louis VIII, she became regent upon his early death and kept the French nobles in line until her son Louis IX came of age.

Louis IX (1214–1270)
The overly pious King of France, his mediation between Henry III and Simon de Montfort was ineffective and ultimately disastrous.

Charles of Anjou (1226 – 1285)
The youngest brother of Louis IX, he found good use for the Montfort sons during his conquest of Italy and Sicily.

Alfonso X (1221–1284)
The King of Castile, he wanted to extend his influence beyond the southern reaches and challenged Richard of Cornwall for the crown of Germany.

English Nobility
Descended from the Normans and Continentals who followed William the Conqueror to England in 1066, their French-speaking families were otherwise completely anglicised by the time Henry III came to the throne 150 years later.

William Marshal II (1190–1231)
The son of the legendary knight who saved Henry's throne, he was the first husband of Eleanor de Montfort.

Ranulf de Blondeville (1170–1232)
The Earl of Chester, his decision to release the earldom of Leicester set up the young Simon de Montfort in England.

Hubert de Burgh (d. 1243)
A father figure to Henry during his minority, the king turned against him with a vengeance after coming of age.

Peter des Roches (d. 1238)
Originally from Touraine and officially the Bishop of Winchester, he was Henry's other father figure and Hubert's rival for the king's favour.

Hugh Despenser (1223–1265)
One of Simon's trusted coterie of the reform movement, he was the justiciar when he too fell at Evesham.

Peter de Montfort (1205–1265)
This unrelated Montfort was part of Simon's affinity and joined him as one of the original seven confederates united against the king.

Roger Bigod (1209–1270)
The Earl of Norfolk and the last survivor of the seven confederates, he kept a decidedly middle course through most of the reform period.

Hugh Bigod (1211–1266)
Roger's brother, he was another confederate and the first justiciar appointed during the reform period. He later became an ardent royalist.

Richard de Clare (1222–1262)
A confederate and the Earl of Gloucester, he was the first major defection from the ranks of the reformers.

Gilbert de Clare (1243–1295)
Richard's son and heir, he was the only major baron to fight and win on both sides of the struggle.

John de Warenne (1231–1304)
The Earl of Surrey. He kept flip-flopping like most of the barons. First he opposed the reform movement, then joined it, opposed it, joined it, and finally deserted it.

The **Marchers** were a group of English lords who ruled over the borderlands of Wales and England. They included a Kentish man by birth, **Roger Leybourne** (1215–1271), and his brother-in-law **Roger Clifford** (1243–1282), both of whom first helped Montfort sweep into power, then deserted him. The king had to buy the support of **Roger Mortimer** (1231–1282), but it proved invaluable.

English Clergy
The Church became a major political force during Henry's reign, thanks to the arrival of the mendicant orders and the widespread opposition to the papacy's demand for money.

Robert Grosseteste (1175–1253)
The Bishop of Lincoln. A scholar and philosopher, his theories on the nature of government had enormous influence on Simon de Montfort and other reformers.

Adam Marsh (1200–1259)
This Franciscan lecturer at Oxford became a spiritual adviser for the royal family and for Simon and Eleanor de Montfort.

Walter de Cantilupe (1195–1266)
The Bishop of Worcester and spiritual head of the reform movement, he remained by Simon's side to the end.

Thomas de Cantilupe (1218–1282)
The nephew of Walter and chancellor of Oxford, he skilfully represented the Montfortians before the French, but was rehabilitated after Evesham.

Stephen Berksted (d. 1287)
The Bishop of Chichester who, together with Montfort and Gilbert de Clare, completed the triumvirate ruling in Henry's name.

Timeline

1204   Philip II of France completes the seizure Normandy from King John; the Earl of Leicester dies, his nephew Simon de Montfort (III) standing to inherit the earldom

1207   Henry Plantagenet is born in Winchester

1208   Probable birth year of Simon de Montfort (IV); the Albigensian Crusade in southern France begins

1209   Richard of Cornwall is born

1213   Battle of Muret, Simon de Montfort III defeats an army under Peter II of Aragon

1214   Battle of Bouvines, England loses Normandy forever; the future Louis IX is born

1215   John is forced to accept Magna Carta, rewards Ranulf, Earl of Chester, for his support by giving him Leicester; Eleanor Plantagenet is born

1216   Beginning of the Barons' War with French intervention; John dies, Henry is crowned in Gloucester

1217   The French invasion force leaves England

1218   Simon de Montfort's father is killed during the siege of Toulouse

1219   William Marshall I dies; struggle over the regency commences between Hubert de Burgh and the Poitevin faction under Peter des Roches

1220   Henry's mother Isabella of Angoulême marries Hugh Lusignan

1221   Simon de Montfort's mother Alice dies

1222   Richard de Clare is born

1223   A plot by the Poitevins fails; Hubert de Burgh becomes Henry's supreme adviser; Philip II dies and his son becomes Louis VIII

1224   William Marshal II marries Eleanor Plantagenet; Eleanor of Provence is born

1225   Louis VIII seizes Poitou from England; Hugh Lusignan fails to take Gascony

1226   The Albigensian Crusade is reignited; Louis VIII dies of dysentery, his son becoming Louis IX

1227   Henry declares himself of age

1230   Simon de Montfort arrives in England, joins Henry's failed invasion force in Brittany, asks Ranulf for the return of Leicester

1231   William Marshal II dies; Richard of Cornwall marries Isabel Marshal; Ranulf renounces all claims to Leicester in Simon's favour; Peter des Roches returns

1232   Hubert de Burgh falls from power, leaving the Poitevins again in control of Henry's court; Ranulf dies

1233   A baronial party under Richard Marshal rises up against Henry and the Poitevins

1234   Richard Marshal is killed at the instigation of Peter des Roches; downfall of the Poitevins; Eleanor makes an ill-advised settlement with the Marshal estate and becomes a bride of Christ; Louis IX marries Margaret of Provence

1235   Henry's sister Isabella marries Frederick II of the Holy Roman Empire; Henry of Almain is born; Robert Grosseteste is made the Bishop of Lincoln

1236   Henry marries Eleanor of Provence, her uncle William of Savoy becomes his principal adviser

1238   Simon de Montfort marries Eleanor Marshal, provoking outcry throughout England; Simon goes to Rome to ask for a dispensation; Henry de Montfort is born; Peter des Roches dies; Henry's sister Joan, Queen of Scotland, dies

1239   Henry officially makes Simon the Earl of Leicester; the future Edward I is born; Henry denounces Simon and Eleanor and drives them from the country; William of Savoy dies

1240 Simon leaves for the holy land on crusade; Simon de Montfort (V) is born

1241 Peter of Savoy comes to England and joins the council; Eleanor of Castile is born; Gilbert Marshal dies; Henry's sister Isabella, wife of Frederick II, dies

1242 Henry's invasion of Poitou at the instigation of his mother and stepfather is roundly defeated by Louis IX; birth of Amaury de Montfort

1243 The Montforts return to England; Boniface of Savoy becomes the Archbishop of Canterbury; Hubert de Burgh dies

1244 The first stab at reform with the 'Paper Constitution' under the leadership of Robert Grosseteste; Henry grants Kenilworth Castle to the Montforts; Guy de Montfort and Gilbert de Clare are born

1245 Henry commences the reconstruction of Westminster Abbey; his second son Edmund is born; the two remaining Marshal sons die

1246 Isabella of Angoulême dies

1247 Henry's half-siblings the Lusignans arrive in England; William de Valence is married to a Marshal heiress

1248 Simon is appointed viceroy for Gascony

1249 Louis IX embarks on crusade, and Hugh Lusignan dies during the landing in Egypt

1250 Louis' army is destroyed and he is taken prisoner and ransomed, returning to France after four years; Henry vows to go on crusade; Aymer Lusignan is elected the Bishop of Winchester; Frederick II dies

1252 Henry turns against Simon's administration in Gascony and orders him to stand trial; Simon is acquitted by a baronial court; Blanche of Castile dies

1253 Henry goes to Gascony but asks for Simon's help in reasserting control; Robert Grosseteste dies

1254 Edward is married to Eleanor of Castile; Henry meets his brother-in-law Louis for the first time; reunion of the Provencal sisters in Paris

1255 The 'Sicilian business' begins in earnest; Edmund is declared the King of Sicily; the Jews of Lincoln are condemned

1257   Richard of Cornwall is elected King of the Romans; Welsh
        raids commence; the onset of famine following rains

1258   The barons march on Henry, demanding he institute
        reforms; the Provisions of Oxford are drawn up and the
        Lusignans are expelled

1259   Richard of Cornwall returns to England and takes the oath
        to the Provisions of Oxford; Simon and Richard de Clare
        fall out; the bachelors march on Parliament; the Provisions
        of Westminster are enacted, promising reforms for local
        concerns; Simon and Edward become allies; Henry and his
        court leave for Paris to sign a peace treaty with France

1260   Henry shows no intention of returning to England to hold
        parliament in February as required by the Provisions;
        Simon insists that the parliament be held even without
        the king and is backed by Edward; Henry returns in April
        and wins over Edward, ordering Simon to stand trial on
        sedition, but an incursion by the Welsh delays it; Simon
        and Richard de Clare come to an accommodation at the
        October parliament; Aymer Lusignan dies

1261   William de Valence returns to England; Henry reveals
        a papal bull absolving him of his oath to the Provisions
        of Oxford; the barons unite against him and summon a
        parliament without the king's approval; Richard de Clare
        deserts to the king and baronial resistance collapses; Simon
        goes into exile in France

1262   Richard de Clare dies; Henry goes to France for arbitration
        with Simon before Queen Margaret but the arbitration is
        suspended after a plague strikes his court and nearly kills
        the king; Simon briefly returns to England with a papal
        bull supporting the Provisions of Oxford; Henry's palace at
        Westminster burns down

1263   Simon returns and leads an army that targets the Savoyards
        and isolates Henry in London; Edward robs the New Temple;
        Queen Eleanor attempts to escape to Windsor and is turned
        back by the mob; Henry capitulates; Simon convinces Louis
        of the justness of the Provisions but his support dwindles
        after Edward bribes away many of his leading supporters;
        both sides agree to allow Louis to arbitrate their dispute

1264 Louis nullifies the Provisions; civil war breaks out; Henry and Edward are captured at the Battle of Lewes; Simon summons a parliament that approves a constitutional monarchy and fortifies the south-east coast against an impending invasion by Queen Eleanor; attempts at arbitration through a papal legate come to nothing; the invasion force melts away

1265 Simon summons a parliament that includes representatives of the towns; he marches west to deal with his disaffected partner Gilbert de Clare; Edward escapes and joins up with Clare, and together they hem in Simon's smaller army at Evesham in August; the slain include Simon, his son Henry, Hugh Despenser and Peter de Montfort; the newly freed Henry orders the dispossession of the Montfortian survivors; Queen Eleanor returns to England; Edmund becomes Earl of Leicester; Eleanor and her children go into exile in France

1266 The Dictum of Kenilworth offers peace and the Montfortians are slowly reabsorbed; Walter de Cantilupe dies; Hugh Bigod dies

1267 Gilbert de Clare turns against his royalist partners and seizes London but is convinced to stand down

1268 Peter of Savoy dies

1269 Henry's official ceremony translating the body of Edward the Confessor into the new environs of Westminster Abbey takes place

1270 Louis leaves on another crusade and dies shortly after arriving; Edward continues what is left of the crusade; Roger Bigod dies

1271 Roger Leybourne dies; Henry of Almain is hacked to death in a church by Guy de Montfort

1272 Richard of Cornwall and Henry III die

1274 Edward returns to England and is crowned

1275 Eleanor de Montfort dies near Paris

1276 Edward captures his cousins Amaury and Eleanor de Montfort on their way to Wales

1278 Edward allows Llywelyn, the Prince of Wales, to marry the young Eleanor

1282 Amaury is released; Eleanor dies in childbirth; Llywelyn dies in a skirmish; Edward places their baby daughter Gwenllian in a convent; Roger Mortimer dies

1285   The future Edward II is born

1287   Guy de Montfort is captured in battle

1290   Eleanor of Castile dies

1291   Eleanor of Provence dies; Guy de Montfort dies in prison in Sicily

1295   Edward organises the 'Model' parliament

1296   Edmund dies

1297   The barons march on Edward over his duplicity on taxation

1300   Amaury de Montfort dies

1307   Edward dies; succeeded by Edward II

1327   Edward II is deposed by his wife and the namesake grandson of Roger Mortimer and later murdered; Edward's closest advisers, the son and grandson of Hugh Despenser, are executed

1337   Gwenllian dies

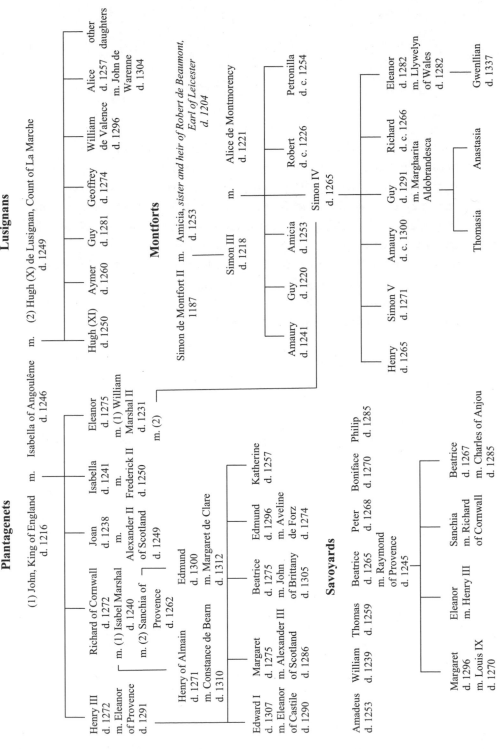

The key families.

Note on money, lineage and births

The only coin in circulation during Henry's reign was the silver penny (he tried to introduce a gold penny, with typically disastrous results). There were 240 pennies in a pound (£), which was a currency of account. The mark was another currency of account in widespread use during the thirteenth century, generally worth two-thirds of a pound. For simplification purposes, all payments in marks have been converted to pounds, hence the sometimes odd configurations like £6,667 (10,000 marks).

It was common for the men of the Montfort family to carry the names Amaury, Simon and Guy. This makes it difficult to pinpoint their exact number through succeeding generations. The Simon de Montfort of this biography has been designated IV in the line, in keeping with the previous two biographies.

Since the births of ordinary and even most highborn individuals went unrecorded in medieval chronicles, the years given in the previous sections have been more or less gleaned from the records available.

Mainland Europe during Simon de Montfort's lifetime.

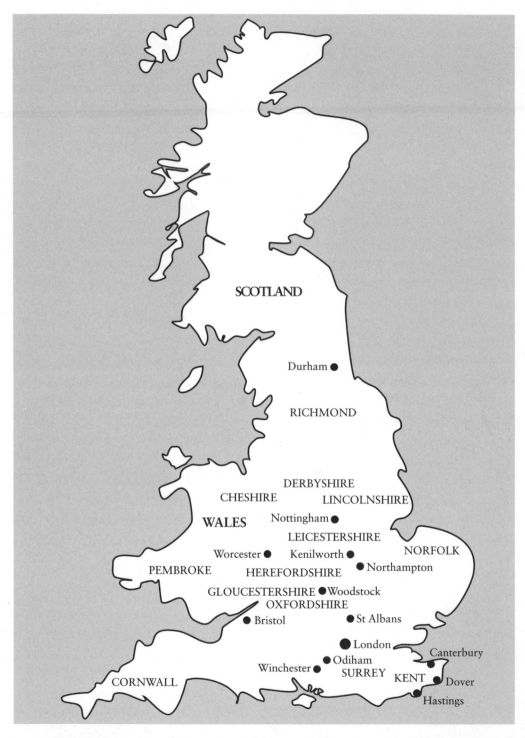

The British Isles during the thirteenth century, with key locations highlighted.

All the Thunder and Lightning in the World

Like any major river at the height of summer, the Thames offers a retreat for those eager to take their meals outdoors. In July 1258, the King of England was just such a person. It had been a troublesome year, a troublesome few years really, and he needed a respite. He was a man of exquisite tastes, and we can be sure that Henry, the third with that name after the Norman Conquest, had taken care in choosing his dinner before setting out, even the ingredients that went into it. He was also a temperamental and finicky sort, and if his attendants knew what was good for them, they would have his boat stocked and ready by the time he left his palace at Westminster.

There is no record of who accompanied the king on this excursion. Most likely the queen was not at his side. Their insular court had been marked by infighting between their relatives, with hers coming out on top of his in the latest round. A vindictive man by nature, Henry had once cut off her income after she became involved in an earlier dispute between their greedy in-laws.

Their son also missed the trip. He was apt to switch from this side of the family to that one, all in a bid to ease the strict controls his parents imposed on him. He certainly needed a firm hand. Almost twenty now, he had a reputation for violence and hanging out with the wrong sort of people. There were already whispers that England would rue the day this man became king.

Henry was beset by more than just family problems, however. The Welsh were making incursions at will, and rather than mobilising to beat them back, his barons had decided to take him on instead. Some of them had even formed a confederation for the purpose of ousting his half-brothers, four arrogant bullies who did what they wanted with impunity. The barons not only succeeded in driving them out of the country, but forced the king to accept certain measures, or reforms to be more precise, that basically straitjacketed him.

No more would he be free to choose his own councillors and officials or summon Parliament whenever he felt like it. Now everything would be done according to provisions, rules set down in writing, much the way the barons had forced his father to accept Magna Carta. The barons had even dared to march up to him in armour as if to suggest he was in their power. With kingship now no more than a cipher, he was in the way.

These events weren't going to ruin his dinner. Time and again the king had sworn to uphold the provisions of Magna Carta and then just as easily ignored them. Only there was no ignoring the weather in England, and on top of everything else, incessant rains the previous year had ruined crops and led to famine throughout the realm. Now it was threatening his outing on the water. Suddenly there was a thunderclap and that put an end to it. And things were about to get worse.

Everyone knew that the king was terrified of thunder and lightning. He had been crowned as a boy, during equally troubled times, and in a way the insecurities of that period never left him. His crew knew right away to make for the nearest landing. It happened to belong to a stately palace where, of all the dumb luck, the Earl of Leicester was just then residing.

He was the king's brother-in-law, married to his sister, and so unrelated to the other quarrelling family members. Although he owed everything to Henry, he had been a thorn in his side ever since the king humiliated him at a public gathering twenty years earlier. Now, as part of this baronial confederation, he was clearly out to get him. But on this occasion, Simon de Montfort readily came out to meet his lord and show him all due deference.

Seeing Henry still trembling, Simon assured him that the storm had passed and there was nothing more to be afraid of. The king, no doubt looking older than his fifty years, drew back and uttered words profound enough to be quoted in full:

The thunder and lightning I fear beyond measure, but by the head of God, I fear you more than all the thunder and lightning in the world!

Simon tried to assure him that he was his friend, one who was ever faithful to him and the kingdom of England. It was the king's enemies, his false flatterers, he said, that he ought to fear.

Matthew Paris, the chronicler who reported this interview, died the following summer. A scathing advocate of reform, he did not live to see the tumultuous years that followed, as the court faction struggled to regain power. He could not know that Henry came very near to nipping the whole movement in the bud as one reformer after another fell by the wayside. All but one, Simon de Montfort, and the king's innate fear of him, so prophetically recounted on that steamy summer day, would end in a clash of wills and armies, and ultimately in one of the most compelling and dramatic periods in English history.

1

Steel and Wax
1208–1231

It is thanks to the feud between Simon and Henry that we know as much as we do about Montfort's beginnings in England. In the summer of 1262 the king had sought to destroy him politically before the French court, where he was held in high regard, and brought all manner of charges against him in yet another failed attempt at arbitration. Simon's replies show that dissatisfaction and a lack of grace, literally speaking, marked their relationship from the very beginning:

> The king says that he has done me great goodness in that he took me for his man, because I was not the oldest. And so that one may know what the goodness was, my brother released to me all the right that he had in our father's inheritance in England (the earldom of Leicester), if I could secure it, in the same manner that I released to him the heritage which I had in France. And I went to England, and prayed the king that he would restore to me my father's inheritance. And he answered that he could not do it because he had given it to the Earl of Chester and his heirs by his charter. Upon this I returned without finding grace.

In all probability, neither Henry nor anyone privy to their dispute knew much about Simon's life before he came to England, not unless they asked his older brother Amaury. They would have the chance to do so when he came to England to witness Henry invest Simon with the earldom of Leicester, indicating his suit with the king had eventually paid off. This, of course, raises the question why Amaury, as the eldest, did not receive the earldom himself, and what was behind the claim of this French family for acceptance among the higher nobility of England.

That chapter begins with another Simon, their grandfather and number two in the line, who belonged to a noble clan in northern France. The founder of that clan, another Amaury, was charged in the early part of the eleventh century with building ramparts around a castle overlooking a strategic trade route thirty miles west of Paris, near the border that separates Normandy from Ile-de-France. This fortress, or Mont Fort, became the seat of his descendants, none of whom it seems took any noticeable part in the Norman Conquest of 1066. About a hundred years later, Simon II married into a family that did, the Beaumonts, becoming the brother-in-law of Robert, 4th Earl of Leicester. When Robert de Beaumont died childless in 1204, his estates were divided between his two sisters. The widow of Simon II, Amicia, inherited the half of Leicester with the earldom. With her eldest son dead and the second one a clergyman, she claimed the estates for her third son, naturally, another Simon.

This Simon, the father of ours, had just returned from the Fourth Crusade, where he vigorously opposed the sack of Constantinople and other Christian cities. His appeal to King John for the return of the Leicester estates was successful, but they were confiscated in 1207, presumably because of outstanding debts, and eventually ended up in the possession of the Earl of Chester. By that time a new crusade had been launched, one that would forever make Simon III a lasting figure of fear and contempt.

Like all religions grown too big for the pasture, medieval Christianity was beset by heresy, most prominently Catharism in the south of France. The Cathars, or 'pure ones', subscribed to a dualist offshoot with beginnings, oddly enough, in Bulgaria. For them, Good and Evil were represented as Spirit and Matter. As a material being, mankind was essentially evil in so far as the skin trapped a spirit hankering to get out and join the heavenly host elsewhere. If all this smacked of Christianity in its purest form, that's what made the Cathars pure. They had seen the light, but only allegorically since light itself was matter.

Where they really had it good was in the way they went about absolving the sins that accumulated in a material world. Like Catholicism, Catharism also discouraged carnal pleasures like sex, but only because procreation led to the creation of more skins, more trapped souls. Their absolution consisted of 'consolation', a ritual involving the touch of the hand of a Good Man, a believer who had already been imbued with the Holy Spirit. While Catholics received repeated absolution, if they could afford it, Cathars got only one, so it had to count. Once imbued, no meat, no sex, no shoes, only door-to-door preaching. Since most people couldn't handle such a life, they were usually given consolation on their deathbed. It was a life of sin with a clear conscience, and the only thing the Good Men and Women asked for in return was that the others kiss the ground they walked on.

So Catharism wasn't too far off ordinary Christianity. To be sure, the Cathars accepted and revered Christ, but only in spiritual form. Jesus the man, Mary the virgin, all that was superfluous nonsense since it implied they were once skins. To worship material things like holy blood, the Holy Grail, even the True Cross, that most evil of all instruments, was total blasphemy. Priests and bishops, by now entrenched and isolated from the masses, addicted to gold embroidery, silver chalices and speaking in a language the flock couldn't understand, were the real heretics.

Naturally, the Church of Rome found all this unsettling, more so because the Cathars insisted on thumbing their noses at all the popes who tried to win them back. Then came the most feared pontiff of the Middle Ages, Innocent III, who revelled in making kings grovel before him. Convinced of his place next to God, he at first stuck to persuasion. Then, in January 1208, one of his emissaries was murdered by a Cathar sympathiser. He had enough and ordered an army of Christian soldiers to muster and skin these heathens for good.

It became known as the Albigensian Crusade after the city of Albi, a hotbed of heresy in a region where it seemed every lord was named Raymond. Although crusades were by their nature cruel, this one would receive special notice for the order 'kill them all, God will know his own', which supposedly accompanied the massacre of 20,000 people in Beziers during the initial onslaught. Simon III didn't become the leader of the crusade until after this slaughter, mostly because no one else wanted the job, and while he maimed, hanged and burned people alive, the other side did so as well, notably Raymond, the Count of Foix. His chief regret was he didn't have the chance to chop up more priests.

Simon III was no more brutal or depraved than this Raymond or that one, but he came to stand for everything terrible about the crusade because he was the better general and more inspired leader. Starting out with the most meagre of forces, he captured one stronghold after another, ensuring that the cycle of violence and reprisals continued. He seemed to be everywhere at once, but as his victories grew, so did local resistance and hatred for his winning ways. For the people of Languedoc, whether Christian or Cathar, he was loathed for being an invader from the north. For being a successful invader, he was the Antichrist.

The Christian overlords in the south came to see Montfort as a threat to their feudal hierarchy, which for 90 per cent of the population meant a life of poverty, exhaustion and starvation. In September 1213, King Peter II of Aragon, the darling of the papacy after he turned back the Moors, led an allied army to crush the fiendish horde from the north at Muret. Peter, courageous but a bit warped, had put on ordinary armour so he could face Simon man to man. The duel between these two warrior giants of the Christian world, both described as tall and immensely strong, never came to pass because Peter suddenly shouted out he was the king and would take on all comers. The French knights gladly took him up on the challenge and wiped him and his entourage out to a man. The Spaniards were routed and Montfort won another victory against the odds. Whatever came after Antichrist, he was certainly it.

Reversals inevitably set in and even he began to question whose side the Lord was on. The pope, though troubled by the mess he himself had created, tried to cheer him on by calling him the Earl of Leicester and pressuring John to restore his estates. When Raymond, Count of Toulouse and John's brother-in-law, whose inexplicable cowering and double dealing had contributed much to the general misery, returned from exile in England, Montfort was off to besiege that city yet again. In June 1218, he had just heard Mass, had just witnessed the lifting of the holy host, when he received word his brother had been wounded. Riding to his aid, he was struck on the head by a stone, shattering his skull. He was probably in his mid-fifties.

The townspeople cheered and sang songs, even rubbed it in by insisting the stone had been launched from a mangonel manned by women and girls. Whoever was responsible, Simon de Montfort, the scourge of the Albigensians, was dead. But it was a false sense of security, for it was only a matter of time before the French monarchy got involved. Raymond's son Raymond would later try his own hand at burning heretics in a desperate attempt to stave off the greater power, but in the end the people of Languedoc lost not only their heresy, but their independence as well.

Beyond Languedoc, where most of the fighting took place, Simon III was hailed for his personal courage and readiness to seek consensus, two traits clearly passed on to his son. One English annalist compared his warlike skills to those of Mars, his beauty to that of Paris, and his morals to those of Cato. Another jotted down a rumour that in 1210 a council of barons had deposed John and elected Simon III as their king instead. The kings of France were certainly grateful to him. His zealous use of fire and sword allowed them to extend their authority further south. Probably the most grateful were the Christian worshippers offended by the thought that their sacred rituals and pilgrimages were deemed the work of the devil.

It was now up to Montfort's sons to carry on the crusade. As he would show in a later crusade, Amaury lacked the overall ability his father possessed. He eventually arranged a settlement with the papacy and French court for the territory that nominally came under his control and retired to the family seat at Montfort l'Amaury. His younger brother Guy continued to fight until he died in captivity in 1220, leaving behind two daughters. His father had arranged for him to marry the heiress of Bigorre, a county on the slopes of the Pyrenees that served as a buffer against the Spanish kingdoms and their sympathies for the heretics. It won't be the last we hear of this little county.

Another member of the crusading family never far from the action was their mother, Alice de Montmorency. Like the Montforts, hers was a distinguished noble family that claimed Charlemagne as an ancestor. One of her grandmothers was a natural daughter of Henry I, making our Simon de Montfort also a descendent of

William the Conqueror. Her brother Mathieu, the constable of France, played a leading part in the victory at Bouvines in 1214, which finished English power on the Continent for good. Her access to the court in Paris enabled her to raise funds and troops for her husband. Her piety was as fiery and militant as his was and she shared in his counsels and determination to root out unbelievers. One of her daughters, Amicia, who had been betrothed to Peter of Aragon's son James during sunnier days, founded a convent at Montargis. The other, Petronilla, would become an abbess after being consigned to a nunnery by Alice herself, shortly before her death in 1221.

According to a chronicler of the crusade, Simon III and Alice had 'numerous children' with them during the siege of Toulouse, presumably including two boys, Simon and Robert. Nothing is known about when or where they were born, because neither was the eldest son and they therefore stood to inherit nothing as far as chroniclers were concerned. Tradition has it that Robert was the younger of the two and died before reaching manhood.

Simon was probably not older than ten when his father perished. His name does not appear in a family charter of 1207, but he was old enough to give his consent to a grant made by his mother in 1217. Lacking all other evidence, the crusade year of 1208 is the one usually given for his birth. He was certainly orphaned before he reached adolescence, and whatever he remembered of his parents and their vigorous pursuit of heresy no doubt left a lasting impression on him.

There is no mention of his whereabouts after the deaths of his parents. He might have spent time at court as a boyhood companion of the future Louis IX. The later attempts by Louis to intercede on Simon's behalf suggest a friendship that went way back. In all likelihood, Simon returned with Amaury north, then south again when the crusade reignited. In England he was famed as a warrior long before his later generalship confirmed it. He could have made a name for himself in knightly tournaments, which were more like mock battles than the jousts we have come to know, but the only possible proving grounds for his skills in warfare were the campaigns in the south. It also helped to be the son and namesake of the great Simon de Montfort.

While we cannot be sure of his education, Simon clearly appreciated the value of learning and made sure his own children were well educated. He learned to read Latin, which was no mean feat for a layman in those days. It was reported that he did not know English when he first stepped ashore, and while this implies that he learned it to some degree later on, he would not have used it much. French was the language of the court and nobility, and his own French, which bespoke the region of Ile-de-France, no doubt lent a pleasing air to the anglicised dialect of his contemporaries. His 'pleasant and courteous way' of speaking noted by one chronicler, and they were always jotting down his sound bites, certainly stands at odds to the modern tendency to see him as imperious or insolent.

The oratorical skills that stood him in good stead later on were about to receive their first test. The wars in the south were finally concluded and Simon was a man of about twenty. Amaury, as the oldest surviving brother, had first claim to the earldom of Leicester, but his status as a French peer ended any hopes of him becoming an English one as well. Simon was a different story. With no land binding him to the King of France, he had nothing to lose by supplicating to the King of England. Amaury agreed to relinquish his claim for a price and sent his brother on his way with one of his knights to accompany him. In early 1230, Simon arrived in England and met the man who, for the next three and a half decades, would reward him, exasperate him, betray him, and probably, when it was all said and done, even mystify him. That most unique among English monarchs, Henry III.

Henry Plantagenet was born on 1 October 1207 in Winchester, but he was nearly as French as Montfort was, perhaps more so in terms of art, food and fashion. The only trace of Anglo-Saxon blood in his veins came from his great-great-grandmother Matilda, the wife of Henry I. Henry III was about the same age as Simon when his father too died in the midst of a revolt against the established authority. John's death from dysentery in 1216, after watching all his Crown jewels get washed away, was no more glorious than Simon's father getting his skull split open by a bunch of women two years later. Neither Henry nor Simon left any record of their feelings about their fathers, but both spent their lifetimes dealing with the legacies they inherited from them.

Like Simon, Henry was orphaned at an early age. His mother Isabella had been denied any active role as queen and little changed once she became queen dowager. Miffed, she left for her native Angoulême, never to return, although she was far from finished in his life. By twelve, Henry was in the hands of tutors and regents who would instruct him on the meaning of kingship.

He was said to have made a pretty prince during his makeshift coronation in Gloucester. True, he had a drooping eyelid, but he still had some growing to do. Important was that the lad showed much dignity under the circumstances, and reassured all his new subjects when he swore to abide by the liberties granted in Magna Carta, which had been so abhorrent to his father and other absolutists. Of course, John had also sworn to abide, but only long enough to regroup and counter-attack. Time would tell what was in the boy's mind as his high-pitched voice repeated the oath.

The most pressing problem for the regency council led by the famed knight William Marshal was to clear the country of invaders. The rebellious barons had invited the son of the French king, the future Louis VIII, to be their liege after John reneged on his oath. Louis, one of the most humourless men who ever lived, occupied London and refused to budge even with John suddenly out of the picture. His presence was a threat to Henry, who otherwise would have to be confined to a monastery or, more likely, done away with. Louis was adamant on staying put even after losing the military advantage, so in the end he was bought out. Henry's throne was safe, but he would grumble years later about that buyout. The generosity, almost lavishness, he would become famous for tended to obscure the ingratitude he was equally capable of showing.

As his drooping eyelid became more pronounced, his councillors began to worry about the wilful and impatient youth who chafed under their authority. He could be charming, ingratiating, eager to please and learn when things went his way. When, inevitably, they didn't, he would snarl and throw a fit. One word often used to describe him was 'simple', and in his case it had three meanings. It meant that he was frank and candid, which could evoke either relief or alarm in his listeners. In more charitable terms, simple also described his almost infectious childlike innocence, how he loved Christmas and family and toying with little details because it gave him such pleasure. But just as often as not, it meant he was simple-minded, and much of what he did during his long reign easily justified that label.

Yet even that didn't tell the whole story, for Henry was intelligent, ambitious and shrewd, and those who might add visionary to his talents would suggest that the problem was he kept biting off more than he could chew.

He was never more at his simplistic best than when it came to his dreams of being a great warrior. Twice he led an army to France to recover the English possessions lost by his father, and each attempt ended in failure. It hardly mattered that he wasn't cut out to be a warrior. He fumed and spluttered that it was all the work of traitors. Taking stock of his second defeat, he knew what he needed was a personal standard to strike fear into the hearts of his enemies. So he hired renowned craftsman Edward of Westminster to design him a royal banner showing a dragon's head with demonic eyes and a tongue that appeared to flick in the wind, almost as if it were real. Indeed, he won his next foray into the field under it, but it was mostly downhill after that.

Henry never reconciled to his father losing Normandy to the French and made it almost his life's mission to get it back. It got harder after Louis VIII, still stewing over his failure to be crowned King of England, seized Poitou from him in 1225, two years before Henry assumed the full powers of kingship. Louis might have finished the English off completely on the Continent had the renewed crusade against the Albigensians not led to his death from dysentery. With his twelve-year-old son Louis IX now on the throne, the nobles of northern France saw their chance to gain more autonomy and promised to support a landing from across the Channel.

Henry was putting together his invasion force when a young Frenchman arrived and asked him for something he couldn't give him. As Amaury de Montfort had been informed, the Earl of Chester was in possession of the lands and title of Leicester. Henry was not adverse to Simon working out some agreement with the older man and offered to take him into his service, at the respectable sum of £267 a year, until such an agreement could be reached.

In his deposition, Simon claimed he returned without finding grace, but the king had shown he was more than willing to cooperate. Henry has often been accused of bestowing gifts indiscriminately on newcomers at court, yet rarely did he give anything that didn't somehow strengthen his position. His keen eye probably recognised that this young man had something of his father's soldierly skills in him. The Montfort family connections in and around Normandy, moreover, might prove useful in winning the province back from the French. Behind the amiable munificence always stood a king looking out for his own interests.

The invasion was botched from the outset. Henry couldn't bring himself to strike first, and the French nobles, led by the caretaker Duke of Brittany, Peter of Dreux, were spooked by the determination of the queen dowager, Blanche of Castile, to quell their disaffection. Feeling lonely in his indecisiveness, Henry simply marched to Nantes and back, entertaining the locals along the way to win their favour. A bout of dysentery and a Welsh uprising forced him homeward in October 1230. He left command of the army to the namesake son of William Marshal, the man most responsible for saving Henry's throne. When the younger Marshal next went home, only to die suddenly, command fell to Ranulf de Blondeville, the Earl of Chester.

Ranulf was sixty at the time but had managed what turned out to be the only real skirmishing on that expedition. He was at his castle in Brittany when Simon approached him to sign over his half of Leicester. If Simon's claim was arguably tenuous, Ranulf's was non-existent. He had received the lands from John as a reward for standing by him after most of the baronage, including the younger Marshal, rose up in rebellion. His total holdings were massive and, since he was childless, he knew they would be eventually divided up among his sisters and their families. Simon was, moreover, family too, as his father and Ranulf were first cousins. To continue Simon's account:

The following year my lord the king crossed to Brittany and with him the Earl of Chester who held my inheritance. And I went to the earl at the castle of St James-de-Breuvron which he held. There I prayed him that I could find his grace to have my inheritance and he, graciously, agreed and in the following August took me

with him to England, and asked the king to receive my homage
for the inheritance of my father, to which, as he said, I had greater
right than he, and all the gift the king had given him in this he
renounced, and so he received my homage.

Henry received them in August 1231, while he was in the Marches
trying to deal with a new, more vigorous leader of the Welsh, who
showed what stuff he was made of by publicly hanging an English
lord he caught in his wife's chamber. Henry had no stomach for the
guerrilla warfare of his enemy and was content to build a castle to
guard against further encroachment. Simon was fortunate to find
him in a giving mood. The king had just made Richard Marshal,
the difficult brother and heir of William II, the Earl of Pembroke.
He had already made his own brother Richard Earl of Cornwall,
and now he gave him land to back up the title. When the young
Frenchman showed up with Ranulf's agreement, Henry had to
decide whether to dispense with a third earldom all in the matter
of a month. He chose to hedge. Simon could take possession of his
family's half of Leicester, but the title would have to come later, if
at all.

Henry had good reasons for holding back the title. There were
less than a dozen earls throughout the realm and the title still
evoked the prestige that went with being an earl during the heyday
of the Anglo-Saxon era. The other earls would take it amiss to find
this unknown alien suddenly within their midst, enjoying similar
privileges such as the 'third penny', their entitlement to one-third of
the revenue generated by the courts within an earldom. Of perhaps
more immediate concern to Henry was to find out what kind of
man this Montfort really was before elevating him into the ranks
of the higher nobility.

The king depended on his earls and other barons to keep the
peace and prosperity. While England was enjoying both when
Simon arrived, the properties he inherited had been exploited and
neglected under the care of Ranulf's custodians. They consisted of
twelve estates scattered around the Midlands and the south-western
part of the country, all part of a feudal system that would have
been familiar to him since it had been imported by the Normans.

As its Latin roots indicate, feudalism was a hierarchy of tenancies with the king at the top. He owned all secular land in the realm, some of which he kept for himself and his family, called the royal demesne, and the rest he farmed out to the leading men around him, his barons. These tenants-in-chief, as they were known, held their land from him in return for putting a body of knights in the field for military service. The knights were their tenants, and they in turn imposed similar requirements for services, military or otherwise, on their own tenants, and down the line it went. Anybody who was a tenant was basically the 'man' of his 'lord'. The relationship was cemented by the man paying homage to his lord, an official act of sworn allegiance. Those not directly beneath the king swore their allegiance to him by taking an oath of fealty.

These ceremonious acts of loyalty were designed to keep society tightly knit and make sure everybody knew their place, but cracks had already developed before Henry became king. A 'bastard' form of feudalism had crept in with the realisation that merit was just as important as loyalty. Men with skills and personal qualities were being retained in the service of lords who were not their own, simply because they were rewarded better. Naturally this led to all kinds of conflicts of interest and priorities, but it enabled lords to create more dynamic affinities and gave people of promise greater opportunities and mobility.

At the end of the day, however, the lord was still master, and inasmuch as the king had a say in their lives, so too did they meddle in the lives of their own tenants. They held their own private courts, where they lorded over everything from marriage and inheritance to service and discipline. Steps were begun under Henry's grandfather Henry II to break the monopolies of these courts, mainly by allowing tenants to bring suit in the king's court. The tenants who stood the best chance of besting their lords were freeholders, those families with land between forty and a hundred acres. They weren't exactly the gentry, but they had it much better off than the peasants, who formed the vast majority of tenants. Peasant families held considerably less acreage and subsisted almost entirely on bread and porridge.

Life could get even worse for the more than 50 per cent of peasants who were unfree. They not only owed their lords rent like the others, which could be paid in cash or products, but labour service as well. They were required to till their master's fields and shuck his corn and draw his water. While this service could be exempted in return for more cash or products, unfree peasants had no legal rights outside their local court. If their lord said they owed three days a week and not two, then three it was. Freeholders and free peasants, on the other hand, could take their cases all the way up to the king, theoretically at least. This didn't mean that the unfree took it lying down. They constantly raised challenges over their legal status, and in many cases their lords were happy to be rid of them because they had already discovered the economic benefits of outsourcing.

There was certainly money to be made in the thirteenth century. More and more wool, from upwards of ten million sheep, was being exported to Flanders and this fuelled imports of commodities like wine, silk and spices. New markets and towns were founded to accommodate all this trade and they provided opportunities for excess labour from the countryside. There were people aplenty across England, for the population had doubled since the Normans arrived, to around four million. The booming prosperity naturally didn't affect all of them, especially with farm output struggling to keep everybody fed. It was a harsh reminder that most of the people of that age woke up every morning at the mercy of market forces and the weather. Anybody with an income of £10 a year was doing very well, but a common labourer, with an average wage of a penny a day, would be lucky to make £1 in a good year.

Major landowners were eager to maintain their exalted station in life and drove their peasants hard to make it possible. The richest earldoms at this time were Cornwall, with an annual income of at least £5,000, followed by Gloucester and Pembroke with about £3,500 each. Leicester was not the poorest earldom, but it brought in no more than £500. That money had to go to upkeep, infrastructure, wages, feasting and entertainment. Simon then needed whatever might be left to pay off the debt he had accumulated in acquiring his estates.

There was the medieval equivalent of an estate tax, the £50 he owed to the Crown for taking possession of his half of Leicester. He was in debt to Ranulf for £200, which could have been either a starter loan or else the old earl, for all his kindness, did nothing for free. Finally, there was £500 to Amaury for renouncing his claim. Altogether it was one and a half times his yearly income and would burden him for decades to come.

To establish himself as the Lord of Leicester, Simon had to appoint several officials, including a seneschal to administer his estates and bailiffs to supervise them locally. For political power, he needed an affinity, a following of barons and knights who worked together in support of each other. Some, like him, had been a part of Ranulf's affinity; others happened to be neighbours. It cost him to keep them in his service, whether it concerned a grant of land or intervening for them at court. In his lifetime Montfort's affinity never exceeded more than a dozen, modest compared to other ones, but his would remain steadfastly loyal to the end over three decades later.

He also had to go about winning over those new subjects not under his immediate control, the townsfolk, freeholders and peasants for whom he was now the link to the court. The king had his own rights and privileges within each earldom and the locals would turn to Simon to keep the sheriff and other Crown officials from being too assertive in their duties. His authority would in large part rest on his ability to get along and show leadership. Both were in evidence in what was his first official act, his order that all the Jews in his half of Leicester leave.

The Jews had arrived in England with William the Conqueror to help monetise the wool trade. The Church's intolerance of usury practised by Christians had allowed them to monopolise moneylending by the start of Henry's reign. This was a vital service in a cash-starved economy, but their faith and their interest rates, which Henry capped at 43 per cent per annum, generated much hostility. Since the Jews were the property of the Crown, the king protected them, although that didn't always save them from massacres and expulsions, as had occurred under Richard the Lionheart. The king was more attentive when it came to ensuring their debts were collected, because legally the money belonged to him. He wouldn't take it all in one swoop, just tax them whenever he needed extra cash. Called a tallage, it was a nice way of describing his cut, and Henry would exploit this advantage until he literally bled them dry.

Not a vicious man like his father John, and certainly a more pious one, Henry latched on to a proposal by the clergy in 1231 to establish safe houses for converting the Jews through persuasion instead of violence. Their expulsion from local communities, the argument ran, would upset their livelihood and complacency, forcing them to seek shelter, and salvation, in one of these conversion homes. It would be good for their souls and Henry's. Simon claimed he was expelling the Leicester Jews for the good of his own soul and those of everyone who came before and after him until the end of the world.

Like most of the king's schemes, however, nothing much came of these shelters. Henry could hardly afford a mass conversion that would rob him of his tallage and stick him with thousands of hungry souls to feed. He could allow magnates like Simon to move against the Jews in their dominions because, in the case of Leicester anyway, it concerned a handful of families at most.

If Henry permitted this action, and his Christian subjects welcomed it, Montfort was no doubt driven from within both by his parents, who had little regard for anyone denying the incarnation of the Almighty, and by Robert Grosseteste, the local archdeacon and future Bishop of Lincoln. Thirty years older than Montfort, he was a man of considerable learning, and his political and spiritual influence on Simon would be enormous until his death in 1253.

Grosseteste studied in Paris and Oxford, later becoming the first chancellor of the latter. His knowledge of Greek, Aristotle and mathematics was impressive enough. Where he learned Hebrew is anybody's guess, though it was a delicate matter in an age where a person could be hanged for converting to Judaism. An impatient stickler for detail and biblical imagery, Grosseteste had very definite ideas about the place of Jews in the world. Simon may have been the Lord of Leicester, but every move he made would be under the watchful glare and boundless energy of the exacting churchman.

How the Jews were driven from Leicester, from their miserable hovels next to the ruins of the old Roman wall, is unrecorded, but the ethnic cleansing of the twentieth century, unmatched in the astronomical number of people forced from their homes, suggests it could not have been a pleasant ordeal. In the end, they did not find shelter in Henry's conversion home, rather across the line that separated the two halves of Leicester. Simon's elderly great-aunt Margaret, the sister of his grandmother Amicia, had offered them refuge. At the time she was engaged in a dispute with her young kinsman over the exact partition between their inheritances. Whether she sympathised with the Jews or else welcomed them merely to spite the haughty newcomer is a matter of conjecture.

One person who might have thought that she acted out of sympathy was Grosseteste. He had immense respect for her and was deeply in debt to her for similar acts of kindness. Eager to return the favour, he saw the expulsion of the Jews as an opportunity to give her some beneficial advice. Telling her that Simon had done what he did to end usury, he was anxious that the Jewish families not continue as before under Margaret's protection. He hurled missives from the Bible to show it was the duty of all people of her rank to prevent them from 'oppressing' Christians with their moneylending operations and to insist that they seek physical labour instead.

Margaret's response is unknown, but her dispute with Montfort continued up to her death in 1235. By then he was securely established in Leicester, and Margaret's heir, now the Earl of Winchester, was largely absent. Simon's debts, however, were as pervasive as ever. The surest way out of such predicament, as true then as in any age, was to marry well. The king had a say about whom his leading men and women married, and never was there an English monarch who relished the role of matchmaker as much as Henry did.

2

More of the Great Bounty
1232–1238

Simon was fortunate that his entrée to the court was through the Earl of Chester. Ranulf had been in a struggle with Henry's leading councillor, Hubert de Burgh, for some time, going back to the minority. In his position as justiciar, Hubert was keen on centralising the power of the court, meaning his own power, and magnates like Ranulf saw this as an infringement on their local rights and privileges. Hubert was not above promoting his own men and family, and more importantly himself, even taking a Scottish princess for his third wife. When Henry made him Earl of Kent, that was it. He came from a humble background and did not deserve such honours on par with all the great noble families.

This 1st Earl of Kent had played a role as crucial as anyone in preserving the throne for Henry. As the keeper of Dover, Hubert held off all attempts by Prince Louis to take that vital link to the Continent. When Louis' wife Blanche of Castile made one last attempt to supply him with reinforcements, Hubert took a small flotilla and overpowered the French transport ships near Sandwich on 24 August 1217, arguably the first great victory at sea for the Royal Navy. After William Marshal I died in 1219, he ousted the foreign faction led by Peter des Roches, the French-born militant Bishop of Winchester and tutor to Henry, and virtually ruled alone until the king came of age.

Hubert's undoing was inevitable and the Normandy expedition provided the occasion for it. He saw, as many barons did, that there was as much to lose as to gain by getting Normandy back. The English barons who had lost their possessions in France after the partition were compensated with the lands of Normans seized in England. The only way to win back the allegiance of these Normans was to give them their English possessions back, and for the Normans with English possessions in France to do likewise. Neither side was disposed to disgorging in this manner, but Henry, for all his love of detail, would always cover his ears to whatever he didn't want to hear. He would win Normandy back no matter what and gave the order to assemble the men and ships.

Wearing a silky white suit and gloves, Henry arrived in Portsmouth in October 1229 only to discover there would be no D-Day after all. The army was too small and the fleet even smaller. The king, in his wrath, turned on the justiciar, calling him a traitor and drawing his sword. Hubert had to be saved by Ranulf, who was perhaps more interested in protecting Henry from himself. De Burgh got the message and made sure the fleet was ready to sail in the spring. This time there were too many ships, but an impressive army of 450 knights had been ferried over, only to be squandered by the king's inability to rise to the occasion. The outcome was a disaster, the Welsh intervention following it was a disaster, and the Treasury was empty. It was at that time that Peter des Roches reappeared on the scene wondering if everything was all right.

It took a lot to move Henry against someone he had trusted all his life. Only when the leading barons, all of whom had grudges against Hubert for one thing or another, were ready to let him stew did Henry finally turn him out. Interestingly, just before his fall, Hubert had obtained a life grant from the king to protect his position. Far from luring him into letting his guard down, something John would have done, it shows Henry was determined to stick to him to the last.

He subsequently hounded the old man, until Ranulf again had to step in to save the king from himself. It was more of the simple Henry, always ready to play out his vindictiveness for all to see. Roches was happy to let the king throw a tantrum. He was busy reconstituting the court and administration to include his foreign cronies, called Poitevins for their origins in and around Poitou, all of whom were eager to get back what Hubert had taken from them.

Their actions in 1233 precipitated the next crisis of Henry's regime. The Poitevins had the king dispossess certain men of their property without the due process stipulated in Magna Carta. Roches reassured Henry that a real king was a law unto himself, which was just what Henry wanted to hear. Battle lines were drawn when the seizures touched too close to Richard Marshal, the new Earl of Pembroke, whom Henry had recently elevated despite misgivings about his loyalty. In the skirmishes that followed, Henry got the worst of it. The Archbishop of Canterbury, Edmund of Abingdon, arranged for the king to beat a hasty retreat, but things had already gone too far and Marshal was killed in April 1234 fighting off an attack in Ireland, instigated by the Poitevins.

Knowing he had gotten himself in over his head, Henry humbled himself and confessed he had arbitrarily denied his subjects their rights. In reality, he was only sorry for getting caught. He hated getting caught, hated when people put him in embarrassing situations. He not only dismissed Roches and his circle but, as with Hubert, went the extra mile to ruin their reputations.

Simon's association with the Poitevins through Ranulf, who died in October 1232, and his status as a foreigner at court, could have made him an easy target. He survived their disgrace unscathed, probably because he was still a newcomer and not directly implicated in their schemes. However he managed it, he was in a perfect position to fill the vacuum that was left and would begin his rise as one of Henry's most trusted courtiers.

It had begun not even a year into receiving the king's bounty when, in July 1232, Henry granted Montfort all the lands confiscated from the Normans within his fief. Like all kings, Henry used, had to use, patronage of this sort to sustain the loyalty of his baronage. While these extra lands in Leicester never brought in more than £100 a year, anything helped at a time when most barons were mortgaged to the hilt and quite often depended on the king for gifts.

This could be in the form of more land and manors, even castles, or a herd of deer and timbers of freshly felled oak. The king might forgive a debt or award a wardship, meaning the income from the ward's lands. The complicated business of giving and receiving, promising and rewarding, would in time create a maddening situation between these two men that could only have one possible outcome.

For now, Simon was on his way, witnessing the king's charters and sitting in on council meetings. Perhaps the most pressing issue before the council in the mid-1230s was finding a wife for Henry. Several candidates had been discussed, usually with the intention of strengthening England's position against France. If Henry had his way, he would have made one of the Scottish princesses his wife. Hubert ruined that for him by snatching up the oldest of the girls for himself, as there was no way the council could countenance the king as the brother-in-law of one of his own subjects. (Henry, as we shall see, had no such qualms.) The king would later accuse Hubert of scaring off one potential wife by describing him as an impotent leper. True or not, he was keeping in character by letting the whole world hear about it.

The marriage market took an upswing in 1235. After three days of debate, the council agreed to wed Henry's sister Isabella to the Holy Roman Emperor, Frederick II. She was twenty at the time and beautiful. He was forty, bald, covered with red hair and twice widowed. Henry hoped an alliance with this learned and contentious ruler, who didn't bow lightly before popes, would put added pressure on France to come to terms about Normandy. It didn't, and Henry was forced to pay Frederick £20,000 for Isabella's dowry, almost the king's entire revenue for one year. After being 'viewed' and approved by Frederick's ambassadors, she was sent to spend the remaining six years of her young, lonely life in a faraway land, surrounded by strange-speaking eunuchs and concubines and waiting for an older, eccentric man to pay her a visit.

While his sister Isabella was getting married, his brother Richard of Cornwall was trying to get an annulment from his wife Isabel. She was the second of William Marshal's five daughters and had been married first to Gilbert de Clare, the Earl of Gloucester, a man twice her age and one of the original enforcers of Magna Carta. Their solid marriage ended when he died during the ill-fated French expedition, in October 1230, just as Henry and Richard were returning. Rich widows were expected to remarry and Henry would have some say in this. Richard appears to have gone behind his brother's back in courting her and the king was miffed when they suddenly married in March 1231.

Born in 1209, Richard of Cornwall was nine years younger than Isabel. She already had four healthy children, but her first two with

Richard died in infancy. Worried he might be left without an heir, he wrote to Rome for an annulment, but the pope advised him to stick with it. Sure enough, a son, Henry, was born in November 1235 and survived to adulthood. He was destined to be the most tragic figure of this story after the main events were played out.

What bothered Henry most about Richard's marriage was that it was so unnecessary. He had already married their youngest sister Eleanor to William Marshal II, thereby creating an alliance with that wealthy and powerful family. It was in fact for the purpose of Isabel's remarriage that Marshal turned over command in France to Ranulf and returned that spring. He probably overdid it at the wedding feast, because he died less than a week later. Everyone was distraught at his sudden death, especially Henry, who reportedly tore his clothes and lamented that some curse had played a hand.

William and Richard had been friends, brought together by an alliance against Henry in 1227. In that year the king, under Hubert's influence, had ruled against his brother in a dispute over a manor. When Richard insisted on appealing to his peers, Henry ordered him to either quit his claim or the realm. Fearing Hubert would have him locked up, Richard fled to William and Ranulf for support, and together they put up a united front.

William and Ranulf didn't care about Richard's manor. What worried them was Henry's intention, since coming of age, to start reclaiming large swaths of land as part of the royal forests, land they had under their control. Faced with his first armed revolt, Henry did what he would do for the next four decades in similar situations: promise to reform, wait for the barons to go home, then go about with business as usual.

For Richard, one manor was as good as the next. Important was to acquire them, not lose them. He made it clear to Henry that as his brother and heir to the throne he expected to be well endowed. Mindful of this first test of his authority, Henry was careful to keep Richard on his side, making steady grants to him that in time would make him one of the richest earls in England. Greed was clearly Richard's weakness, so the next time he rose up in rebellion, Henry knew exactly what to do.

It turned out to be the Marshal rebellion in 1234. Henry by this time had every right to be sick of this family. At first, Richard stuck by the Marshals, even having Isabel warn her brother about a possible trap. But then characteristically he was bought off by his own brother and the rebellion ended with the death of Marshal and the fall of the Poitevins. Richard's betrayal was viewed contemptuously by Marshal's supporters, ending in the destruction of one of his manors. So deeply aggrieved did he feel by this wanton act that he made sure the man responsible was later arrested and imprisoned in 1236, an incident in which Montfort, by then a leading councillor, had a hand.

With the king now almost thirty, the council was insistent on him taking a wife. He finally settled on Joan of Ponthieu, an heiress whose family lands near Normandy could help him recover through marriage what he couldn't take back in war. A papal dispensation was required because they were fourth cousins, but since these things took months, Henry decided to marry her first and then get the dispensation. Rash moves were something he was famous for, but in this case he wanted to make sure Joan wasn't snatched up by someone else while the papacy considered his request. He and Joan had already been married by proxy and a party was on its way to Rome when Henry, seemingly out of nowhere, changed his mind.

In 1234, twenty-year-old Louis IX of France married thirteen-year-old Margaret, the eldest daughter of the Count of Provence. Louis and his mother, the formidable Blanche of Castile, were determined to cement the gains made by the French monarchy in the south following the end of the Albigensian Crusade. The count had four daughters, all of them reportedly beautiful, and the next oldest, twelve-year-old Eleanor, was available. A well-travelled yarn has her writing a poem about a knight from Cornwall and sending it to Richard in an attempt to snare either him or Henry. While Henry was just the man to fall in love under such circumstances, he saw an alliance with this part of the world more conducive to his big-picture type of thinking.

He jilted Joan and quickly despatched new orders to forget the dispensation. The French were agreeable to the union, because they had the eldest daughter from Provence, and Blanche was ready to offer Joan to someone from her native Castile. Henry's council also viewed the match favourably. If their king were the brother-in-law of the King of France, he might be less inclined to go to war with him. As usual, Henry had them all fooled.

He nevertheless almost blew it by putting business too much at the heart of the matter. Although Provence was impoverished, he demanded £14,000 – not quite what he had been forced to give Frederick for his sister, but stiff enough. He wasn't serious, of course, it's just he had his dignity to think about. His plan was to lower Eleanor's dowry in increments all the way down to a paltry £2,000. That way he would look both dignified and generous. Not until he sent these instructions to his proxies did he realise that others might see it as degrading. He quickly countermanded his previous instructions and ordered them to bring back the girl with a dowry or without. The count and his wife, both poets incidentally, were glad to opt out of paying anything, but eventually settled £7,000 each on her and Margaret.

Where Henry failed as a warrior, he more than made up for it as a wedding and coronation planner. He went to incredible lengths and expense to prepare a glittering wardrobe for his future queen and to redecorate the palace of Westminster, perhaps overeager to outdo what he thought must be the splendour of Provence. He also wanted to erase the scandal of his father, who was still married to another woman when he stole Henry's mother from her intended in 1200. John secured an annulment soon enough and married the twelve-year-old Isabella of Angoulême, who was said to be so beautiful that he couldn't drag himself out of bed to take care of the business of the kingdom. Her coronation in London was a lavish affair, but only for him. Everyone noticed how John glimmered with jewels and gems, but Isabella got none at all and her dresses cost no more than £13 to make. She could have been just another lady waiting on her lord for all anyone knew, and that's pretty much what she became.

Eleanor of Provence was described as *venustissima*, which is not quite so alluring as the 'venus' in the word might suggest, but does indicate she had a physical appeal that included charm and good breeding. When Henry met her and her party at Dover in January 1236, he handed out gold presents to her and her attendants to dispel any notion of parsimony, then accompanied them to Canterbury for the wedding. He was determined that his subjects make a favourable impression on his bride and had London swept and cleaned and decorated for her arrival. They were met by 360 men on horseback led by the mayor, who rode with them from the Tower of London to Westminster, with crowds cheering and trumpets blaring the whole way. After a sumptuous feast of venison and fish, everything not nailed down was claimed by the attending party, even the queen's bed and all its furniture.

The removal of the queen's bed made it clear to Eleanor that, although she was only twelve, her marriage to Henry had to be consummated to make it legally binding. She was fortunate that he was a sensitive soul who would naturally make her feel at ease as much as possible under the circumstances. Their first child would not be born for three years, a clear indication that this man, with his sharp eye for curves, was willing to let his young wife's own curves develop before making the conjugal bed a nightly venue for the royal couple.

Since the beginnings of Norman rule, the Earl of Leicester held the honorary title of Steward of England. Nobody could quite remember what the functions of the steward were apart from holding a wash basin for the king to clean his hands in during banquets. Roger Bigod, the Earl of Norfolk, wanted the honour on this particular occasion and disputed the claim of Leicester to the title. Simon held firm and so held the basin for Henry, perhaps getting his first look up close at the newly crowned Eleanor.

If it seemed to her that he spoke in a familiar accent, there were plenty of people in her train who could tell her why. This was Simon de Montfort, the son of the scourge who had ravished their lands two decades earlier. Provence wasn't as affected as Languedoc, but the whole region was impoverished as a result of the crusade, and if Eleanor came to England with no dowry, Henry had the family of the man holding his wash basin to thank for it.

The leader of her party was her mother's brother William, who came from Savoy, a small province that guarded the western passes to the Alps and therefore to Italy. Henry knew he was making a strategic match by aligning himself to this part of the world, and William was planning to exploit that position in creating opportunities for himself and his family. Blanche of Castile had sensed a similar intention when William brought Margaret to her wedding to Louis IX two years earlier. The queen dowager was having none of him or his relatives and sent them packing right away. Frederick did the same with the English party sent to accompany Henry's sister Isabella, and Richard advised his brother to follow suit, but Henry couldn't get enough of these people from Provence and Savoy. He gave them gifts of money and grants of land, and soon made William the leader of his council.

They were smooth talkers, these Savoyards, but what set them apart from his native-born nobility was their readiness to let Henry do the thing he wanted most: rule with a free hand. While his English barons were always balking and lecturing him, these Frenchmen were just happy to be there, and so they encouraged him when he acted wisely and gently nudged him when he didn't.

The English grumbled that he was playing favourites, but what Henry clearly had in mind was to create a court of his own making, one free of the clan alliances that went back to the Norman Conquest. By marrying a rich English heiress to a penniless Savoyard clerk, he kept the power of her family in check and made the clerk his friend for life. What the barons saw was the king squandering the wealth of the realm on these infernal freeloaders. He even had the audacity at this time to invite the Poitevins back, the same group that only a few years before implicated him in the 'murder' of Richard Marshal. It was almost as if he was thumbing his nose at them.

Simon couldn't begrudge William of Savoy his stellar rise, for he had enjoyed the same trajectory under Henry. Although entitled to Leicester by inheritance, he owed his possessions, his very presence in England, to the king. He started using the title of earl without waiting to be formally invested, a sure sign of favour that could only provoke resentment among his peers, and he was identified as one of the 'infamous and mistrusted' councillors responsible for all that was then wrong in the kingdom.

This included the arrival of Otto, a papal legate whom Henry had summoned to prop up his royal dignity. The other nobles were angry that the king should have taken this step without consulting them, especially when he then proceeded to demean his royal dignity by worshiping the ground Otto walked on. They were in for an even bigger surprise when Henry invited them to a great council, or parliament as it was coming to be known, and asked for a tax to offset the costs of his wedding and his sister's dowry. It was typical of the king. He only consulted them when he wanted money.

Richard of Cornwall was among the barons who deplored the state of the realm and figured it was as good a time as any to go abroad. Taking the cross to go on crusade, he began the arduous task of raising money for it, mostly by selling off woods. Montfort was also eager to go to Jerusalem, but whatever plans he may have had to join Richard's retinue were quashed by an incident at court that engulfed him in the worst of Henry's failings. If the king surrounded himself with foreigners who only took and never gave, then this particular Frenchman was about to take the biggest prize of them all.

There was another Eleanor at Henry's wedding, his youngest sister. She was a woman of about twenty and everyone knew she was a widow. Simon, as everyone also knew, had been recently rebuffed in his pursuit of two other widows. They were much older than him, unlikely to produce an heir, so he was clearly after their fortunes. Both women were countesses on the Continent, holders of vast dominions, and when word reached the French court that this newly instated English lord was trying to get his hands on their goods, he was sent scurrying back over the Channel. So concerned were the French by his intentions that they hauled the second of the two women, Joanna of Flanders, into court to swear that she had not married Montfort, nor would she. If she had suffered any embarrassment through his attentions, the man she did marry would get him back soon enough for it.

The young widow Eleanor would have been pleased by the attention. She was only nine in 1224 when she was married to William Marshal II, then a widower in his mid-thirties. The union provoked all kinds of debate, for the age of consent was twelve and princesses were not ordinarily given in marriage to commoners. They generally went to foreign potentates to create useful alliances, as had been the case with Eleanor's two older sisters Isabella, the empress, and Joan, the Queen of Scotland.

In William's case, the king was anxious to keep him from marrying a woman that might put all his wealth and manors into the hands of a foreign family. He was so rich that Henry didn't even have to provide his sister with a marriage portion, the lands and assets conferred on a girl by her family to secure her children in marriage, and he bragged about it in the letter he wrote to the papacy justifying the match. The ten manors he eventually settled on her as a marriage portion cost him nothing, for they had been seized from a French nobleman and given to William to hold anyway.

That was just Henry's predilection for braggadocio, because he was clearly concerned about the child's welfare after her wedding. In 1230 Eleanor accompanied her husband and brother on the expedition to France. When she became seasick during the voyage, Henry, who was leading an army to the Continent, had his ship drop anchor at the nearest landfall to give her time to recover while ordering the rest of the fleet to continue.

The fifteen-year-old Eleanor even being on the expedition was probably more Henry's decision than William's. The king was hoping to secure the support of his mother Isabella of Angoulême and her second husband Hugh Lusignan, the Count of La Marche, in his showdown with the French. A reunion between mother and daughter, who had not seen each other since Eleanor was three, could somehow help. It didn't.

William Marshal's unexpected death after their return from France should have left Eleanor in a comfortable state. In the absence of children, widows were generally entitled to a dower equal to one-third of their husband's estates. The Marshal family holdings in Ireland alone were worth at least £3,000 a year, but Richard Marshal, the new Earl of Pembroke, was decidedly uncooperative in honouring his sister-in-law's rights. He even went so far as to insist that the marriage portion Henry gave her become part of any settlement. Finally Marshal offered her £400 a year to be done with the business. It was far short of the £1,000 she was entitled to, but, at Henry's urging, she accepted.

His reasons were good at the time. Besides being a tidy sum, it was £400 more than she could hope to get out of the obstinate Marshal. Magna Carta stipulated a settlement period of forty days for the allocation of a dower, and here it was over one year and still no progress had been made. The sheer vastness of the estates, and the need to assess them, gave Marshal plenty of excuses for stalling. In the end, Henry felt it was better for Eleanor to get whatever she could and he would make himself surety for the payments.

Henry seems to have forgotten that his kingdom teetered on bankruptcy that year, forcing him to ask his barons for an 'aid', or tax. Marshal was already in arrears with his payments to Eleanor when he rose up in arms against the king. In 1234 he was dead, and Gilbert, the brother who succeeded him as Earl of Pembroke, was unlikely to prove any more cooperative. It was in this atmosphere of exasperation that Eleanor took a step that changed her life.

She became a nun. Well, sort of. Together with her former governess, a widow of austere devotion, Eleanor swore an oath of perpetual widowhood to Edmund of Abingdon, the Archbishop of Canterbury. He sealed the act by placing a ring on her finger, thus making her a bride of Christ. She was not really a nun because she had neglected to take the veil as well, but the ring meant that she was expected to be chaste and virtuous.

She had a spiritual side to be sure. In the wake of her husband's death, she visited religious houses in search of comfort and would do so for the rest of her life. Becoming a bride of Christ, however, was clearly a political move. The archbishop was the architect of the peace deal between Henry and the Marshal faction and he might have prevailed upon the young woman to swear she would never remarry as a concession to the Marshals. This way, the family could rest assured that none of the estates she held from them came into the hands of a future husband.

In fact, whatever consent Eleanor gave probably owed to fears that she would have to remarry to better serve the interests of the Crown. Like any king, Henry would have preferred to keep his sister available for such purposes, despite the longing of his two other sisters for home, but he had been caught in a bad way by the rebellion and wanted to end it any way he could.

Harried as he was in the 1230s, Henry remained close to Eleanor. He made her gifts of venison for her table and timber for her manors. He lent her money and forgave her debts, all of which indicated that the ring on her finger wasn't keeping her from enjoying the courtly life. Her status as a princess and nun doubtlessly made her vulnerable to the same snipes that Simon received for being a foreigner and upstart. At Henry's wedding, when another Eleanor replaced her in her brother's affections, she might have noticed some snickering every time the young Frenchman holding the king's water basin glanced at her. He had already made a play for two widows above his station. Would he try for a third?

Eleanor and Simon had probably met before in the comings and goings of the court. Each familiar with the controversy that surrounded the other, the attraction between these two headstrong, high-spirited individuals had to be mutual. Beyond interests like religion and learning, they were supreme organisers with phenomenal energy, not afraid to speak their minds or stand up to authority. For Simon, marriage to Eleanor would make him the brother-in-law of a king, an empress and the Queen of Scotland, a signal that he had truly arrived. For her part, Eleanor would get a man full of ability and courage who would stick up for her and not let bullies like the Marshals push her around. Her brother, nice guy though he was, simply did not have the backbone to shove back.

But there was still the little matter of her vow of chastity. Even in that devotional age, she and Simon were especially pious and the thought of leaving her oath by the wayside troubled them. At some point in her widowhood, however, Eleanor was overcome by the desire to become a mother, and Simon, for all his pursuit of older widows, needed a younger one to give him heirs and therefore make the future of his earldom worth the time and effort. The sexual tension between these two ambitious people, both described as enormously attractive, would eventually lead Eleanor to slip off her ring for good.

Fortunately for them, Henry was a romantic who could sympathise with their dilemma, and nothing gave him more pleasure than helping people who turned to him. Of course, arranging a marriage for them was not going to be easy, not by a long shot. There was bound to be a firestorm from all quarters, starting with the Church. As with annulling Henry's marriage to Joan of Ponthieu, a dispensation would be required from the pope, but those were easily bought. The bigger problem would be the reaction of the Archbishop of Canterbury. Even if the primate had talked Eleanor into taking her vow, he was a stern taskmaster who would surely consider it a personal affront if she sidestepped it now.

The way was open when the archbishop, fed up with Otto and his own monks, left for Rome to complain about them to the pope. On 6 January 1238, in a little chapel built privately by Henry so he could enjoy Mass without actually having to get out of bed, the king joined Simon and Eleanor in holy matrimony while his chaplain officiated. Simon was grateful to receive her, it was said. His peers, however, were livid.

Apart from having no clue they were even a couple, the barons saw the clandestine nature of the marriage as more of the king at his worst. He consistently used poor judgement in matters affecting the realm, mostly because he failed to seek their advice, and he promoted aliens without 'give' or anything useful to offer. No one could miss the irony that these were the same issues that propelled Simon to the forefront of the revolution that toppled Henry twenty-five years later.

Henry had faced rebellion twice before, in 1227 at the hands of William Marshal II, and in 1234 at the hands of Richard Marshal. Now, in 1238, it was Gilbert Marshal's turn to call the king to account, only he wasn't the leader. Rather it was Richard of Cornwall, who felt especially aggrieved because Eleanor was his sister, too. His opposition during those earlier occasions had been more temperamental than threatening, but this time he meant business. Henry was sufficiently unnerved to send out orders to his port wardens countermanding whatever scheme his brother might cook up.

The ill feelings reached such a pitch that Otto had to step in and arrange a compromise that showed just how desperate a situation Henry found himself in. A series of provisions, presumably reforms meant to rein in the king's whimsical rule, were drawn up and sealed but never implemented because Richard, characteristically, withdrew his opposition at the last minute. Officially, Simon had pacified him with the argument that the marriage was what his sister wanted, as if that really mattered in those days. Clearly, Richard had been bought off. A huge sum of money, nearly £4,000, was sent eastwards in preparation for his crusade, all of it sent by Henry from the tax he levied the previous year.

That tax had been the source of a furious debate, with the magnates giving way only after Henry promised to include them in his counsels and spend the money wisely. He reneged on both accounts, but would pay a price as, for the next thirty years, all of his subsequent requests for a tax were refused by them. Richard, however, would continue to profit from his own wily behaviour until he eventually became his brother's banker. The terms he was able to dictate in that capacity ensured he never needed to rebel again.

The king and his brother could afford to be cavalier, for now anyway, but Simon enjoyed no such luxury. He set off for Rome to get the dispensation, carrying with him a glowing reference from Henry and an undetermined sum of money. At least £300 of it came from an alderman in Leicester, who apparently cut down some trees Montfort was planning to sell. When Simon insisted he pay for them, the alderman complained to everyone that it was extortion. Robert Grosseteste intervened, advising Montfort not to let severity get the best of him: 'Do not let your conduct be harsh and inflexible. Instead let your goodness and mercy triumph over judgement.' Montfort had immense respect for Grosseteste, but he probably couldn't help wondering how the bishop would react if somebody cut down his woods.

Simon left around the end of March, which coincided with the departure of a group of English knights sent to fight under Frederick. Apparently he stopped on the way to meet the emperor, now his brother-in-law, for he obtained letters of support from him. The Archbishop of Canterbury was still present at the papal court in Rome and tried to quash Simon's plea, but however much money did the trick, the dispensation was granted in May 1238. Montfort then betook himself back to Frederick, where he saw some service with the English contingent at the siege of Brescia, and perhaps met for the first time John Mansel, later to become Henry's most trusted adviser and Simon's shrewdest enemy.

The archbishop's own pleas were rejected by the Curia and he returned in a worse mood than ever. An apocryphal story has him later fleeing the country because he refused to be reconciled to the marriage, but not before standing on a hill and cursing any Montfort offspring. Simon arrived in October and immediately proceeded to Kenilworth Castle, where Eleanor, who was pregnant when he left, had gone for her confinement. The question of whether she was expecting when they got married seems to have been answered when she gave birth to a son over ten months later, on 26 November 1238. Henry received word while he was with his court at Woodstock and quickly set out on the thirty-five miles to Kenilworth to share in the happy occasion. He gave his consent for the child to be named after him and, we can guess, stood as godfather when he was baptised.

The rite itself was performed by the Bishop of Lichfield, who had earned Henry's displeasure because of his close relations with Richard Marshal. The prelate saw his chance to patch things up with the king by baptising his nephew, but he had no more than lifted the baby out of the font before he was overcome by a severe illness. He died the day after Christmas.

Otherwise the year had been remarkably successful for the couple. They had wed, weathered the storm surrounding their marriage, remained high in the king's favour and welcomed the arrival of a healthy son. Henry made it clear that he planned to confer the title of Earl of Leicester on Simon early the next year. The Montforts, it would seem, had more of the great bounty to look forward to.

3

The Churching
1239–1243

It was Henry himself who explained the nature of kingship in a way everyone could understand: 'If I am rich, you are rich. If I am poor, you are poor.' This arrangement, naturally, worked better when they were all rich, and Henry tried to be accommodating. He never pressed his barons to pay the debts they owed him, Simon being a good example. The £50 'relief' for taking possession of his half of Leicester was still outstanding and would be forgiven entirely in the mid-1240s. But the king wasn't nearly as rich as his ancestors. When William I conquered England in 1066, he took a whopping 17 per cent of the landed income for himself, but this resource had been much depleted through patronage since that time. Now Henry had a wife and trove of in-laws to support, all of them eager to share in the great bounty, just as Henry was eager to pursue his enjoyment of building, redecorating, and the good life in general.

Montfort too had a wife and family now, and if anything his marriage to Eleanor should have relieved some of his financial problems. Her income from her Marshal dower, including the £400 settlement for the Irish lands, totalled nearly £1,000, twice as much as his Leicester holdings. But they were both aware that this money, when it was paid, was due her alone, and that all such payments would cease if she predeceased him. Henry had again neglected to provide her with a marriage portion, perhaps thinking he was more than generous by allowing them to marry in the first place. That left only Simon's property to bequeath to their children, which would clearly not be enough if they were to have as many children as Simon's mother (six) or Eleanor's (fourteen).

More worrisome was the problem of Simon's debts, which only seemed to have accumulated since he first stepped ashore in England. Henry had advanced him £1,565 for his trip to Rome, and his older brother Amaury, who was expected to arrive to make a final renunciation of any claim to the earldom, was also seeking 'pacification' before he left on crusade. The king had been most kind to his sister during her widowhood, with regular gifts of deer and wine, £1,000 in loans, and the castle of Odiham for her personal home. His gift to Eleanor that Christmas included a robe and surcoat made of gold and silk, meant for her to wear at her churching, that very public display of thanks given by a woman for a safe childbirth.

His own gift to Simon would be his official investiture as the Earl of Leicester at the great feast of Candlemas, held on 2 February 1239 in Winchester. It had taken nearly eight years of unwavering support, where Montfort's loyalty to the king had always outstripped that of the native-born magnates. Sensitive as usual to appearances, Henry wasn't merely rewarding him for good service, rather giving him a rank more becoming to the husband of a princess. The timing was opportune, for Simon was chosen among the noblemen to witness the baptism of the heir to the throne four months later.

The newborn was called Edward, named after Henry's idol Edward the Confessor, the last king to die in his bed before the Conquest. Unlike his Norman predecessors, Henry considered himself to be an English king and not just the King of England. He basically had no choice. His uncle Richard could scoff at his island subjects as 'You English' because he spent nearly his whole reign abroad. Save for those few months of gallivanting around in France, Henry had spent all his life in England. What drove him to worship the Confessor rather than the Lionheart were the traits they seemingly had in common, namely piety and the semblance of lording over a peaceful land. It would be hoped that the new Edward looked nothing like his namesake, however, whose long white hair and beard and bony fingers made him resemble a wizard emerging from Middle Earth.

The age of registering births at the local church was still a hundred years in the future. Births not considered major events at the time went unrecorded, like those of Simon and Eleanor. As the heir to the throne, Edward's birth on 17 June 1239 easily qualified as an event worth remembering. Even more intriguing is the fact that the date of his conception can probably be pinpointed as well, thanks to an attempt on his father's life.

The story goes back, as most seem to during this period, to Richard Marshal's uprising. In 1235 a clerk who bragged about killing Marshal in Ireland was himself slain at his lodgings close to the royal palace. William de Marisco, whose father had been suspected of leading Marshal to his death, felt the clerk was standing in the way of his family's rehabilitation, and so killed him with a group of horsemen one night and fled. Since that definitely removed any chance of rehabilitation, Marisco turned to piracy before coming up with a scheme to kill the king.

The assassin he sent first confronted Henry at the court in Woodstock. Pretending to be mad, he shouted and claimed that the king had usurped the throne from him. Henry pitied the man and ordered his attendants to stop beating him and let him go. Later that night he crept into Henry's chamber with a knife. When the king was nowhere to be found, he started ranting and making all kinds of commotion until one of the queen's ladies-in-waiting alerted the attendants. He was later hanged, drawn and quartered along with Marisco and fifteen others.

Describing the scene, Matthew Paris ascribes to Providence the good fortune that Henry, on that night of 9 September 1238, was sleeping with the queen, nine months and eleven days before the arrival of baby Edward. It's possible in this light to see his conception taking place just as the madman sank his 'naked knife' into the empty bed of the king. It goes a long way towards symbolising the birth of a man whose violent nature was unnerving even in that age.

For all his love of Edward the Confessor, Henry had to know that it was his failure to give England an heir that led to the great Norman oppression. And so the birth of this healthy boy with the English name was greeted with celebration throughout the land. Gifts arrived in abundance, but the king had to go and bungle the occasion by sniping that some locations had scrimped on value and quantity. True to form, he saw nothing unseemly about asking for more.

It was an indication that he was starting to feel squeezed by his financial situation, and when the king felt squeezed, his response was to lash out at those he felt responsible. He didn't care who they were and what the ramifications could be. As it happens, he chose what should have been the most dignified event of the year, his wife's churching, to humiliate two people who would show him in time they were ready to give as good as they got.

The royal churching took place on 9 August 1239. Noble ladies, accompanied by their husbands, gathered from all over to witness the queen's purification. The dramatic scene described by Matthew Paris has Simon and Eleanor just arriving when Henry turns on them in a fury. He calls Simon an excommunicated man, snarls he 'defiled' Eleanor before their marriage, and forbids both of them from attending the ceremony. Stunned, they return to their lodgings at the palace of the late Bishop of Winchester, only to discover that the king has had them ejected. More bewildered than ever, they return to the ceremony, begging pardon for what they know not, but Henry levels even more charges at Simon. Paris quotes his words as follows:

You seduced my sister before marriage, and when I found it out, I gave her to you in marriage, although against my will, in order to avoid scandal; and, that her vow might not impede the marriage, you went to Rome, and by costly presents and great promises you bribed the Roman court to grant you permission to do what was unlawful. The Archbishop of Canterbury here present knows this, and intimated the truth of the matter to the pope, but truth was overcome by bribes; and on your failing to pay the money you promised, you were excommunicated; and to increase the mass of your wickedness, you, by false evidence, named me as your security, without consulting me, and when I know nothing at all of the matter.

Paris was well known at the court and his vivid account, whether the words are verbatim or not, suggests he was present at this spectacular episode. But he was a lover of gossip and scandal and would naturally give the seduction aspect of the king's argument precedence. In a modern novel, seduction is also the reason given for Henry's fit, only it was his own Eleanor that Simon defiled. The queen betrays this secret to the archbishop, who then informs Henry about it. Indeed, the archbishop is made to look like a snitch in Paris' version of the events. Perhaps it was payback time for Eleanor de Montfort breaking the vow of celibacy she had solemnly sworn before him.

Simon himself recalled the event twenty-three years later for the French court. In his account, it was the money that set Henry off:

> The King of England honoured me by giving me his sister; but shortly afterwards he was incensed by a debt which my lord Thomas, Count of Flanders, was claiming from me and for which he sued me at the court of Rome. The king wished me to pay; to which I replied that I was ready to do so, if I was legally the debtor; but I asked that justice should be done to me, as to the poorest man in the kingdom. He refused, with ugly and shameful words which it would be painful to recall.

This Thomas was another of the queen's uncles from Savoy. He was due to arrive at court in a week's time, seemingly only to visit and not to replace his brother William, who had left on a mission to shore up support for the papacy in its growing squabble with the emperor. Henry had tried to win William back by making him the new Bishop of Winchester, only the monks wouldn't have him, declaring he was a 'man of blood'. Henry would never see William again. He was poisoned in Viterbo that autumn, just as he was about to assume command of the papal army. The king was inconsolable. He ripped off his clothes and threw them into the fire, wailing to high heaven over his misfortune.

Thomas had recently become the Count of Flanders by marrying Joanna, the second of the widows Simon had courted. The match had been approved by the French court as part of its alliance with the papacy in the growing turf war in Italy between Pope Gregory IX and Emperor Frederick II. Technically, Provence was in Frederick's sphere of influence and he needed to keep the Western passes of the Alps, which crossed through Savoy, open to his troops. The French presumptuously considered Provence now to be in their sphere thanks to Louis' marriage to Margaret of Provence.

Henry was caught between a rock and a hard place, inasmuch as he was the brother-in-law of both Frederick and Louis. His despatch of English knights to serve in the emperor's army the year before had infuriated the pope, and Thomas was sure to bring that matter up during his visit. Henry was justifiably nervous and went out to meet Thomas with such warmth and humility that it drew derision from onlookers.

It was through the papacy and the murky world of medieval finance that Thomas became Simon's creditor. Eight years earlier Simon agreed to give Ranulf £200 for the return of the earldom of Leicester. When Ranulf's estate was settled, the money was assigned to Peter of Dreux, the French noble who talked Henry into making a stab at Normandy in 1230. Henry seems to have been bewitched by an alliance with this man, who held Brittany by right of his wife, and it ended up costing him £13,000 in subsidies before Peter went crawling back to the French. Henry didn't bear any grudges and even invited him to be one of Edward's godfathers. If Peter exchanged any words with Simon during that occasion, it was likely about the money he owed him, because Peter was planning to join Amaury on crusade and needed all the funds he could collect.

He had already taken steps to recover it by suing Montfort at the court in Rome. At first, the Curia tried threatening Simon with excommunication, then arranged for Thomas, now their point man in the war with Frederick, to assume the loan, probably at a reduced rate. Only it wasn't £200 anymore but £1,400, and that was just for Thomas. Peter was still claiming more than £300 as he looked at Simon across the baby in the font. Officially, the original amount was swollen seven times over by interest, but in all likelihood it included whatever was still outstanding for the purchase of the marital dispensation, money which, presumably, Simon said the king was good for. After all, they were family now.

When Henry learned of this, he went berserk and allowed old resentments about his sister's marriage to get the better of him. Only he didn't just target Simon for bribing the pope (which Henry knew about) and naming him as security (which, perhaps, he didn't), he also dragged his sister into it by insinuating, for all to hear, that she had broken her vow of chastity before she got married. There's no way of knowing if this was the archbishop's way of getting back at the Montforts or it was a concerted effort by the papacy and Savoyards to brand Simon a deadbeat and get rid of him because of his friendliness to Frederick. Even Queen Eleanor is disturbingly quiet in the record.

Conspiracy theories aside, Henry was notoriously prone to temper tantrums, and the long list of charges easily reflects a man sputtering out of control rather than a staged event. What was beyond doubt to those witnessing this particularly shabby episode was that neither Simon nor Eleanor were welcome at court any longer, and even then Henry wasn't through. Montfort continued:

> Then, the same day that he had invited us to the queen's churching, he ordered the men of the commune of London to arrest me at the inn where I was lodging and to take me off to the Tower; but Richard, who was there, would not allow that to happen at that moment. Seeing his great wrath and that he would not listen to reason, I left the country.

Richard's intervention was much like the role that Ranulf used to play when it was Hubert in the king's bad graces. He wasn't saving Simon from Henry as much as Henry from himself, and perhaps hoping to spare his sister any more humiliation. As Simon mentioned, he and Eleanor took a boat and left for France immediately, where presumably they stayed with his relatives. So quick and sudden was their exile that they were forced to leave their son behind with his wet nurse.

Simon poured his heart out in a letter to Grosseteste, who had only recently rebuked him for severity towards his alderman. The bishop promised to take the matter up with Henry and advised him not to despair. A little misery was a good thing now and then:

> For suffering is to the righteous what pruning is to the vines. May you, then, in keeping with what your name means, endure suffering humbly and obediently, and thereby climbed the steps of humility, as is consistent with the proper understanding of your surname, to the peak of the mighty mountain (mons fortis) ...

If Grosseteste approached Henry on his behalf, nothing had come of it by Christmas that year. At that time the king sent orders to his proctors in Rome to give 'our beloved uncle' Thomas their full support against one 'S. de Montfort'.

Little comfort though it was, Montfort wasn't the only member of the council purged that season. Two others were also dismissed, reportedly because both refused to sanction the king's intention of giving Uncle Thomas a cut of the duties on each sack of wool from England that passed through Flanders. Henry then went after Hubert de Burgh again, confirming once and for all that he was simply in a peevish mood. The charges against Simon paled in comparison to what Hubert had to endure, including the claim that he had even tried to slit the king's throat. The old man could do little more than just roll his eyes at the outlandish nonsense and let Henry help himself to his remaining possessions.

The tense atmosphere at court and the death of his wife Isabel in childbirth in January 1240 meant Richard resolved to finally set off on crusade. Among the lords sworn to accompany him was Isabel's brother Gilbert Marshal, but since he too had fallen out with the king, he was determined to reconcile before departing. Henry, however, was having none of it. Even though Marshal was grieving for his sister, Henry levelled accusations at him so demeaning that Paris thought it better not to record them. Not until the following year did he and the king make up. By then he had missed the crusade, and he was killed shortly afterward at a tournament in Hertford, one Henry had expressly forbidden.

Simon returned to England in April 1240 to raise money for his own crusade and to bring his young son Henry back to his mother. He found the king happy to see him, but that was just Henry being unable to make up his mind whether to support the emperor or the pope. Frederick had written him a curt letter, expressing surprise that Henry didn't oppose the pope's excommunication of him despite them being brothers-in-law. He also strenuously objected to Otto using England as a bank for the papacy and advised his expulsion. Henry was sufficiently frightened to plead with the pope for leniency towards Frederick, but the pontiff merely snapped that the English were hopeless.

Richard tried to steer a neutral course by departing for the east from Marseille, where he was the guest of Henry's father-in-law, the

Count of Provence. Montfort showed where he stood on the matter by deciding to go directly overland through Italy as Frederick's guest. Eleanor, who had given birth in France to their second son Simon, accompanied him with their two children even though she was pregnant again. Frederick lent them a palace at Brindisi, where presumably Eleanor and her sister Isabella were reunited. The only thing known for sure is that Isabella met Richard one more time, while he was on his way home from crusade, but only after they were granted permission by Frederick. She would die the next year in childbirth.

For the unwarlike Richard, the crusade provided ample opportunity to bring his true gifts of wheeling and dealing to bear. In November 1239 Amaury de Montfort, never able to live up to his father's legend, got himself captured in Gaza when he tried to emulate a secretive but successful raid carried out a week earlier by Peter of Dreux. Already close to fifty years old at the time, his imprisonment was made all the harsher when he refused to name names to the sultan. He would spend nearly eighteen months locked away before Richard used his wealth to ransom him and the eighty other captured French knights, as well as arranging the burials of those not so fortunate.

It would be the last time the Montfort brothers saw each other. Amaury accompanied Richard homeward through Frederick's territories before falling ill in Rome, barely two months into his release, and died there in June 1241.

The only thing Simon is known to have achieved in the Holy Land was making a good impression. Somewhere around the time Amaury died, a petition was sent to Frederick asking him to name Simon the governor of the region until the emperor's son grew up. Nothing is quite as remarkable about this man as the ease with which he convinced others of his leadership qualities. In this case, it also helped that the Lord of Tyre was his cousin, Philip de Montfort, the son of the elder Simon's brother Guy, another renowned crusader, killed in 1228 during the second phase of the Albigensian Crusade. Philip was part of the efforts by a local faction, the Ibelins, to wrest more control from the emperor, and figured this Anglo-French nobleman, already three times a guest at Frederick's court, would have some influence. In the end nothing came of the proposal and Simon returned in the autumn of 1241 with the Duke of Burgundy. He probably had to go in that direction because Henry was in the region, at the head of a shaky coalition to recover Poitou from the French.

The king had been lured into making a second attempt at regaining England's Continental empire by his mother Isabella. She had left England in 1218 to give her eight-year-old daughter Joan in marriage to Hugh Lusignan, the Count of La Marche. He was the son of the same Hugh that Isabella herself was supposed to marry when John whisked her away, losing that Continental empire in the process. Thirty-two years old at the time, Isabella could see that if she joined her homeland of Angoulême to La Marche, marrying Hugh Junior in place of her daughter, she would finally get to play a role in the affairs around her, something John always denied her.

The regency council was not at all happy about her scheme and gave in only after she refused to return her daughter otherwise. Joan was retrieved and married to the King of Scotland, but she would yearn for her family, in a way her mother never did, till her dying days. When she died in March 1238, it was in the arms of Henry and Richard. These two had just made up following their spat over Simon and Eleanor's marriage, and Joan's illness had helped to bring them closer together.

It was strange that Henry should have trusted his mother at all. In 1225 Louis VIII had seized Poitou from England and had invited Hugh to do the same with Gascony. Richard of Cornwall was then sixteen years old, but as the official overlord of Gascony he had been sent there with an army to beat his stepfather back. Then, in 1230, Henry had been counting on Isabella and Hugh helping him to retake Normandy and Poitou, but like the other French nobles, they followed his lead: when he feasted, they feasted; when he went home, they went home.

Isabella and Hugh had nine children and were already receiving a pension from the French monarchy to coexist in peace. Louis IX upset all that by investing his brother Alphonse with Poitou, technically making him superior to Hugh, who was twice his age. Isabella, a former queen but now a countess, had also been snubbed by her rival Blanche of Castile, now queen dowager. Their pride wounded, Hugh and Isabella began putting together a coalition of disaffected nobles and potentates that included Henry's cousin Raymond, the Count of Toulouse, King James I of Aragon, and naturally Peter of Dreux.

The King of England was approached because he was family and had a legal claim to Poitou. They would be happy to recover it for him if he covered the costs. He didn't have to raise an army or even put in an appearance. All he had to do was send money, meaning barrels full of silver pennies, since that was the only currency in circulation. Henry, however, loved being in the thick of things and couldn't resist a chance to redeem himself after his inglorious march on the Continent twelve years earlier. He would come with an armed contingent, and, yes, bring the silver.

In order to get the money, Henry had to call a parliament to ask the barons for a tax. They first asked what had happened to the last tax. He should still have it since they did not authorise him to spend it. More worrisome to them was the five-year truce with France. The king should at least wait until it expired before going ahead with this scheme. When he got nowhere with the barons as a group, he summoned them the next day, one by one, as 'penitents going to confession'. He was unable to win all of them over and probably didn't know why he even bothered. As usual, they were against everything he took in hand. He was forced to fill his barrels with money taken from Ireland, the Jews and the monasteries. With thirty barrels of silver thus collected, the fleet sailed with 150 knights in May 1242.

The expedition also included Queen Eleanor and six earls. A writ was sent out to a seventh earl, Simon de Montfort, to join them at the mouth of the Gironde. He did, but told the king he was not inclined to do him any favours until 'several acts of injustice' were redressed. He was still nursing a grudge after Henry distrained his lands to pay off Thomas of Savoy without giving him a proper hearing. Henry agreed to compensate him and threw in an extra £70 to secure his service.

Neither Simon nor the other military men present, mainly the earls of Salisbury and Norfolk, could save what was clearly a doomed enterprise from the start. Peter of Dreux had already betrayed their plans, so by the time Henry announced he was annulling the truce, Louis had already raised an army and was swallowing up Hugh's castles. Before Henry knew it, the French were ready to swallow him up as well. He turned on Hugh, demanding that the man he called 'father' produce the army he had promised him. Hugh merely shrugged that he had made no promises, and that if he had it was all his wife's doing.

Richard could sense a hopeless cause much faster than Henry. Dressing up as a pilgrim, he went to ask Louis for a truce. He was well received by the French, grateful that he had rescued so many of them from the Holy Land. Also, with it being a Sunday Louis had no choice but to grant him a truce, although only for that day. Fair enough, said Richard, and he raced back to camp to tell Henry words to the effect of 'Let's get the hell out of here!'

Louis gave them their one day and took off in pursuit. A fierce rearguard action in the vineyards, where Montfort was named among those to distinguish themselves, allowed Henry to make good his escape. It was the only real skirmish of the campaign, which was otherwise even more pathetic than the expedition of 1230. Henry came, he looked, he retreated, and didn't stop until he reached Bordeaux, losing all of his treasure and dignity along the way. He might have been driven into the sea had the French army not been decimated by dysentery.

Disgusted by the king's ineptitude, Simon told him that he should be taken away and locked up like Charles the Simple. He even suggested they use a house in Windsor, where the windows were safely barred with iron. For Henry it was an unforgiveable, if well-deserved, insult, and he made sure to recall it in the charges he levelled against Simon twenty years later in front of, oddly enough, Louis.

'Father' was nowhere to be seen. Hugh had secretly gone over to the King of France under terms that not only forced him to surrender some castles and his pension, but ordered him and that other traitor Peter of Dreux to attack their ally Raymond of Toulouse. So Henry got no help from the southern quarter, either.

He then alienated Richard in a fiasco typical of his weathercock nature. All tears for Richard securing the one-day truce, Henry granted him Gascony as his reward. The queen was dismayed that he could do something so rash and urged him to revoke it. The resulting quarrel grew so heated that Richard left in disgust, and nearly didn't make it when his ship foundered in a storm. Other barons also began going home, but Simon was among those that stayed behind.

Also there in Bordeaux were Henry's allies Raymond and James. As a boy, James had been betrothed to Simon's sister Amicia and was living with the Montforts, perhaps playing with young Simon, when his father Peter and Raymond's father Raymond teamed up against Simon's father Simon at the Battle of Muret and got the worst of it. Now the sons were teaming up to have a sneaky sort of revenge by whispering to Henry that he would be best rid of Simon. Henry seems to have appreciated the fact that Montfort had remained with him while Richard and other barons took off, and disregarded their advice, no doubt much to his chagrin later.

Henry was thinking of renewing operations when Raymond made his peace with Louis, and he finally gave up all hope of ever recovering Poitou. He concluded another five-year truce with Louis and left, all told spending £40,000 on another wasted adventure. The one good thing to come out of it was a marriage. It had been arranged for Raymond to marry Sanchia of Provence, Margaret and Eleanor's sister, thereby uniting Toulouse and Provence against further encroachment by France. There was no way that it could go forward after Raymond's useless performance, so Henry wanted Sanchia for Richard. That way two of the four Provencal daughters would be married into the English royal family, as compared to one, albeit the eldest, for the French family. Where he couldn't beat Louis in the field, he would do so at the altar. Nothing, moreover, gave Henry more pleasure than festivities like weddings, so in September 1243 he returned to England with the queen in not such a depressed state of mind as his recent misfortunes might suggest.

Richard had met Sanchia when he stopped in Provence on his way to crusade. Described as incomparably beautiful, Sanchia was as far apart in age from Richard as Eleanor was from Henry. The marriage was arranged by the latest Savoyard to join Henry's court, Peter of Savoy, another uncle and the smoothest talker of them all. So captivated was Henry by this 'little Charlemagne', as Peter was known, that he gave him the honour of Richmond outright, a gift meant to have gone to Peter of Dreux before he reneged on every deal he ever made. Peter of Savoy had help in arranging the marriage from Peter d'Aigueblanche, a Savoyard protégé raised by the king to become Bishop of Hereford. He would guide Henry through the worst of his foreign policy decisions in the next decade.

The wedding took place at Westminster in November 1243. A magnificent feast was prepared, much of it paid for by the Jews. One in particular, Aaron of York, was forced to contribute £3 in gold and £2,800 in silver, but neither he nor his family received an invitation. The bride was accompanied by her mother, Beatrice, another beauty and the sister of all these uncles at court. Not surprisingly, Henry seems to have been quite taken with his mother-in-law. He made gifts to her, loans to her husband, and didn't take it at all amiss when she brought up the financial situation of Simon and Eleanor. She considered it unfair that the king should lavish so much land and offices on her brothers, men he had only just met, but had not even bothered to provide his sister with a marriage portion.

How Beatrice became involved is a matter of conjecture. Perhaps the Montforts approached her, perhaps her daughter the queen was grateful to Simon for sticking firmly by her husband's side, all insults aside, when she was gravely ill after giving birth in Bordeaux. She could also anticipate that a man with Montfort's military skill was going to be needed back in France if they were ever going to secure Gascony for little Edward someday. However Beatrice came to take up the matter, her charm worked magic. Henry promised to give the Montforts £333 annually as a marriage portion and pardoned nearly £2,000 worth of debts. He also cancelled £110 they owed to the family of the recently deceased David of Oxford. Given Simon's denouncement of usury, his resort to Jewish moneylending in this case was an indication of how desperate their financial situation was.

The king also made himself surety again for the payment of Eleanor's dower, which had passed to the next Marshal brother, Walter, and had gone unpaid while they were abroad. An even grander display of affection was granting them custody of Kenilworth Castle, one of the greatest in the Midlands, as their home.

Henry may have been in a giving mood, but he knew he was going to have a fight on his hands with the barons. He came back from his ignoble failure in Poitou with a debt of £15,000 and he was about to embark on a great building program that included Westminster Abbey. Parliament had denied him a tax before he left for France and they would probably refuse another request without him making concessions, something he found counter to true kingship. He would need a core group of councillors he could depend on, and Simon had proven his loyalty unflinchingly before Henry shamelessly humiliated him at the churching. It would be just like Henry to think that was all in the past now, that everything could be just as it was before. Perhaps it could, but it was still going to cost him.

4

On the Margins of Favour
1244–1248

Simon and Eleanor returned to England after nearly four years abroad with a growing brood of children. The eldest, Henry, was five, followed by another Simon, who was born in France around April 1240. Both boys were with their mother in Italy waiting for their father to return from crusade. Amaury was born sometime in 1242 or 1243, making him their first child after brother Amaury's death and Simon's return from the Holy Land. The fourth son, Guy, could not have been born much later than 1244 if we assume he had to be around twenty when later given posts of responsibility under his father. In addition there were three more children: a daughter who died in childbirth, and Richard and Eleanor, both of whom were probably born around the turn of the next decade.

The records offer only glimpses of their upbringing and education. It was normal among noble families of the thirteenth century to place the boys for some time in the households of other peers and churchmen. Henry, as the eldest and heir, was put under the care and guidance of Grosseteste, both for learning letters and good manners. Amaury, destined to be the most scholarly of the boys, joined him as part of his preparation for a career in the Church. Both he and Henry left behind evidence that they wrote in an elegant hand, a rare achievement in an age where the ability to write was unusual even for many who could read.

Later events would show the second son, Simon, to be clumsy, unreliable and inept in matters of importance, more like his uncle Henry than his namesake father. On the other hand, the warlike Guy was every bit his father and mother in temperament and purpose.

All four boys would be a source of pride and disappointment for their parents, and fodder for their enemies, but to the end and beyond they remained fiercely loyal to one another.

Eleanor, we can be sure, ran the household, which usually involved keeping everyone fed. Grain always topped the list of stores in her accounts. Most of the bread baked from it, unleavened in those days, was consumed directly, but slices were left to harden to form plates. When soaked with gravy, they made nice handouts for the poor waiting outside.

Next on the list came wine for the family and their guests, while servants were given beer brewed from whatever cereal was available. Hops had yet to be discovered, so spices like pepper or fennel were usually added for zest. Meals were typically of fish like herring, cod or whale, accompanied by peas and onions boiled into a nice gruel. Apples and assorted dried fruit formed dessert. Eleanor's accounts show other purchases like poultry, eggs, milk, cheese, rice, cinnamon, ginger and almonds, as well as garments, parchment and other household accessories.

Much of what we know about family life in the Montfort household comes from the letters of Adam Marsh, a cleric based in Oxford who turned his back on his family's high political standing to join the Franciscan order in 1232. The Franciscans had arrived in England eight years earlier and gained many converts with their pastoral approach to salvation. Many noble families were drawn to their teachings of poverty and good works, if only because they asked for nothing in return. The Montforts were introduced to Marsh through Grosseteste and he soon became both a friend and spiritual counsellor.

Marsh did not hold back from chiding the Montforts for what he considered marital insubordination. To Simon he wrote, 'Better is a patient man than a strong man, and he who can rule his own temper than he who storms a city.' Eleanor, in particular, he took to task for failing to be obedient and submissive. She was too assertive, too quick to anger and too lavish in her dress. He warned her about reports of improprieties that are 'soiling your reputation not a little', and advised her to follow 'the example of praiseworthy matrons'.

Admonitions like these – and Marsh lectured everyone – have

been used in modern days to paint Eleanor as something of a shrew. Some of these letters have their origins in a particularly difficult time for the Montforts. It seems that Simon was beginning to feel pangs of conscience about his marriage, an indication that, even if he didn't seduce Eleanor directly, he definitely had a hand in breaking her vow of celibacy. How much of this owed to the inward-looking preaching of the friars cannot be determined, but it does suggest a deeply introspective individual conscientious of his mark on the world. His desire for penance would lead him not only to take the cross again, but also to abstain from sexual relations with his wife. That would help to explain the nearly six-year gap between the ages of the older and younger children.

Eleanor was as devotional as he was and probably shared the same doubts, for she also took the cross with him. It wasn't only family squabbles, however, that Marsh concerned himself with. He gave the couple reports about their children's progress in Grosseteste's household. When the good bishop asked if he might not retain the services of Eleanor's cook, she told Marsh that she would be happy to put any of her staff at his disposal.

A nice vignette of a medieval family going to church can be found on Palm Sunday 1245 when Simon and Eleanor took their two eldest boys to Waverly Abbey, not nine miles away from their home at Odiham Castle, to listen to the sermon and watch the procession. It was a rare occasion indeed for the monks to welcome a woman in their environs, a princess no less, and they were honoured by her gift of an altar cloth, later followed by £45 which they used to buy an additional 150 acres of land. The abbot remained a firm friend of the family until the end.

As with any couple, then or now, their marriage endured almost steady financial strain. Henry helped here and there with gifts of wine and deer, and in 1245 he sold the wardship of the newborn Umfraville heir to the Montforts for £333 a year, basically offsetting the £333 Henry agreed to pay as a marriage portion. This entitled the Montforts to the profits of the Umfraville estates until the ward, who lived with them, came of age twenty years later. Wardships were lucrative forms of patronage, and Richard of Cornwall, already one of the richest men in the kingdom, was angry he didn't get this one.

But Richard was no warrior and Henry needed one like Montfort for the expedition he was planning against Wales that autumn. Simon went, but Henry could again bring himself to do no more than build a castle and unleash his Irish irregulars on the unfortunate inhabitants. Richard actually lent Henry £2,000 to undertake the campaign and lost four of his household in the fighting, but he was still defamed in the ranks for favouring the Welsh, supposedly because the king denied him, again at the urging of the queen, another major land grant.

Money was fine, but what Simon and Eleanor really wanted, what every family wanted, was land. They would have at least four boys to provide for and so little of their combined wealth could be passed on to them. Instead of constantly fighting with the Marshals over the dower payment, they wanted Henry to simply offer them something comparable in land, and he had to have plenty available. At least three dozen Savoyards, total strangers to the realm, had come and received land from the king, and Peter of Savoy for one was given the lands of Richmond under extraordinary conditions. He was allowed to give or bequeath them to any of his brothers or kinsmen, later expanded to include anyone at all. By contrast Eleanor was forbidden to do anything with her dower manors other than collect the rent. Even selling the woods to raise cash was forbidden.

Things then got worse when Walter Marshal died at the end of 1245, and he was followed to his grave by his brother Anselm not even a month later. And like that, the stock of Marshal boys, five in all, had died childless. The estate was divided among the sisters and their heirs, many married into the families of the higher nobility. The Earl of Norfolk was a Marshal grandson, and so too were the earls of Gloucester, Surrey and Derby. They stood to inherit the wealth of these lands, many of them in Ireland, 30 per cent of which should have gone to Eleanor fourteen years earlier.

When Henry was unable to cover the defaulted payments of her dower, he advised the Montforts to sue the heirs. So they did in 1247, but no verdict was given in the case. Henry probably quashed it out of fear he would lose the support of the four earls above if they were forced to disgorge any of the estate to one of their own. By encouraging his sister and brother-in-law to take action, then denying them satisfaction, Henry had greatly offended them. The king made them look foolish in front of their peers, and so himself weak and pathetic in their eyes. Henry's incompetence in this matter, his unwillingness to make good his sister's claims once and for all, would remain a flashpoint throughout all the troubles ahead.

His own financial difficulties were understandably of more concern to him. Forced to ask Parliament for another tax on movables, he himself presented his case to the assembly of bishops, abbots, earls and barons. He needed to make war on Scotland, he insisted, and the quasi-war in Poitou had nearly bankrupted him. Parliament's reply was to set up a committee of twelve, including Richard and Simon, to draw up terms.

Since Henry had disregarded the last set of conditions imposed on him, this time the barons upped the ante. They wanted to restore the offices of justiciar, which was still vacant after ten years, and chancellor, which had more or less lapsed after the king unceremoniously deprived Ralph Neville of the great seal six years earlier in 1238. Neville had recently died, and the magnates missed the way he zealously guarded the seal as a check on Henry's personal rule.

They also demanded that four councillors serve as 'preservers of liberties' by maintaining a continuous watch over the king. Last but not least, these men were to be chosen by 'common consent', not by the king alone. The reason, they added, was because the chancellor had received the seal 'by the common counsel of the kingdom'.

Such was the 'paper constitution' of 1244. Even if its origins went back to 1238, to the baronial crisis caused by Simon and Eleanor's marriage, it was a truly revolutionary attempt to 'bridle' the king with constitutional controls. Parliament was telling the king they were not happy with the way he was doing business, that with all due respect he needed their advice and active involvement in order to ensure the security and greatness of the kingdom. In simpler terms, if we are rich, you are rich; if we are poor, you are poor. From now on, there would be no overt favouritism, no overseas misadventures, no taxation without the consent of Parliament.

Henry's first reaction had to be disbelief. Of all the effrontery, of course Neville had been given the great seal by common counsel.

Henry had only been a boy then, eleven years old, and the country was ruled by a regency council. It was an insult to think that at thirty-seven years of age he was still not fit to choose his own ministers. But he knew he had his work cut out for him if he was going to get any money without retreating from the benevolent absolutism that marked his rule. He tried to break up the united front by lobbying the barons and prelates for six straight days, even producing a letter from the pope pleading on his behalf. At one point he formed his own committee, also including Simon, to soften up the bishops and abbots, but Parliament remained evasive to his entreaties. The king didn't get his tax and the paper constitution remained just that: paper.

Unwilling to yield even a little to parliamentary control, Henry was again forced to fall back on his feudal rights. As king, he had the right to call out the army any time. Those who didn't want to go could pay a scutage in lieu of military service. That had been the case in Poitou when his silver ran out. Now he demanded a feudal aid, which was a special tax for matters that affected the king personally. When Richard the Lionheart got himself captured fifty years earlier, England had to raise a true king's ransom of £100,000 to free him. Henry didn't want that much, just £1 per knight, to save up for the marriage of his five-year-old daughter Margaret to the future Alexander III of Scotland. The nobles and clergy could live with it, inasmuch as it averted war with their northerly neighbour and payment was easy to avoid in any case. With approximately 6,000 knights scattered about the realm, the aid should have raised £6,000, but it's unlikely if even half this figure reached the exchequer.

Royal revenue at this time was about £36,500 a year, ten times what a rich earl might earn, and not all of it was wasted on misadventures and favourites. Henry's court was spending £20 per day on food and drink alone. Parliament had to know that if they did not make up any shortfalls, he would exploit other, less savoury sources. With the Jews he was merciless, taxing them at will under the threat of imprisonment or expulsion. His sheriffs were given ever higher increments of money due to the Crown to fill and were ordered not to disappoint at the exchequer. The country was flooded with eyres, those circuit-style courts meant to mete out local justice but which instead levied fines left and right to generate revenue. It was a classic catch-22 situation. Parliament wasn't going to vote him any money until he stopped these abuses, but he wasn't going to stop them until they gave him money.

The magnates and bishops who rejected his plea generally had access to him when he wasn't holding a grudge against them. That wasn't the case for minor barons and clerics, whose disaffection included an ever-swelling bureaucracy. When the offices of justiciar and chancellor were filled, there was always a chance of seeking redress through them, if only in exchange for favours. Now they had to run the gauntlet of an insular court surrounded by professional clerks with beady eyes and stiff necks, a truly shadowy government. It's very likely that when the king put in an appearance at Parliament before these middling lords, when they finally had him in their grasps, their reaction was indicative of a future, unruly House of Commons. 'Explain yourself, sir!'

If Simon enjoyed watching the king squirm, he kept it to himself. As part of rehabilitating himself in the eyes of his brother-in-law, Henry exempted him from paying his share of the feudal aid and resumed making gifts of deer and timber to him and Eleanor. Montfort's ambiguous role in the paper constitution, however, demonstrated that he was his own man now. He was ready to reciprocate service for favours, but no more. Sobered by Henry disposing of him on a whim, he would never again be one of his intimates or a steadfast member of the court. He had moved closer to the spiritual world of friends like Adam Marsh and Robert Grosseteste, the Bishop of Lincoln, and it was the latter's lead in denying the king his tax that perhaps showed him the possibilities of reform and defiance.

The king had found out what it was like to tangle with a man like Grosseteste when a church benefice in his diocese became vacant and he gave it to John Mansel, a wily clerk who had taken a hold of his imagination much the way the Savoyards had. Mansel seemed to have that effect on people. When his leg was crushed during the Poitou campaign, two poets saw fit to glorify his sacrifice, with one of them threatening the surgeons if poor John never walked again. Others, however, despised him for his crafty brilliance and the ease with which he collected favour after favour from the king.

This benefice was just one of many already given to Mansel, and Grosseteste was angry because he felt the king was encroaching on his authority. Henry tried to justify himself by saying it was what the pope wanted, but the bishop refused to back down. Seeing that he was growing 'unbecomingly violent', Henry gave in, which was just as well for Mansel, as the king found him another rich church in no time.

Henry spent much of these years quarrelling with churchmen. Following the death of Peter des Roches in 1238, the bishopric of Winchester went vacant for six years because he refused to accept the man chosen by the monks for the post. He was none other than Ralph Neville, his former chancellor and keeper of the seal, whom he now denounced as 'impetuous, passionate and perverse'. The monks next tried to install William Raleigh, the Bishop of Norwich, in the post, a man called 'wise and circumspect' by Matthew Paris despite having four Jews hanged for allegedly circumcising a Christian boy. He was another close associate of Henry's who fell into disfavour when he refused to let the king decide who was going to be bishop. Their dispute dragged on for years, with Henry locking Raleigh out of Winchester and sending his attendants to bully the monks. It took papal intervention to reconcile them, and while Henry's principles may have been in earnest, he was nevertheless content to pocket all the money of the diocese that went to the Crown in the absence of a bishop.

Where he did get his way was in the case of the successor for Edmund of Abingdon, the Archbishop of Canterbury who, weary of the struggles of this world, died in 1240 in self-imposed exile in France. Henry wanted to give the office to the last of his wife's uncles to come and reap the bounty of England, twenty-five-year-old Boniface of Savoy, the youngest and most handsome of the lot. He was an incredibly odd choice given the choleric old men who preceded him, but the monks, on probation after endlessly fighting with Edmund, could only shake their heads in protest. The pope, who was in the process of deposing Frederick, welcomed the young warlike cleric among the senior prelates of Christianity and detained him for his own uses for several years. Just how warlike the English clergy would discover when Boniface finally settled down in the late 1240s to run his diocese.

It took the underhanded actions of the papacy, in fact, to unite Henry and his barons and prelates for the last time in his reign. The issue, of course, was money and how much of it was being siphoned out of England by the Church – as much as £45,000 a year by Grosseteste's estimate. Going back to Henry's minority, the pope had been in the habit of filling Church offices in England with his Italian friends and relatives as an easy way for them to make a living. In 1231 resentment against this practice led one local knight and a group of followers to ride around in the night harassing these foreign churchmen. Henry, who was forever grateful to the papacy for saving his throne, was scandalised and, as usual, tried to pin the blame on Hubert de Burgh. But as the papacy's struggle with the empire demanded ever more money, Pope Gregory IX got caught secretly trying to recruit the monks of Peterborough as his private fundraisers, leading Matthew Paris to describe him as a 'common brazen-faced strumpet'. Gregory was now dead, hustled into his grave by the emperor imprisoning his legates, including Otto, and razing a castle belonging to his favourite relations.

In 1244 the new pope, Innocent IV, was even more brazen. He sent an agent by the name of Master Martin to England to demand the money outright. Martin didn't even waste time on formalities. Any prelate bearing less than £20 was turned out and he installed his own family members in newly created vacancies. When the Abbot of Peterborough refused to cave, Martin ratted on him. The abbot was ordered to appear before the pope, who subjected him to such abuse and insults that the old man withered away in grief.

The barons had enough of the unpleasant little clerk and decided to take matters into their own hands. A group of them, gathered for a tournament in Dunstable, sent an envoy to tell Martin he had three days to leave the country or be cut to pieces. Thoroughly frightened, Martin asked Henry to ensure his safe passage. At first, Henry told him to go to hell, then figured the sooner they were rid of him the better. He had his steward of the palace escort the trembling clerk to the coast with the advice to never return.

At the March parliament in 1246, the king sent a letter to Innocent complaining about all this extortion. The barons and clergymen who didn't think he had it in him were soon disappointed, however.

At the next parliament, held in July, Henry completely gave in, presumably at the prodding of his brother, who had been bought off again. Years before, Richard had received the papal privilege of collecting money for his crusade. Now, in the wake of Henry's unusual obstinacy, the papacy granted Richard this privilege again, even though he had no intention of ever going back to the Holy Land. With his usual efficiency, he hired an Italian agent to run a network of friars to work the countryside, persuading people to take the cross, regardless of age, sex or health, then release them from their vow for a fee. In this way, he collected as much as £1,000 a year. The Earl of Salisbury also received the privilege, but collected far less money. He complained about it to the pope, not least because he did plan to go back.

Richard's betrayal was especially shocking because the barons had sent their own protest to the pope about the extortion and his name topped the list. Second came Simon's name, ahead of other leading nobles, probably only to emphasise his position as the king's brother-in-law. Otherwise he was little involved at court. The gifts of deer and timber again lapsed, suggesting Henry was peeved that he didn't want to assume a bigger role. In 1247 he undertook a secret mission to France for Henry which to this day has remained secret. He was back in October for the king's favourite holiday, the feast of St Edward, and the truly special event Henry had concocted for it.

He had acquired a crystal vial of holy blood, authenticated by the masters of the Templars and Hospitallers, even the patriarch of Jerusalem himself, and he planned to dedicate it to the Confessor. As usual, he went all out, fasting and praying the night before and then appearing in humble sackcloth at St Paul's the next morning bearing the vial high above his head. He carried it barefoot the mile or so to Westminster, never taking his eyes off the blood or heaven, even across uneven patches of road. The whole point was to keep up with Louis and the French, whose collection of relics had grown to include a piece of the True Cross and the Crown of Thorns itself. There was also a political purpose to the escapade, one that didn't bode well for the kingdom or for Simon and Eleanor in particular.

In 1246 Isabella of Angoulême died, virtually walled up inside a nunnery after being implicated in a plot to poison Louis. Since the Lusignans were now thoroughly disgraced, five of their nine children made their way to England at the invitation of their half-brother, the king. Henry immediately married two of them into the English nobility. Alice was given to the young Earl of Surrey and William de Valence to Joan de Munchensi, a Marshal granddaughter who stood to inherit a huge slice of the contested estate. Henry knighted William as part of the holy blood ceremony to let everyone know he was the new favourite.

By all accounts, the Lusignan siblings were an ill-bred, ill-tempered lot. Guy announced their presence with authority by arranging a tournament against Richard de Clare, Earl of Gloucester and Richard of Cornwall's stepson. Peter of Savoy had done the same after his arrival in 1241 when he challenged Roger Bigod, the Earl of Norfolk, to a tournament to see who was superior, the English or the aliens. Worried the aliens would get the worst of it, Henry tried to rig that match, but had to settle for cancelling it when his intrigues got nowhere. This latest one he also forbade, but William de Valence, the youngest of the brothers, was eager to show off his skills and entered another tournament. Only his daring showed he had been worth knighting, for he was thrown to the ground and kept there.

Henry was determined to promote the Lusignans at court, both to keep a firm hold over events in France and because he could be absolutely assured of their loyalty. He had thought the same could be said about the Savoyards, and then his mother-in-law Beatrice blindsided him by marrying her youngest daughter Beatrice to Louis' youngest brother Charles of Anjou, thereby evening the score. Two daughters for England, two daughters for France. She even twisted the knife by turning sixteen castles in Provence over to Louis, even though Henry had been maintaining them at a cost of £2,700 a year. When word of his displeasure reached her ears, Beatrice dismissed it with singular ingratitude, muttering that her only regret was that she had married any of her daughters to the English.

To top it off, Beatrice's brother Boniface, the Archbishop of Canterbury, had the gall to annul one of Henry's appointments. Only the sweet nothings of his queen could save her family from his fury, and just in time too, because Peter of Savoy had arranged for two nondescript ladies from Provence to step ashore in the footprints of the Lusignans to be united in marriage with two young English noblemen. But it was only a matter of time before the sophisticated Frenchmen of Savoy clashed with the uncouth Frenchmen of Lusignan, pitting the king's family against the queen's. For now, the Savoyards were too savvy to voice anything openly, but that other Frenchman, Simon de Montfort, was a different matter, especially now that William was given a chunk of the Marshal estate at his wife's expense. The chance of any immediate confrontation was averted when, in 1248, Simon again took the cross, and this time Eleanor did so as well.

Unlike the previous crusade, there was a sense of urgency to this one because in 1244 Jerusalem had been overrun by an Asiatic people who themselves had been driven from their homeland by the Mongols. Simon's cousin Philip, who had tried to make him the governor of that territory, was one of the few to escape alive. The pope put out a call to liberate Jerusalem yet again, and Louis, thankful to have recovered from a near-fatal illness, vowed to go.

Simon and Eleanor may have been motivated by a desire to quell any lingering pangs of conscience about their marriage, but Simon's military standing and experience made him the best choice to lead the English contingent. Yet he did not go because Henry had another important assignment for him. It was a turn of events that would have a catastrophic effect on their already brittle relationship. In the end, it was the Earl of Salisbury who led the English forces. And he didn't return.

5

The Trial
1249–1253

Henry did more than just lick his wounds after being chased off the field by Louis in 1242. He had been in danger of losing control over Gascony even before he tried to retake Poitou. This last sliver of the old Angevin empire of his grandparents Henry II and Eleanor of Aquitaine was like a 'patchwork quilt' of feuds and alliances, home to an endless turf war conducted by rival clans. He spent his more than one year in the region trying to buy off the local petty lords. One of these was Gaston de Bearn, who showed up with his 'monstrous' mother and troop of knights for a handout. It cost Henry £20 a day for their loyalty, but Gaston and his men no sooner pocketed the money than they got back on their horses and again ravaged the countryside at will. All the disorder and pillaging made the province vulnerable to the ambitions of the Spanish kingdoms in the south or, worse, of the French in the north. Henry knew he had to make it secure if he and Queen Eleanor were going to give it to Edward someday and thereby continue the fiction of the Angevin empire.

The king and queen turned to Simon to instil order down there, and for several other reasons. First and foremost was his fame as a warrior, a clear indication that they knew only a force of arms could achieve peace in the region. As the king's brother-in-law, Montfort's authority, together with his family name, would undoubtedly carry more weight and fear than the Crown officials who came before him. Just as important was to know the people you were up against, and no one at court had more experience in the south of France than Simon.

That familiarity, however, was a drawback in inducing him to take the job. He knew it was going to be an arduous slog and saw no sense in commencing any enterprise in which he was not fully empowered to bring to a successful conclusion, much the way his father had balked before assuming command of the crusading army against the Cathars. He demanded a fixed term of seven years to run the duchy with adequate support in men and money, and he wanted it in writing. His terms were stiff, but that was no problem for Queen Eleanor if we can believe another yarn about her. When a copy of Magna Carta was accidentally burned, it was said she rejoiced in believing that the provisions contained therein had also gone up in smoke. Just burn the agreement with Simon and it no longer applied.

Simon's first task was to neutralise any external threats. The truce with France was extended and an agreement reached with the King of Navarre to submit his dispute with Henry to arbitration. The regional metropolis, Bordeaux, was ruled at that time by two hostile families that had concluded their own truce before he arrived, so he was able to take his force of knights around the countryside to lay down the law. There would be no more seizing collateral without a court order ('the beginning of all wars' in his opinion) or carrying around arms. His proscription of highwaymen, who were otherwise known as noblemen, met with fierce resistance. He had two petty lords arrested and held in lieu of trial for heavy ransoms, which was the medieval version of a fine. The biggest brigand of them all, Gaston de Bearn, he chose to isolate for the time being, leading to gripes from townspeople who wanted him locked away.

They were also irked when informed they would have to go to him to swear fealty to the king instead of the other way around. Now he was running roughshod over their rights, too, they claimed. But Montfort made it clear that he was there to recover the king's rights, and they were just going to have to cooperate until that happened. When he returned to England for Christmas, he was hailed by Henry and the court for bringing the unruly land under control. In the eyes of Matthew Paris, he had showed himself worthy of his father in all respects.

He remained in England until June 1249, crossing over with Salisbury's contingent on its way to the crusade. He had no sooner returned to Gascony and gone to bed when fighting broke out between the rival families in Bordeaux on the eve of the mayoral election. He managed to quell the disturbance, but was accused by one family, the Delsolers, of favouring the other, the Colombines. As in any feudal relationship, the Delsolers had the right to appeal their case to the overlord of the duchy, Henry, who acted on the advice of his council and ordered Simon to return the vineyards and property he had seized from them. Henry then took a more sober view after hearing the Colombine side of the story and agreed to have the Delsolers stand trial, though not without adding his concerns in a very informative letter to his 'faithful and beloved Simon de Montfort':

> Act energetically and unremittingly, see that no excessive indulgence encourages the criminals to begin again, but that the punishment be not greater than the offence, as befits a consistent and just judge. Finally, in order that the hostages shall be secure while the process is pending, we have found them safe-conducts, so do not treat them as suspects, that the judge himself be not suspected.

Henry may have been worried that Simon was proceeding too high-handedly, but one outside observer, a chaplain in the service of Louis' brother Alphonse of Poitiers, was impressed that the province had been tamed. He had come to take up matters of litigation for his patron, who was away on crusade, and wrote him that 'all obey Montfort and dare undertake naught against him'. Simon knew better even as he followed the chaplain back to France, where he went to represent Henry at *parlement* in Paris. On 26 March 1250, he wrote to the king, in what is the only letter of his to survive, explaining that all in fact was not well:

> Sir, I have heard for certain that some knights of Gascony have provided themselves with everything to demand their lands by war. And they are certainly leagued together, they and their friends; and I fully understand that they will begin soon to overrun the land; but what force they will have I cannot as yet be at all sure. And because the great men of the land bear me such

ill will, because I uphold your rights and those of the poor against them, there would be danger and shame to me, and great damage to you, if I were to return to the land without instructions from you and without speaking to you.

Henry knew exactly to whom he was referring. At the end of the preceding year, Simon had captured Gaston de Bearn and despatched him to England for trial. Since this was the same man who had ravaged the king's territory after freely taking his money, Simon might have thought Henry would deal with him severely. But in an incredible blunder so characteristic of Henry, he pardoned and released Gaston on his word to conduct himself with noblesse. He may have been swayed by his wife, who was Gaston's cousin, or he was hoping to win him and the other troublemakers over by showing the kind hand of the king as opposed to the backhand of his viceroy. The result was catastrophic, as Simon now found he had a guerrilla war on his hands, and as usual the peasants were made to suffer the most. He continued in his letter:

One cannot stay such men by an army in the kind of war which they will make, for they will do nothing but rob the land, and burn and plunder, and put the people to ransom, and ride by night like thieves by twenty or thirty or forty, in different parts; wherefore it is needful in every way, if you please, that I should speak to you, before I go into the country. For I heard that they have given you to understand many sinister things of me; they will tell you soon that I was the cause of their war. Therefore, sir, if you please, do not take it amiss if, when I have finished your business in this Parliament of Paris, which is going well, thank God, I return towards you to know your advice, ready to do that which you command me.

Despite the king's unwelcome interference, Simon insisted on consulting him before taking his next course of action. What came out of the meeting was more money to deal with the insurgency. All the Irish revenues, plus £3,500 raised from loans, Jewish tallages and London rents, were put at his disposal. This was soon followed by another letter from Henry with rumours that more trouble was brewing, that a certain noble brigand was using his castle above a valley to relieve traders and pilgrims alike of their possessions. Simon seized the fortress and razed it to the ground, but by then Gaston had already forged an alliance with another robber baron and struck. Finding himself completely without resources, Montfort made a mad dash for England, 'ingloriously' as Paris describes it. In January 1251, thirteen years after becoming the king's brother-in-law, Simon told Henry that the war was lost without more assistance. He reminded him whom they were dealing with:

> My lord king, you must recall that when you were last in Gascony, you turned to those whom you considered your faithful subjects, yet they did not stretch forth the hand of assistance as they ought. Neither did they have any mercy on you when you were fleeing from the treachery and persecution of the French king, nor on the queen in her pregnancy, when she was lying ill and then gave birth, but extorted money from you and allowed you to lose your territory and honour.

By this time, Henry was clearly worried that things were getting out of hand, especially the costs, and he wasn't always so inclined to believe the man he put in charge: 'I will not refuse effective assistance to you, who are fighting so vigorously for me. But loud cries of complaint have reached me, that you unbecomingly imprison those who come to you in a peaceable way, and those whom you send for as if in good faith, and that you put them to death when in your power.' Simon advised the king to again recall his own experience with them: 'My lord, their treachery which you have experienced renders them unworthy of belief.'

The king gave him another £2,000, but appointed two officials just the same to go to Gascony to audit his accounts. Simon took the funds and, with some more raised from Leicester and his other properties, hired 300 irregulars from nearby Brabant, who thirsted after the blood of their neighbours like 'leeches'. Although the Gascons were eventually forced to submit again, they now included a league of disaffected citizens whose spokesman was none other than the crafty Gaston.

In their name, Bearn sent a letter to Henry's officials, indicating that all the problems were the work of one man, and it wasn't him. Henry, always susceptible to the last person he spoke to, was disturbed by this and other complaints about Montfort. When at the end of 1251 Simon and Eleanor accompanied her half-brother Guy Lusignan to Dover, they found the king waiting, not to greet them, but Guy. This very public snub was more of the shabby Henry, for he had to know that his sister had given birth to a daughter in Bordeaux who subsequently died. Unlike the infamous churching, however, they were not barred from attending the Christmas court and subsequent wedding of eleven-year-old Princess Margaret to Alexander III of Scotland in York. While there, they found an unexpected ally in Queen Eleanor.

It happened when Henry refused to reimburse Montfort for the cost of the castles in Gascony, as he was required to do under their contract. Only after Simon threatened to alienate them did the queen step in and convince her husband to abide by the terms. She was all for Simon's firm rule, if that was what it took to secure the duchy for Edward.

The Montforts and the queen also shared a close association with Adam Marsh, who would provide the couple with spiritual advice and information about the king's mood during his tenure as viceroy. Already at the outset Marsh had taken Simon to task for acting too brusquely, as when he whisked away the parish priest of Odiham to serve with him overseas. 'This priest will be long separated from his parishioners,' the friar wrote, 'and he has not given any proof of his affection or zeal.'

Simon's response is unknown, but he might have justified his action by pointing out that he never wanted to go to Gascony, either. In another missive, Marsh rhetorically asks, 'What does it profit to guard the peace of your own fellow citizens and not guard the peace of your household?' While the exact nature of Simon's alleged offence here is unclear, it's likely Marsh was reproaching him for sacrificing too much to bring about a successful end to his mission, and his family and tenants back home were paying the price.

Aggrieved as he might feel, Montfort was admonished to try and see things from Henry's point of view. It was absurd to think the king should wait the seven years of their contract before dealing with the complaints that were flooding in. Whether or not they were all the fault of Gaston, they had to be dealt with now. Simon was being accused of extorting all kinds of wealth from them, supposedly for the king but in fact keeping it all for himself, and, worse, of detaining, imprisoning and even starving certain nobles to death. Faced with such charges, Simon refused to understand how the king could even consider them.

'How is it, my lord king, that you believe those who have been convicted of treachery rather than me your faithful subject; and thus institute an inquiry into my actions?'

Henry thought he could only benefit from a closer look at the facts.

'If everything is clear, what harm will the scrutiny do you? Indeed, your glory will be greater still,' he replied.

Humbled by this logic, not to mention another subsidy, Simon could only grumble as Henry despatched a commission to investigate the charges. What they found was a country at war, with Gaston of course in the lead, but they were able to arrange a truce after the Gascons, led by the irritable Archbishop of Bordeaux, agreed to come to England and present their charges in person.

Simon could forget about any glory now. The king, beside himself with anger, no longer addressed him as 'our faithful and beloved Simon de Montfort', not even 'S. de Montfort', only 'the Earl of Leicester'. He ordered him to appear before him and the magnates to answer the charges. The man who had sent the chief instigator of the war to England for trial would stand trial instead.

It opened on 9 May 1252 in the refectory of Westminster Abbey and ran for five weeks. Just as the Gascons sought safety in numbers with their parade of witnesses, so Simon made sure the audience included plenty of his peers, men such as the earls of Cornwall and Gloucester. The king's commissioners started off by declaring that Simon had treated some of the Gascons 'with great inhumanity', but that they deserved it. Hearing this, the Archbishop of Bordeaux at first demanded judgement, then threatened to find another lord for the land besides Henry if the king did not get rid of the 'exterminating earl'.

Henry was inclined to find in favour of the Gascons but, fearing the reaction of his brother and the other nobles, settled for verbally abusing Montfort. Adam Marsh, who was present at the trial, says Simon took it stoically with the 'mature wisdom of a great-hearted soul'. Matthew Paris, who was not there, contradicts that assessment by claiming that he shot back and reminded the king in front of everyone how he had advised him to 'crush' the Gascons.

Since the king obviously had no more faith in him, Simon demanded that he repay the money he had expended on behalf of his service in that infernal land. Worked up into another one of his uncontrollable fits, Henry again forgot he was facing one man he would have done well not to call names.

'I will not observe my promises to you, an unworthy traitor, for it is allowed to break one's agreement when the other party breaks theirs, and to deal without shame with those who are so shameless.'

Traitor? Shameless? The whole gallery must have been dead silent as Simon glared at the king and let him and all those present know that some people were indeed born luckier than others.

'It is your fortune to be sheltered by the name and dignity of king, else you would rue the day for uttering those words to me.'

Henry, by now probably gnashing his teeth and clawing at the air, would have ordered him hauled away and locked up for all but threatening his life, but knew his brother Richard and the other earls would never permit it. And Simon wasn't even through yet.

'Who would believe you are Christian?' he scoffed at the king in front of the others. 'Have you ever confessed?'

'Yes!' snapped Henry.

'Ach, what's the use of confession without repentance and atonement?'

Simon knew that to go after Henry's religion was to go after his heart and soul. The king, however, was easily his equal when it came to a sharp wit and tongue to match.

'I never repented any act so much as permitting you to enter England to gain land and honours and grow fat and insolent!'

Richard and the other nobles and prelates could see no good coming from this heated exchange and brought it to an end. They were unanimous for Simon, but mostly for political reasons. Richard, who had saved Gascony from his stepfather Hugh Lusignan over a quarter of a century earlier, was still fuming over the way the king had deprived him of it. The queen wanted the province sufficiently tamed for Edward to take over there as overlord and made sure her uncle Peter of Savoy took Simon's side.

Another baron Simon could depend on for support was Peter de Montfort, whose Norman ancestors had settled in Warwickshire after the Conquest. Peter had served down in Gascony and saw for himself what ruling the place was like. Although not related, these two Montforts would form the most loyal and enduring bond of the entire reform period.

Henry was forced to accept the verdict of his council. Then, typically, he changed his mind and launched into another bitter attack, at which point Simon realised the king was simply out to get him. He offered to go back and rule the province by mercy alone or resign his office with full indemnity and free of any guilt or reprisals. Henry rejected both out of hand. He ordered him and the Gascon party to observe a truce until he himself got there and squared everything out.

Finally, he looked at his brother-in-law and snarled, 'Go back to Gascony, you who are so fond of war and strife, and reap its rewards like your father before you.'

The jibe was meant for the pleasure of his Gascon audience, who would have known that the elder Montfort had met his death fighting in the south and so could take heart that maybe the son would, too. Simon cheerfully took it in stride.

'Yes, with pleasure, and I won't return until I make them your footstool.' This despite Henry being an ungrateful wretch, he added.

He left in June 1252, taking his eldest son, thirteen-year-old Henry, with him. Eleanor stayed behind to await the birth of her seventh child, their only surviving daughter, Eleanor. Her anxiety over her husband's ordeal is reflected in the greetings she sends to Grosseteste at this time, where she commends 'her lord, herself and her children' to the bishop in 'this time of fear and danger'. While her brother may have been making life unbearable for her family, she could at least count on the support and friendship of her sister-in-law. After the birth, the queen sent one of her nurses to care for Eleanor and included a gift of jewellery for her, which must have pleased her despite Marsh's admonitions that she dress more informally.

Part of the queen's sympathy may have had to do with the

fact that she was going through her own rough patch with the king. She had recently overstepped her authority in granting a Church appointment, which only angered Henry, but when she got Grosseteste to back her up it infuriated him, leading him to observe that a 'woman's arrogance' needed restraining. What certainly needed restraining was the queen's greedy side, and in October 1252 he had one of her clerks locked up apparently for conducting some shady business for her at the Jewish exchequer. The real blow came a month later when the inevitable quarrel between her relatives and his finally broke out.

After years of struggle, Henry had forced the monks of Winchester to elect his own candidate bishop, in this case his half-brother Aymer, a disagreeable ignoramus who, the king insisted, would enlighten the Church 'like the sun, with the rays of his noble and royal extraction'. Henry expected Aymer to rubber stamp his requests in Parliament, unlike that ungrateful Boniface, who was presuming to act like an independent Archbishop of Canterbury. And yet when he asked the bishops to subsidise the crusade he had sworn to undertake two years earlier, Aymer sided with Grosseteste in denying him. It was little wonder Henry was seeing traitors all around him.

It wasn't even a month later that Aymer showed his true colours by declaring a turf war against Boniface and sending his henchmen to rough up one of the archbishop's officials. Boniface was something of a bully himself, and in one notorious incident he had aroused the people of London against him after his inspection visit to St Bartholomew's turned into a riot. The archbishop had struck a sub-prior and denounced him and the other canons as 'English traitors'. In the ensuing scuffle, Boniface revealed he was wearing armour underneath his cloak. He had come there to do battle and was ready to take on all religious houses that dared to defy him.

He was at the papal court justifying his ruthlessness when Aymer made his move. Hurrying back to England, Boniface found his fellow Frenchman was made of the same tenacious stuff and refused to back down. That set off a chain of events that pitted Lusignans against Savoyards, one group of alien relatives against the other. Henry was more furious at the queen than at Aymer, presuming, rightly, that her Savoyards had been getting a free ride for too long.

He cut off her queen's gold and placed her under house arrest in Winchester, as if to remind her that his half-brother, ruffian though he was, was there to stay. She was soon freed on condition that she help restore peace in the family. An exchange of valuable presents did the trick, but the jealousy between the French factions never fully went away until civil war united them in a conflict that was mostly about them.

The Gascons, meanwhile, spent their remaining time in England feasting and rejoicing that their nemesis would be cut to pieces the minute he returned. When they returned, however, they found that Simon had raised a mercenary force from among his friends and relatives and was ready to 'take vengeance for the defamation of his character'. He stationed an ambush to catch them unawares, but the Gascons got the better of the fight and captured one of his leading knights. Upon receiving the report, Simon didn't even wait for his followers to get mounted, but hurled himself directly into the fray. Wholly outnumbered, he was nearly captured himself, but with the help of the men he had rescued he beat off the enemy, taking five of their nobles prisoner.

But the Gascons were relentless and forced him to surrender them when they encircled him at a poorly provisioned castle. It goes without saying that the king's new commissioners arrived to find the country at war again, and they demanded that Simon above all cease and desist. Tell that to them was his reply. The commissioners came ready to relieve him of his command, and did so, telling the Gascons they were not to obey him. Simon scoffed at their orders. Not until Henry had fulfilled his contractual obligations would he give up command. With that, he raced off to besiege another stronghold.

Since he wouldn't go quietly, Henry thought about declaring him a traitor, therefore disinheriting him and seizing his lands. Simon had some idea that was his plan all along; that way he could give his earldom to one of his relatives. The impasse was broken when the king was made to understand that his only realistic option was to buy Montfort out of his contract. And so he offered him £4,667 plus the payment of his debts to clear out and sign everything over to Edward.

It was a generous settlement that Henry insisted had been imposed on him. In his complaint to Louis ten years later, he insinuated that Simon deliberately rekindled the war just to strengthen his bargaining position. If that were the case, the Gascons certainly didn't help the king any by trying to cut his viceroy to pieces. In fact, they showed where they really stood the minute Simon left by throwing in their lot with the new King of Castile, Alfonso X, who started pressing his own claim to Gascony through his lineage back to Henry II and Eleanor of Aquitaine. Gaston, of course, was behind the switch of allegiance, leaving Henry to look like a stooge.

It was a surprising turn of events given that Gaston had sworn his game all along had been to get rid of Simon. Now he wanted to get rid of Henry as well, and it was all due to a little strip of land in the foothills of the Pyrenees that bordered Gaston's county of Bearn. When Simon arrived in 1248, this strip called Bigorre was being ruled by Simon's sister-in-law Perronelle. Her third husband had been Simon's older brother Guy, who left her with two small daughters when he died three decades earlier fighting in the Albigensian Crusade. The eldest daughter had a son named Esquivat, who was in line to succeed his grandmother. But Perronelle had married two more times after Guy, and her daughter by her last husband was married to none other than Gaston. Together they eagerly pressed her claim for Bigorre before and after Perronelle died in 1251, declaring that her marriage to Guy had been invalid because she never got an annulment from her second husband.

To be sure, Perronelle made a mess of everything with a will that pleased next to nobody. While Simon was in Gascony, he came to his family's assistance and kept their obnoxious neighbours at bay. Now that he was gone, Gaston began his depredations again to force Esquivat out. It was when he learned that Henry was anxious to strengthen Gascony by holding on to Bigorre for himself, by paying Esquivat for staying put and doing homage to him, that Gaston decided it was time to jettison the English king and come to an agreement with the Spanish one.

Henry was now convinced that only his personal intervention could save his hold over the province. He made plans to set sail in the spring of 1253, but Parliament again denied him funds for the expedition. While that may not have surprised him, what he heard from a delegation of bishops led by Boniface and his new friend

Aymer must have dumbfounded him. They would accede to his request for funds if he would stop interfering in elections affecting the Church. Boniface and Aymer were demanding that he stop doing the very thing that landed them in their cushy positions. The only thing that saved the two ingrates from the king's fearful temper was his gift for sardonic irony: 'It is true and I am sadly grieved that I have acted as I have; it ought therefore to be arranged that what has been done should be remedied, that you should resign what you have unjustly obtained, lest you suffer eternal condemnation, and I will take care to promote no one that is not worthy of it.'

Boniface showed his own sharp wit when he rejoined, 'My lord king, we do not make mention of what is past, only the future.'

At last, casting aside the petty squabbling, the Church granted Henry a subsidy for his crusade and from the barons he got another feudal aid of £2 per knight, this one for the knighting of his heir. In return, Henry again promised to faithfully observe Magna Carta, solemnly declaring that anyone who didn't 'be extinguished and stink in hell'.

It wasn't until later that summer that Henry gathered a force ready to subdue his insolent overseas subjects. Landing on 20 August 1253, he immediately launched a war against the treacherous Gaston, using the same strategy of containment that Simon had employed. Apparently he summoned his former viceroy to join him, but got no response. In October he wrote him a second time, in a letter that once again shows the king was ready to let bygones be bygones: 'We command and request you to come to Gascony and discuss matters with us; if you think that it befits neither our honour nor yours to remain with us, you can withdraw when you please, without incurring our indignation.'

Of course, Henry was in no way sorry over his treatment of his brother-in-law. His campaign had stalled and he needed Simon to bring both his expertise and reinforcements, men only too willing to thrash the Gascons. He also knew the French were making overtures to him at a time when all of France, indeed all of Europe, was reeling in the wake of an enormous catastrophe.

Louis' crusade, so meticulously planned and orchestrated, had been an unmitigated disaster, costing him more in men, materiel and prestige than all of Henry's misadventures combined. The King of France had decided to march on Jerusalem through Egypt and got his 15,000 men ashore at Damietta in June 1249. At that point his only notable loss was old Hugh Lusignan, Isabella's husband, whose death on the beachhead was mourned by few.

The crusaders were soon bogged down by the Nile and debauchery set in. Finally Louis made for Cairo in March 1250. An advance force led by his hot-headed brother Robert of Artois and the Earl of Salisbury, who did not get along, was entrapped and slaughtered, while the rest of the army, decimated by hunger and disease, was harassed and destroyed all the way back to Damietta. Louis and his two surviving brothers, Alphonse of Poitiers and Charles of Anjou, were captured and ransomed for a sum equal to his entire revenue for one year. They left with the remains of their force for the Holy Land, together with Queen Margaret, who gave birth in the midst of all this madness. Another notorious member of the expedition, Peter of Dreux, was broken by the experience and died during the voyage home.

Louis spent the rest of his time abroad as little more than a pawn between Saracen factions. His mother Blanche of Castile had to deal with the calamity on the home front, including a new crusade, this one launched by an elderly Hungarian mystic claiming Mary Mother of Jesus had told him to raise an army for the purpose of reclaiming Louis from the infidel. Inside his clasped hands were her written instructions, which he said he was ready to reveal once these affairs were brought to a happy ending. So many peasants and riffraff flocked to his side that Blanche thought he might be on to something and encouraged his efforts. Inevitably riots broke out wherever they swarmed with their knives and sticks, and Blanche was forced to reverse herself, now ordering their destruction. A butcher put an end to the Hungarian with an axe in his head and the others were forcibly dispersed, told to go back to tending their sheep or do whatever it was they did. When a crowd of them approached Bordeaux, Simon asked on whose authority they were marching. God and Mary, they announced. Right. Be gone, he told them, before he unleashed his troops and the entire city on them.

For Blanche, the misfortunes continued when a ship laden with the king's ransom money went down to the bottom of the Mediterranean. In November 1252, she died in a nunnery, worn out by the mess her son had created. The French council, despairing of anyone now fit to run the country, turned to Simon. They asked him to be their seneschal, something like an official adviser, because they admired his 'fidelity and nobleness of mind', not to mention his father, who was still highly esteemed in France. Despite the heap of rewards they promised him, he turned the offer down because 'no man can properly serve two masters'.

It took more than fealty to bring him back into the king's service. Robert Grosseteste implored Simon to forget Henry's impetuous words and instead remember all the good things he had done for him, like making him the Earl of Leicester and giving him his sister in marriage. Out of respect for the bishop, who was as much a father confessor as a friend, Simon rejoined the king in 'the spirit of charity and humility', aside from the hard bargain he drove.

To compensate Montfort for his losses and expenses in Gascony, Henry agreed to pay £500 up front plus £400 in an annual, land-convertible fee, payable by local sheriffs instead of being doled out, one could only hope, by a perennially empty exchequer. This not only raised his and Eleanor's income to £2,350 a year, but he also got Henry to give them lifetime possession of the castles of Odiham and Kenilworth. For Henry, it was worth it, for Simon's return kick-started what would become his only truly successful military adventure, flown under his sparkling red banner with the fiery dragon's tongue flickering in the wind.

It would take several more months of diplomacy before Edward was safely installed as the new overlord. Simon had long since left Gascony by then, never to return. Although never officially vindicated, his fiercest critic in England finally saw what he had been up against after he removed himself from the snug environs of his painted green rooms at Westminster. Henry readily adopted the same tactics on his own campaign, thereby hinting that his real problem with Simon all along had been spiralling costs. It was costing him a fortune to quell a mutinous province that barely brought him £2,000 to begin with, but rather than letting Simon finish what he set out to do, Henry had panicked and turned against him.

The first time he was tossed aside, at the queen's churching, Simon fled for fear of the king. This time, at his trial, he showed nothing but contempt for him, almost daring him to exert his authority over him. And yet Henry wanted him back again, and was ready to reward him substantially for it, because he was already hatching another grandiose scheme, the success of which would depend on the French and a man steely enough to deal with them. Simon's background and prestige in France made him Henry's best bet to pull it off, but as usual, the turn of events ensured that the cooperation between these two utterly dissimilar individuals, one made of steel, the other wax, would end in bad faith and recriminations and both of them appealing to Louis for justice.

6

Shifting Alliances
1254–1255

Before leaving to subdue Gascony, Henry appointed his wife as regent of the kingdom, a sure sign that their recent troubles were behind them. To assist her in this undertaking would be her brother-in-law Richard of Cornwall, in so far as he could stand the sight of her. The queen had been thwarting his greed of late, and he was still smarting over being deprived of Gascony at her urging. Eleanor was thirty and pregnant at the time, her first birth in almost eight years, and Henry wanted his brother available just in case. He might not have bothered, for the queen, far from lying in and hoping for the best, was determined to keep abreast of all the nuggets of royal patronage that cropped up. She was delivered of a daughter in November 1253, celebrated her churching in January 1254 and went right back to work running the regency, even lording over a major parliament that was summoned for the same reason that all parliaments were summoned during that age. Henry wanted money.

The magnates and clergy no doubt guessed why they were being summoned, but certainly not the contents of the king's letter, read aloud by the regency. The King of Castile, Henry had written, was planning to invade Gascony with an army of Christians and Moors, and after he conquered it, England and Ireland were next. Outlandish as the claim was, Parliament declared its readiness to come to his rescue with men and arms, but no money. Worse, they refused to speak for the rest of the political community, hinting that the knights, freeholders and priests were in a restless mood.

In response, someone, probably Richard, devised a plan to have representatives of these orders elected directly in the shires and sent to Parliament after Easter to hear the king's case in person. Surely their patriotic fervour would stir them into action. It didn't, mostly because they feared their local sheriffs more than they did the Moors. They wanted the king to tend to problems at home instead of his personal matters overseas.

Henry didn't help his case any by asking his queen and family to come and join him, which was odd if war was imminent. Then Simon showed up from the Continent and told the assembly that, as far as he knew, all was quiet again in Gascony. It looked like the king was trying to hoodwink Parliament into giving him money for a purpose he wasn't prepared to come clean about. And yet this parliament goes down as one of the great innovations in the development of democracy, for it was the first such elected assembly of its kind in England. It was a political landmark born out of deceit.

The king got no money in the end, and the turnout of the feudal host to come to his aid was decidedly mute. When the queen left England in May 1254, only forty knights accompanied her. She also took along fourteen-year-old Edward, her daughter Beatrice and Boniface, who never missed an excuse to leave the country. Of all the ironies in this twisted tale, this one truly stands out. Ten years later, the feudal host turned out in the thousands to answer Simon's summons to thwart a projected invasion from the Continent, led by the queen herself.

Henry had sent for his children because the diplomatic efforts begun before his own departure had finally paid off. He knew the insurgency would never end until the King of Castile cut off all support to the irascible Gaston. Since Alfonso had two siblings about the same age as Edward and Beatrice, favourite councillor John Mansel, later joined by the slippery Savoyard Peter d'Aigueblanche, was entrusted with the task of creating an alliance with Castile through the marriage of these four children.

Much to Henry's frustration, Alfonso took his time with the offer. His troop movements were actually aimed at neighbouring Navarre, but he was happy to let the King of England think they were meant for him. That way, he could impose terms for the alliance, and impose them he did. Henry could keep Beatrice, but he was to send Edward to Castile to marry Alfonso's half-sister, naturally another Eleanor. To make sure his sister was well provided for, Edward was to be endowed with lands worth at least £10,000 a year, an incredible sum that required Henry to give him not only Gascony, but Ireland, the Channel Islands, the earldom of Chester and scattered fiefs, cities, and castles everywhere. Henry's most incorrigible critic, Matthew Paris, calls the king 'mutilated' by this great giveaway, but Henry kept the titles for himself and was determined to interfere whenever he saw fit, all but guaranteeing future clashes with his son.

Alfonso also wanted Henry to switch his crusading vow from the Holy Land to North Africa, promising him he could take half of whatever they conquered. Instead of the Moors coming to Henry, he would go to them. Lastly, in what was probably the stiffest term, Alfonso wanted the right to knight Edward. The knighting of the heir to the throne was meant to be an elaborate ceremony in England, on the feast of St Edward no less, and Henry lived for these moments. Do all that, said Alfonso, and he would renounce his claim to Gascony. Swallowing his pride, Henry agreed and sent Edward with a middling entourage to Castile, where his knighting and wedding took place in Las Huelgas in November 1254.

There was one last technicality that Henry needed to wrap up before he could rest easily. Eleanor of Castile's mother was none other than Joan of Ponthieu, the woman Henry had married by proxy nearly twenty years earlier before jilting her to marry his own Eleanor. Since he had stopped the process of acquiring the papal dispensation necessary for that marriage, it was theoretically never valid. Still, he was taking no chances, and to ensure that no one would use it to claim he was still married to Joan, thus making Edward a bastard, Henry had his proctors in Rome go through a convoluted process of getting the pope to officially annul that previous arrangement.

The marriage between Edward and Eleanor did bring the insurgency in Gascony to an end, but Gaston would spend the rest of his days causing no end of grief for Edward as he had done for Henry and Simon. The marriage itself would prove lasting, although Edward had none of the refinements of his father and eagerly exerted his conjugal rights. Eleanor was just thirteen when she miscarried the first time. Henry and Queen Eleanor were moved to suggest that Edward go to Ireland to look after his new lands there and leave his little Spanish princess behind. They talked about Ireland being too wild a land for her, but it was clear who the wild one was in this case, and Edward grew to detest the way his parents preached to him in this manner.

With the province as quiet as it was ever going to be, Henry turned his thoughts to going home. He created quite a bit of grumbling the last time he returned from abroad a decade earlier when he demanded that the nobility and representatives of every borough in the realm receive him at Portsmouth in their best holiday clothes, despite the miserable results he had achieved. His subjects should spare no expense for his procession to London, he added. It was all 'pompous as it was sumptuous', just the way Henry liked it, and now he was planning to outdo that earlier occasion.

If he went homeward overland and met Louis on the way, there was no telling what feasts and fetes awaited him. He also dreamed of seeing the cities and cathedrals of France, important for his building projects back home, but he wisely couched his request in terms of a pilgrimage, first to his mother's grave and then to the shrine of Edmund of Abingdon, the recently canonised former Archbishop of Canterbury. Louis was wary of the new alliance between England and Castile, but he had been sufficiently humbled by his crusading calamity to not deny anybody a pilgrimage; nor could he deny his queen, who had been so instrumental in securing his release from Egyptian captivity, the chance to see her sister again after eighteen years.

The first stop for Henry's retinue, described as a small army, was the Abbey of Fontevrault. For all the trouble and neglect Isabella of Angoulême had represented in his life, he was scandalised to find his mother buried in the churchyard instead of inside like his grandparents Henry and Eleanor and his uncle Richard. He had her remains exhumed and interred next to theirs, four tempestuous people who, like Edmund, never seemed to find much peace of mind in the England of their destiny.

The royal parties met in Orleans and together entered a wildly jubilant Paris in early December 1254. Henry chose the Old Temple for his lodgings precisely because it could fit a small army. He was giddy from all the attention he received and returned the favour by lavishly feeding both the rich and poor alike. While the highlight for Henry was a tour of Sainte-Chapelle, Louis was more moved by the family reunion, which was unique by the standards of any age.

The occasion brought together all four Provencal sisters, two of whom were married to Louis and his brother Charles of Anjou, the other two to Henry and his brother Richard of Cornwall. Of course, there was bound to be tension, since the elder two, Margaret and Eleanor, were queens, while the younger two, Sanchia and Beatrice, were only countesses, and their mother, another countess, was quarrelling with Charles over his attempts to push her out of Provence. All in all, however, the meeting was a spectacular success, Henry's one true foreign policy triumph and one that would serve him well in the coming years when his domestic policy was in a complete shambles.

Grateful though he was to Louis for his hospitality, Henry felt compelled to ask him point blank to return Normandy to him. Louis insisted he would gladly do so, but the peers of France, who shunned the détente, would have none of it. Not wanting Henry to go away completely empty-handed, Louis made him a gift of something the people of England certainly appreciated more than the return of some overseas province that only spelled trouble for them. It was an elephant, the first of its kind seen on the island, and it captivated sightseers at the Tower of London in the short time it was able to survive the harsh English climate.

While Henry was making his way north to Paris, Pope Innocent IV lay bedridden in Naples, agonising over his impending death. He had carried on his predecessor's war against Frederick and succeeded for the most part, but now Frederick was dead and his heirs were proving every bit as determined to rule southern Italy and Sicily as their father had been. Knowing Richard of Cornwall had 'an unquenchable thirst for power and world dignity', Innocent tried to interest him in accepting the vacant crown of Sicily. Richard carefully calculated the costs and logistics and deemed that what the pope was really offering him was the moon.

Charles of Anjou was also approached and gave the matter some thought, but claimed his councillors forbade him to proceed. Innocent finally found a taker, but in the week of his death he learned that Frederick's son Manfred had won a crushing victory over the papal army at Foggia. With a singularly bad conscience, he decided to take it out on the relatives and cronies weeping at his bedside. 'What are you all crying for? Didn't I make you rich?' And so Sinibaldo Fieschi, the pope named Innocent whose other acts included legalising the use of torture in the Inquisition, died a troubled man.

The taker was Henry, of course, and if he was also troubled, his gaiety in Paris revealed none of it. He had signed on to the pope's scheme a year earlier, while the situation in Gascony was still far from settled. It was typical of Henry to start up a major project while his hands were still tied with another. Still, he might not have ever become involved had it not been for those inveterate busybodies, the Savoyards.

Back in 1245, Innocent and the papal court had been safely perched in Lyon as the guests of the soon-to-be local archbishop, Philip of Savoy, another of the brothers. Free to pursue his vendetta against Frederick, Innocent had the emperor excommunicated and deposed. Frederick swore to invade to show who was going to depose whom and demanded that the oldest brother, Count Amadeus of Savoy, open the Alpine passes through his territory. Amadeus, however, had secretly fobbed off the castles guarding the passes on Henry for £1,000 a year, plus a baron in marriage for his daughter. If Frederick wanted to march through, he would have to deal with England, not Savoy.

Like most of Henry's shady foreign dealings, this one was the work of the Savoyard Bishop of Hereford Peter d'Aigueblanche. He had convinced Henry that this was his best way to check the French monarchy after Charles of Anjou waltzed into Provence and claimed it for himself and his wife Beatrice. The real reason, of course, was to extricate the Savoyards from their double dealing between the papacy and the empire and blame it all on somebody else. They were successful in so far as Innocent, when he received Henry's letter protesting against papal exactions, sniffed that the King of England was 'playing the Frederick'.

The emperor never got around to invading before his death in 1250. Innocent eventually returned to Italy and tried to reach some sort of accommodation with Frederick's sons. He wasn't taking any chances and started looking for his own candidate to be the King of Sicily. By the time he made the offer to Henry, he had cast 'a wide net to catch any bird' and the Savoyards were clearly intent on Henry being that bird. They wanted to create a grand alliance between England, Savoy and the papacy that would make them one of the ruling families of Europe.

The pope wouldn't even have to worry about Henry presuming to rule Sicily, because the throne, decided the Savoyards, would go to his ten-year-old son Edmund. Queen Eleanor, always supportive of any idea hatched by her uncles, was ecstatic that her other son would also be a king and threw her weight behind them. Henry too was happy for Edmund, but what really won him over was the chance to commute the crusading vow he made in 1250 in the wake of Louis' imprisonment. All the money being raised from English churches and monasteries for that front would instead be diverted to the inevitable war in Sicily. His clergy wasn't going to like that, but Grosseteste had died the previous year, in October 1253, and the Archbishop of Canterbury was a Savoyard and papal warrior. The barons were guaranteed to roll their eyes over the king again getting himself embroiled in Continental politics, so he would do what he always did in these situations and just ignore them.

Known as the 'Sicilian business', Matthew Paris considered this the crowning example of Henry's simplicity, a gullible king being led into the abyss of his ambitions by the papacy, the Savoyards and his wife. Yet Henry was no tool in this business. It was easy for critics like Paris to see him led astray by fanciful dreams of a Mediterranean empire reminiscent of that of his Norman ancestors. But in the main, what he was really after was a comfortable old age.

Now approaching fifty, Henry revelled in the good life of cosy fires, plenty of food and drink, and giving and receiving presents. All that would be seriously upset on 24 June 1256, the date he had scheduled to depart on crusade. Meeting Louis and listening to him describe his humiliation and anguish in the Holy Land, seeing him shell-shocked into the life of a penitent and ascetic, must have unnerved him. Henry wasn't cut out to be either, much less a martyr, and everyone knew it. The pope's demand for men and money for the Sicilian business was his best bet for getting out of it.

But here, Henry was also showing how much he had learned from the Savoyards when it came to duplicitous diplomacy, because he was assuring Alfonso at this very time of his earnestness in joining his crusade to North Africa. Innocent suspected that Henry was only after a commutation of his vow and at first hedged on whether or not to make the offer to him. It was this failure of firm papal commitment, by Innocent and then his successors, that would prove one of the nails in the coffin of the business.

Simon probably would have frowned on it had he been consulted. Beyond Henry's inability to inspire respect in his own people, let alone the Sicilians, the king was deeply in debt to him for the buyout of Gascony and as surety for Eleanor's dower. Innocent had bound Henry on pain of disinheritance and excommunication, so whatever money he could scrape together in royal revenue would bypass the Montforts in favour of the papacy. On the other hand, the new pope, Alexander IV, started insisting that Henry conclude a peace treaty with France so he could fully concentrate on Sicily. Since that would be an equally gruelling affair, requiring both sides to haggle over hundreds of claims, cross-claims, quitclaims and so forth, Henry would turn to Simon to open negotiations when the time came. His friendship with Louis and standing at the French court were indispensable to be sure, but Henry, whatever else he might think about Simon's leadership skills, certainly valued him as a diplomat. In September 1254 he sent him to Scotland on a secret mission, officially involving the honour of Huntingdon, but probably to obtain some word about his daughter's welfare. In fact, fifteen-year-old Margaret was miserable in her barren castle, with no access to friends or her husband. Shortly after his return, Henry made ready to march north to deal with the situation.

His arrival in England revealed all kinds of anxieties, mostly about his crushing debts, and as usual these problems always brought out the worst in him. The citizens of London made a gift to him of £100, which hardly offset the more than £1,000 he spent entertaining and feeding the Parisians. Considering that the money had been meant specifically for that purpose, he pocketed it and called on the Londoners to now make him a real gift. He then outdid that bit of ingratitude by taxing the city £2,000.

From the Jews he demanded more than £5,000, on top of the

£40,000 they had been forced to give him over the last eight years. Sensing the king would never give them peace, they begged to be allowed to leave the realm rather than submit to his continuing extortion. Their plea moved Henry to make one of his more memorable speeches:

> It is no wonder that I covet money, for it is dreadful to think of the debts in which I am involved. They amount to £200,000 and I am crushed into pieces. I am therefore under the necessity of living on money obtained in all quarters, from whomsoever and in whatever manner I can acquire it.

Having said that, Henry 'sold' the Jews to Richard for £5,000, so that his brother might 'disembowel those whom the king had skinned'.

Although still anxious to convert the Jews, Henry had started aping their repression on the Continent, but whereas Louis burned Talmudic manuscripts, Henry ordered them seized and sold back to their owners at high prices. Nowhere, however, was Henry's gross simplicity on display more than concerning the fate of the Jews of Lincoln.

During August 1255 their community was hounded by a woman who insisted they had kidnapped and crucified her son Hugh as part of a macabre ritual mocking Christianity. She claimed he was playing with some Jewish boys at the time of his disappearance, and allegedly there were marks of crucifixion found on his body when it was later retrieved from a well. Henry was then in the north attending to his daughter and decided to stop in Lincoln on his way home to oversee the case. By the time he arrived in early October, his steward, John of Lexington, had already extracted a confession from a Jew named Copin. The king was anxious to be back in London for his favourite feast day, St Edward's on 13 October, and accepted the confession outright, even overruling John's promise to spare the man's life. Copin was drawn and hanged, while ninety-two more Jews were carted off to London. With the mother still demanding their demise, eighteen were subsequently hanged because they refused to submit to a trial by Christian jury and therefore had to be guilty. The others were eventually released after the intervention of Richard, who now owned them, and the friars, where a change of money as well as piety was said to be involved.

That it was all about blood money can be inferred from the work that soon began on building the angel choir of Lincoln Cathedral, in part with donations collected at the shrine built especially for little Hugh. It so happened that the Bishop of Lincoln elected after Grosseteste's passing was Henry of Lexington, the brother of the man who had forced Copin to confess. If the king saw any conflict of interest in this arrangement, it didn't matter. He had to get back to London in time for the feast and so was eager to be done with the case.

Undoubtedly joining Henry at the table of this feast were two men never seen before by the guests. One was the Bishop of Romagna, who had been sent by Pope Alexander to give little Edmund the ring investing him with the kingdom of Sicily. The bishop reminded Henry that he was liable for all the debts incurred by the papacy in its war with Manfred and for raising an army to fight him. Far from recoiling, Henry immediately began wondering the best way to take an army overland across France. While he was at it, he would ask Louis again to return his lands, and if he refused, he would crush him in the vice soon to be England and Sicily.

The other newcomer was Rostand, a papal nuncio charged with collecting money from religious houses for the prosecution of the Sicilian business. The last nuncio, Martin, had been run out of the realm ten years earlier at the point of a sword, with Henry's blessing no less. Rostand, however, had Henry's full support, like 'a lurking lion', and he came well armed by the pope. His authority included the clause *non obstante* (notwithstanding), meaning he was entitled to act beyond whatever law, indulgence or obstacle might stand in his way. A free hand, in other words.

It was an inflammatory clause, one that had been abused by the papacy in filling clerical offices in England with friends and relations of the pope. To the locals, it seemed as if every parish priest was an Italian who couldn't speak their language and ate some odd sort of food. Often they never even came to England to take up the post, just had the money sent to them.

In the last year of his life, Robert Grosseteste decided to do something about it and refused to allow Innocent to install one of his nephews in his Lincoln diocese. The souls of his parishioners were suffering on account of this misguided policy, he declared, and so with all due reverence, he was compelled to disobey, oppose and resist the pope's command. Pope Innocent was naturally furious that anybody should question his actions and wondered aloud why Henry didn't lock up the 'raving old man'. Because, said one of his cardinals, Grosseteste was a holier man than any of them and it was safer to let the truthfulness of his letter lie dormant and gather dust.

The nephew was provided for elsewhere in the end, but Innocent was haunted by Grosseteste even from beyond the grave. He had been contemplating having the dead man's bones dug up and disposed of when the bishop appeared to him in a dream and dared him to just try it. The pope woke up with a terrible pain in his side and from that day forward never recovered his health.

Rostand's mission was made clear at a meeting of Parliament held in October 1255. The previous assembly had been more of the same old story, with the king asking for money and the barons and clergy demanding the restoration of the offices of justiciar, chancellor, and treasurer, plus a say in filling them. It broke up with the king only agreeing to publicly confirm Magna Carta as he had always done. He was in fact resentful of the way his nobles and bishops kept carping that he observe this charter of liberties, but that they did not see fit to do the same for those under their own vassalages. The reply he got was that as the king he should set the example.

The autumn parliament grew even more contentious because the full extent of the Sicilian business was revealed for the first time and the nuncio standing there was supposed to mean that it was a done deal. Henry didn't ask the barons and clergy for their approval, only for their money, and he started at the top with his brother Richard. The Earl of Cornwall, however, was furious at Henry for allowing the Savoyards, together with John Mansel and Robert Walerand, his two faithful English advisers, to drag him into such an undertaking without consulting them. He flat out refused to give any support and the other barons followed suit.

Actually, they could afford to stand firm, because it was Church money Rostand was really after. The bishops in Parliament knew this, but they were still stunned when they learned that one of their own had conspired with Rostand and Henry to get the money as quickly as possible. It was the Bishop of Hereford, otherwise known as Peter d'Aigueblanche, the most notorious of the Savoyards. He had convinced Henry to give him the seals of some of his fellow prelates, which were then attached to blank sheets. Once in the possession of the pope, they became blank cheques and were used to raise money from Italian merchants. The bishops would have to answer directly to the merchants for both the money and the usurious interest they charged. That Henry would allow himself to be involved in this unscrupulous transaction showed he was serious when he told the Jews he was ready to get money in 'whatever manner' he could.

Grosseteste may have been dead, but there were plenty of prelates who didn't care what arrangements the king had made with the papacy and were ready to defy them both. Taking the lead was the Bishop of London, Fulk Basset, whose prominent family had risen against Henry twenty years earlier during Richard Marshal's rebellion. With a world-weary sigh, he declared he was ready to lose his head rather than subject the Church to such slavery. He was followed by Walter de Cantilupe, the Bishop of Worcester, who had replaced Grosseteste as Simon's spiritual guide. Henry was livid at their intransigence and swore to have Basset removed from his bishopric. Basset told him to do his worst. He was ready to put his helmet on and fight.

The prelate who should have led the opposition against the king and Rostand was Boniface, the Archbishop of Canterbury. He was a Savoyard, it was true, but one who had shown the spirit of steely independence. But he was again absent from the country, on a mission directly connected to the Sicilian business. His older brother Thomas of Savoy, the seasoned sponger and troublemaker, had been cast out of Flanders after his wife Joanna died. After a brief flirtation with his former enemy Frederick, he married a niece of Innocent's and became the principal mover behind entangling Henry in papal affairs. It was he who dangled the commutation of Henry's crusading vow before his eyes, hoping to obtain a nice fief for himself in Edmund's new kingdom in return.

Sticking with the Savoyard plan to gain control of northern

Italy, Thomas moved against the cities of Asti and Turin but got himself captured in the process. Boniface and Peter of Savoy joined their other brother Philip, the Archbishop of Lyon, in an effort to free him. Meanwhile their niece, Queen Eleanor, gathered up what money she could for the rescue mission. This loss of focus by the group that had engineered the business would have dire consequences.

As the grumbling grew, Henry started seeing enemies everywhere. At this same parliament he railed against the man he held responsible for his daughter's miserable state in Scotland. When Roger Bigod, the Earl of Norfolk, stood up for the man, Henry went ballistic and called Roger a traitor. Bigod was the hereditary Marshal of England, having inherited the title from his grandfather after all his uncles, the Marshal boys, died childless, and like Simon, he had a formidable reputation as a warrior. He called the king a liar to his face and dismissed any notion that he could harm him outside the bounds of justice. This was the opening for another demonstration of either Henry's wry wit or endearing simplicity.

'I can seize your corn and sell it,' he chirped.

Roger, a humourless man, warned the king he would cut the head off anyone who tried to take his corn, so Henry settled for calling in his debts. Normally easy-going about the money his barons owed him, he was in such a mood as to use any provocation to fill his coffers. Sometimes there was no provocation at all, as when his agents seized the wine of several merchants in Gascony under the cover of customs. The merchants turned to their new lord, sixteen-year-old Edward, for redress, and the young man brought up their complaint to his father when he landed in England after Parliament dissolved. Henry had been forewarned of the trouble by his agents and already instructed them to make amends. He did, however, take to heart their entreaty not to let his son play the big man.

'Your Majesty, there is only one king in England who has the power to administer justice,' they reminded him.

He hardly needed the reminder. He was still seething over his brother turning against him, and now he was going to put his son in his place. When Edward appeared before him, he wondered aloud whether he was rebelling against him as in the days when the sons of Henry II rebelled against their father. Rebuked again, Edward sulked off, but found that neither his mother nor her Savoyard relatives had any time or money for him these days. Ominously, into that gap fell the Lusignans, Henry's notorious half-brothers, who were continuing to make a nuisance of themselves in their adopted country. Their lawless ways naturally appealed to Edward's violent and grasping nature, and he knew in their company he could always play the big man. Gathering up a large retinue of horsemen, he went tearing off into the English countryside.

7

Famine Before Revolution
1256–1257

Barely a year into the Sicilian business and everything seemed to be going wrong. Boniface was back without the Savoyards any closer to freeing Thomas, and Manfred's position was growing stronger by the day. Alexander was constantly reminding Henry that the commutation of his vow and the ring placed on Edmund's finger didn't come for free. The terms called for Henry to repay papal war debts of more than £90,000 and for raising an army of 8,500 men, both by the autumn of 1256. He had no hope of filling either condition and yet he soldiered on, if only because it was second nature to him to latch onto an unattainable project with tenacious fury. This had the unfortunate consequence of forcing him to cut back on other projects dear to him. His desperation can be seen in his order to the treasurer to find at least £400 so work could continue on the rebuilding of Westminster Abbey.

Henry's poverty also forced him to scrounge and act like a heel in a string of unseemly episodes. As he was returning from Scotland, before his inopportune intervention in the fate of Lincoln's Jewry, he stopped at a church in Durham, ostensibly to pray, but he had been informed in advance that a large amount of money had been deposited there by several bishops and clerics. Henry ordered his attendants to break open the chests and haul the money away. He assured the monks that it was a loan that he would repay, which he did, only without so much as a thank-you.

Later, when an assembly of Cistercian monks refused to hand over their wool supply for the profits of Rostand's mission, Henry summoned an abbot from their order and demanded to know why they were being obstinate. The abbot replied that they preferred the king to follow the example of Louis and ask them for prayers, not money. Henry spelled it out simply to him. 'I require both: your money and your prayers.' The Cistercians were still unmoved, so he slapped a special tax on them *non obstante*.

As Henry well knew, he couldn't hope to get even half the money needed just from the clergy. The laymen would also have to fork over, and since his barons refused him a tax he would have to apply pressure on a more local scale. One convenient source of revenue was the distraint of knighthood, which required anyone owning a certain amount of land to become a knight. Henry hadn't employed it often during his forty years on the throne up to that point, but he now issued a proclamation that landowners worth as little as £15 a year were required to become knights. The idea was to ensure chivalry flourished in England as it did in Italy, but because few people with that income could afford knighthood in terms of time, money and physical prowess, it was only natural to allow them to purchase an exemption.

The money for these exemptions was to be paid to the sheriff, who would then bring it and all the other money due the Crown to the exchequer. Henry's anxious state of mind can be seen in the way he appeared at the exchequer one day and declared that any sheriff who missed the deadline for settling accounts would be henceforth fined: £3 the first day, £7 the second, and £10 on the third. On the fourth day, he would be seized and held for ransom. They were likewise fined for failing to enforce the distraint of knighthood, which was eventually reduced to an income of £10 per year.

The poor sheriff; he never had it easy under any king. He was typically a knight himself, often connected to the court, whose job it was to collect revenue and make payments for the king, and to enforce his orders. Outside of fines, fees and taxes, there was the money from renting and farming royal demesne, fixed in increments known innocuously as 'the farm'. The exchequer would tell him what the farm was and his bailiffs would go out and get it. They were expected to skim something off, but now Henry wanted that and more, so the exchequer began raising their increments beyond justifiably sustainable levels.

The only way the sheriffs could keep up was by throwing their weight around, by touching and sniffing all the goods at the market and checking out every jingling of coins within earshot. Since family, friendship and neighbourly familiarity tended to keep local knights from acting in this manner, the king looked to other counties for his sheriffs. The incentives he offered them were the authority of the title and handouts in the form of food, drink, maybe even a rumble in the hay. The presence of these total strangers, who glowered like thumb breakers and carried an air of menace about them wherever they went, would be instrumental in turning the reform movement into a national upheaval.

The local oppression was compounded by eyres, royal commissions that travelled around the country hearing cases, deciding suits and imposing fines. The last general eyre before the 1250s had collected more than £20,000 under the cover of justice. Most affected by this fleecing were knights and freeholders, and they were in for an even more unpleasant development in the court's pursuit of money.

The Jews had often secured their loans with the land of the borrower. Henry's constant extortion of the Jews forced them to sell the bonds denoting this security in order to raise cash. It seemed to be a concerted effort, for the men who were ready to snap up these bonds, on the cheap of course, were closely connected to the king. Richard of Cornwall, William de Valence and the Lord Edward were among these notorious traffickers. Once they had obtained the bonds, they demanded immediate payment from the borrower. They knew that was impossible in their cash-strapped society. The whole goal was to instigate a suit to seize the land for themselves. Many a knight and freeholder ended up disenfranchised in this seedy manipulation of the only mortgage market in the kingdom.

And it wasn't only Henry alienating the people of the counties. When the sheriff was one of the king's household knights, the magnates tended to respect his authority. This wasn't the case for a minor official whom the magnates didn't know and of whom they certainly weren't afraid. He, of course, was afraid of them, and the magnates took advantage of his fear by infringing on royal rights and rents and by coming down hard on their own tenants without the threat of Crown intervention. Henry always insisted that these men were as much obliged to observe Magna Carta as he was, but being weak and forever preoccupied, he preferred not to confront them, even as they were nibbling away at his farm.

These oppressive landlords included not only the magnates, but the queen as well, who shrugged off all complaints about the misconduct of her stewards. In Simon's case, the only will of his to survive commands his executors to see that 'the poor people of my land are provided for' from his estate, especially those whom 'in the eyes of some I have done harm'. The will was drawn up six months after the reform movement began and Montfort was determined that he and the other magnates do justice to their tenants. His insistence on it, in fact, would lead to the first quarrel among the reformers, some of whom were only interested in Henry putting his house in order.

The extent of Simon's wrongs or any amends he might have made before the reading of the will cannot be gauged. Most likely they occurred during his years in Gascony, when he was striven to raise his own funds in order to fight the insurgency there. Henry had promised to make good the money, but he was still in arrears to him for more than £1,000. There were now six Montfort children to provide for, and the older boys had reached their teens. While the family estates brought in an annual income of nearly £2,500, much of that would not go to their children until Henry fulfilled his promise to replace their fees with land.

The king had also done nothing to find prospective brides for the Montfort boys the way he did for the Savoyards and Lusignans. That situation was made worse by Henry marrying his half-brother William de Valence to a Marshal heiress. A boastful and intemperate man, then about thirty years old, Valence not only claimed dower lands that Eleanor, his forty-year-old half-sister, felt should have gone to her, but also defaulted regularly on his payments of her dower settlement to her.

He was hardly alone there. Margaret de Lacy, the widow of Walter Marshal, received 30 per cent more for her Irish dower than what Eleanor got as the widow of William Marshal II. That was bad enough, but Margaret too defaulted on her share of payments to Eleanor, for seven years no less, until she was finally forced to make good. Henry had not only let her get away with being a deadbeat for so long, but took steps to secure Margaret's dower against other claimants. What trouble he would have saved himself in the future had he shown the same concern for his sister.

Henry's almost perverse preference for his half-brothers can be seen in his order, at the height of the money crunch of the 1250s, that no writ of distraint be issued against any of them. The properties of Richard of Cornwall, Peter of Savoy and Richard de Clare, Earl of Gloucester, were similarly protected. The son of Isabel Marshal, Clare was in his mid-thirties and had risen to join Henry's inner orbit of loyal advisers. He, like nearly all the others so protected, had given his approval to the Sicilian business. The one holdout was his stepfather Richard of Cornwall, and Henry might have been inclined to leave his brother off the list had Richard not become engaged in another major project that was separate from Sicily but just as important for its success.

It began at the end of January 1256 when William of Holland went crashing through the ice during a skirmish in Friesland and ended up with his throat cut. In slicing up Frederick's empire, the papacy had given the title King of the Romans to William, which in reality meant he was the king of the Germans. In practice, he was the king of nothing, because the Germans did what they wanted and, apparently, so did the Frieslanders. Richard, however, was covetous of any crown that didn't have the remoteness of the moon, and decided this one was worth the projected cost. In the end, it cost him less than £20,000, certainly a better bargain than Sicily, and unlike that island, it was unoccupied when Richard went to claim it. Or so he thought.

There were many people outside of England who were none too happy with Henry at that time, and Alfonso of Castile was one of them. He fumed about Henry robbing the wine merchants and stringing him along about crusading together. He threatened to invade Gascony and backed off only after the English envoy reminded him that Henry giving Edward in marriage to Eleanor of Castile was like God giving Jesus Christ to the world.

What was really bothering Alfonso was Richard's candidature for the throne of Germany. He wanted it, too, and since his mother was a Hohenstaufen, a part of Frederick's dynasty, he had more local support. But Richard was richer and able to buy up three of the seven votes in play outright. The decision came down to the elector of Bohemia, Ottokar II, who dithered between both camps until he finally threw in his lot with Richard. All the shady dealings didn't stop a German delegation from informing Richard in January 1257 that his election had been unanimous. Almost as an afterthought, they added that his ability to speak English, which supposedly sounded a lot like German in those days, helped tip the scales in his favour.

Of course, what did it was the money, and here Richard had a lot of help from Henry. For years he had been sponging off both the kingdom as the price for keeping him satisfied and the papacy in the forlorn hope he might put that money to good use for Rome. In the late 1240s, he scored another major windfall when Henry put him in charge of minting new money.

The English silver penny had been filed and clipped of so much metal that many coins were no longer worth the value they were stamped with. The king turned to Richard for the new coinage because there were few men like him with enough start-up capital to get the process going. It was a great success, with more than one million pennies minted over fifteen years, allowing the brothers to split more than £10,000 in profit.

That profit came from people who got far less pennies back than they had to surrender. Many others were impoverished when Henry gave Richard the exclusive right of exchange, with all the commissions that went with it. But where the brothers really hurt the economy was in the huge amount of cash they were draining out of the country in order to fund their throne-buying schemes. The tight money made the general round of extortions only that much more difficult to bear.

Richard had already prepared an elaborate ceremony for his and Sanchia's coronation in Aachen, with fifty ships bringing over the English delegation, when Ottokar went and ruined everything by voting again, this time for Alfonso. Moving quickly up and down the Rhine Valley, Richard lavished gifts and money anywhere he could to win over the people directly. It was basically up to the pope to decide who was going to wear the crown, but Alexander had no more resolve than Ottokar. He was worried that an English King of Germany and an English King of Sicily might gang up on him in the future. On the other hand, he wasn't happy about

Alfonso appealing to Frederick's old base for support, so he told both contenders for the throne to be patient for now.

Even though Alfonso sneered that Richard was only pretending to be king, he didn't help his own case any by never setting foot in Germany. He continued to press his claim and insisted that Henry, his nominal ally, do him justice. Henry assured him he knew nothing about these affairs and reassured him of his willingness to go on crusade with him, which only a fool had to believe at that point. He did finally decide to act on some advice Alfonso had been giving him since the start of their alliance and began exploring a long-standing peace with France.

The prospects for such a peace looked good in 1254 when Louis was showing off his collection of relics to Henry in Paris. Louis waxed on about how the two kings had married two sisters and their brothers the other two, making all their children seem more like brothers and sisters than cousins. The kindred spirit didn't alleviate the lingering mistrust, and Louis wasted no time trying to offset Henry's alliance with Alfonso by arranging a marriage between Castile and France. He even reiterated the one-upmanship of their marriages with the Provencal sisters by boasting that he got Alfonso's daughter for his son, whereas Henry only got his half-sister for Edward. Louis also supported Alfonso's bid for enthronement in Germany because the Sicilian business stirred up fears that England really was out to encircle France, and Richard's candidacy only confirmed it.

Henry was glad to play on those fears, and in February 1256 he sent John Mansel to Paris to make what could only be an embarrassing request coming from somebody of Mansel's legendary slyness. The King of England, he was to tell the assembly, would like permission to march an army across France to Sicily. Fortunately for Mansel, the French beat him to the punch with information that Manfred had just destroyed the papal army, therefore nullifying the need for an English one. Henry was so distraught when he heard this news that he asked a Dominican friar to join his council for the purpose of comforting his sorely taxed mind.

With the deadline looming to start sending money and men to Sicily, all Henry could do was appease the pope by declaring he was ready to seek a treaty with France. Pleased to have peace in one part of the world that he may conduct war in another, Alexander gave him another nine months. As in every other scheme of Henry's, there was no way of avoiding questions about his good faith, and sure enough one of the first major embassies sent to treat with Louis again demanded the return of English possessions. That would definitely ensure peace, Henry's men almost quipped. They had no hope of swaying Louis, who was already fortifying Normandy in response to Richard's encampment on the Rhine, but it was the starting point for Henry to wring two distinct advantages out of his brother-in-law in any deal.

The first would have Henry hold Gascony and some smaller principalities on the Continent as fiefs of Louis. He would become his vassal much in the way Simon and the other English lords were his. True, that meant he would have to get on his knees before the King of France and offer him homage, but it would have the benefit of offering him security. If Alfonso or Gaston or anyone else down there made trouble again, they would now have to answer to Louis as well.

The second advantage would have Louis compensate Henry for Normandy and Poitou. The easiest way was to pay him a fixed amount of money, but there was no way to gauge what the loss of these possessions represented in material terms after more than fifty years. Alexander came up with the best suggestion. Louis would pay Henry enough money to fund a large army of knights. These knights would go on crusade, and if they happened to get no further than Sicily, then that was all right. There would be a lot of haggling over the price, but with the queen and Savoyards actively promoting such a treaty, Henry looked ready, after thirty years of pining away, to give up on his dreams of reclaiming the old Angevin empire. Of course, what his son and heir thought about all of that was an entirely different story.

Edward had been none too happy over being cut down to size over the lordship of Gascony. Henry had given it to him, and so the way he saw it, any moves his father made in the duchy amounted to interference. Since there was no telling Henry that, Edward decided he would conduct his business in secret. Not even a fortnight after sitting down with his father to a magnificent feast thrown by John Mansel, surely the richest English clerk ever, Edward made an agreement with Gaillard de Delsoler to promote their interests in Bordeaux at the expense of the Colombines, thus deliberately counteracting Henry's policy of humouring each side.

The king didn't become aware of it until Delsoler went back to Gascony and bragged about it all over town. Henry was furious, but that didn't slow Edward down. He was next off to Wales to deal with an uprising in a territory that was nominally his as well. This time Henry was more than happy to give him a free hand, even telling him that now was his time to shine. Edward took the encouragement to heart and boasted he would punish the Welsh, maybe even exterminate them. But first, he needed money. Since Henry could only spare him a meagre £350, he went to see his uncle Richard for a loan.

Richard was just then doling out money left and right for his German kingdom, but was still able to come up with just over £2,600 for his nephew. While that piece of business was being transacted, Edward's men overran the neighbouring priory, insulting the monks and beating up the servants, apparently a prelude for what was in store for the Welsh. Their swagger proved no match for the poor weather or ferocity of their opponents, however, and in no time Edward was limping back to court in search of help, but his parents had nothing to give him. All his father's money was going to the pope, all his mother's to freeing Uncle Thomas. In both cases they were labouring for his brother Edmund, and he resented it deeply.

His mother and Peter of Savoy eventually offered him £4,000, not as a gift or a loan but to buy a lucrative wardship given to him by his father. Edward must have found her behaviour appalling, since his steward in Wales and the man largely responsible for the uprising had been her choice. Geoffrey Langley had won the queen's favour through a number of shifty deals, particularly in the notorious Jewish bond market, and she felt he could be trusted to look after her son's interests. He ended up looking after his own, gobbling up the land of impoverished families and coming down hard on the Welsh.

Not finding any satisfaction from the Savoyard side of the family, Edward turned to the Lusignans. The queen loathed her brothers-in-law because their hold on the king had come at her expense. She greedily eyed every wardship and benefice that became available, wanting it for her friends and family. Now her husband was just as likely to give it to one of his brothers. Her uncles may have been freeloaders in equal part, but, with the exception of Boniface, they had done their best to be accommodating in their adopted land. The Lusignans, on the other hand, only rode roughshod over everything in their path and were now teaching her son all their nasty tricks.

Matthew Paris recalls how Edward and his riders would trash or steal whatever they came across, and in one infamous incident the future king had his thugs lop off the ear of a young man and gouge out one of his eyes, all seemingly without any provocation. It happened just after his licking in Wales, so Edward was likely taking his humiliation out on the unfortunate young man. Meanwhile, the Welsh were growing ever bolder in their attacks, causing Edward to once again turn to his father for help.

Henry probably had to wonder what kind of man his son had become. Here he was terrorising innocent people who would become his subjects one day and yet he kept turning tail every time he was confronted with a test of his warlike skills. Fed up, Henry told him to ride forth and win his spurs. He ought to instil fear into the hearts of his enemies so that they never forgot it. Otherwise, he should quit pestering him because Father was busy.

Indeed he was, for he had planned a surprise performance for the parliament convened in the spring of 1257. Richard was there to say farewell, as he was off to rule the Germans, but Henry stole the show by unexpectedly producing his son Edmund, dressed in the local garments of Sicily, and pleading with his subjects not to deny the boy the chance to become king of that island. He then explained all the terms that bound his kingdom for the payment of said throne, to the tune of £94,000, not including interest.

Taking pity on the king, the prelates offered £52,000 on condition that he once again observe Magna Carta and quit impoverishing them on a whim. Henry realised he would never get the full amount if not even that bit of pathetic theatre could sway his nobles and clergy. He therefore appointed Simon and Peter of Savoy to lead a delegation to Rome to renegotiate the terms. For some reason, these two got no further than Paris, and the proctors that did make

1. The ruins of Montfort l'Amaury in northern France, the seat of the family and probable birthplace of Simon de Montfort.

2. This miniature from the *Chroniques de France ou de St Denis* shows Pope Innocent III on the left launching the crusade against the Albigensians, and Simon de Montfort III and his men on the right carrying out the inevitable consequences.

Above: 3. Carcassonne in southern France. Montfort likely spent periods of his boyhood in and around this famed citadel of the Albigensian Crusade after it was conquered by his father.

Left: 4. This miniature shows the first four Plantagenet kings of England: Henry II and Richard I in the upper register, John and Henry III in the lower register.

5. Simon de Montfort's seal offers the only representation of what he looked like. The most that can be ascertained from it is that he was beardless, had an impressive mane of hair, and stood tall in the saddle. A contemporary chronicler described him as a 'strenuous and handsome knight'.

6. Tinted drawing of Robert Grosseteste, the energetic and principled Bishop of Lincoln, whose learning and zeal had tremendous influence on Montfort and other reformers.

Above left: 7. Henry and his newly crowned bride Eleanor of Provence in 1236. The king was of middling height, about five feet and seven inches tall. Eleanor's comparably small stature is indicative of her tender age at the time. *Above right:* 8. This page from Paris' chronicle shows Simon de Montfort's arms drawn inverted near the crease.

9. These two images drawn by Matthew Paris suggest the year to be around 1245, when Henry began rebuilding Westminster Abbey, seen at left, and the First Council of Lyon was convened by Pope Innocent IV, at right, for the purposes of deposing Emperor Frederick II. The papacy's persistent demands for money on this occasion would see Henry, his barons and the English clergy united for the last time during his reign.

ibat fuacliorem cuis qui eceini no po
utolatis iusti. g. dchiluc acetorii si per
em asuccessore ii teber solueqm acur to
mi. q censns acmittecpi ic nono posist

abo ii epoibrtoin teinica q
tellugerir in uniauuo. iusi.
iipuo e ce creo qi ipm iurar
pellenoins ct si ac iui soui

10 & 11. These two scenes show
how difficult life was for the vast
majority of people in the thirteenth
century. The man in the first image
is stealing food from a beggar's
bowl, while the peasant in the
second is trying to construct a
simple hovel for his family on a
layer of sand.

12. This English silver penny
depicting the king came from one
of Richard's mints and was issued
in 1257, around the time Henry
was planning his own disastrous
gold penny mintage.

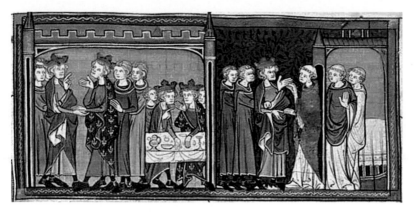

13. Miniature of Henry III visiting Louis IX, and Henry at St Denis. The rapport developed between these two kings, who both ascended the throne when they were boys and who were married to sisters, was instrumental in Henry reasserting his power over the realm.

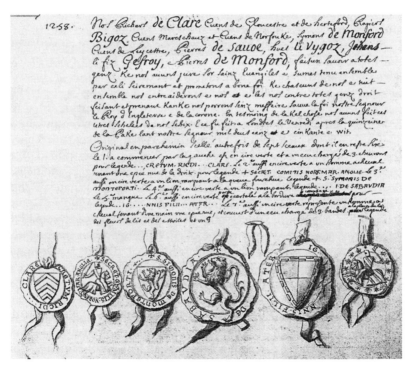

14. The confederation against the king in April 1258. This is an eighteenth-century transcript of a lost original. The seals of six of the seven confederates are shown: Richard de Clare, Roger Bigod, Simon de Montfort, Peter of Savoy, John Fitz-Geoffrey and Peter de Montfort.

15. Montfort dictated his will to his son Henry in January 1259, six months after the reform movement began. It shows a deeply introspective individual eager to make amends for the wrongs he committed and to see that his family is provided for.

16. Westminster Hall at the Houses of Parliament in London, built by King William II (Rufus) just before 1100. Major celebrations and gatherings of state were held here.

Left: 17. This membrane of a genealogical roll shows Henry and his five children: Edward, who struck an alliance with Montfort against his father before switching sides; Margaret, married to the King of Scotland; Edmund, who was given Simon's earldom of Leicester as part of the spoils; Beatrice, married to John, the son of the Duke of Brittany; and Katharine, who died at four years old. Below them is Edward's son, the hopelessly tragic Edward II.

Above left: 18. This image of a jolly friar playing music belies the impact they had in drumming up support for Montfort and his movement.

Above right: 19. Depiction of a messenger receiving instructions. Montfort recognised the importance of communications in his campaigns and employed 'runners' to spread the word.

Above left: 20. The medieval knight represented the warrior class of feudal England. Their value as a political force was first recognised during Henry's reign and carefully cultivated by Montfort in his parliaments. *Above right:* 21. Miniature of a boy being thrown by cattle from London Bridge. In the summer of 1263 a mob gathered on the bridge to harangue and pelt Queen Eleanor as she attempted to flee the unrest by boat.

22. Henry was apt to hole up in the fortified Tower of London whenever tensions with his barons ran high.

23. View of the Downs from Lewes Castle. From here Edward would have seen Montfort's army advancing on the town from the ridge at top. Most of the fighting took place where the houses stand today.

Above left: 24. This imaginary scene from the Battle of Lewes comes from the *Chroniques de France ou de St Denis* and shows Henry on the left facing Simon on the right. Stung by his defeat, the king insisted on surrendering his sword to Gilbert de Clare. *Above right:* 25. Miniature of a bishop preaching. The bishops of England, influenced by Magna Carta and Robert Grosseteste, provided the spiritual support for Montfort's revolution, but never tired of searching for a peaceful solution. *Opposite:* 26. A map depicting the campaigns of 1264 and 1265.

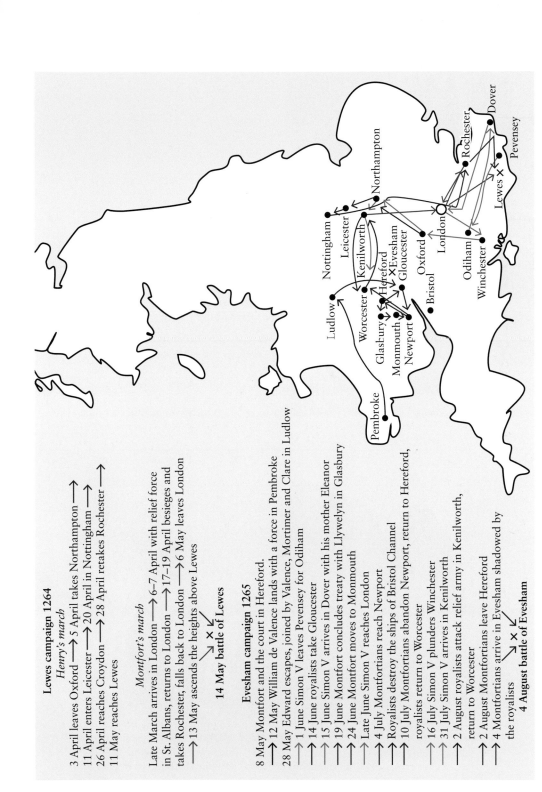

Lewes campaign 1264

Henry's march

3 April leaves Oxford → 5 April takes Northampton →
11 April enters Leicester → 20 April in Nottingham →
26 April reaches Croydon → 28 April retakes Rochester →
11 May reaches Lewes

Montfort's march

Late March arrives in London → 6–7 April with relief force
in St. Albans, returns to London → 17–19 April besieges and
takes Rochester, falls back to London → 6 May leaves London
→ 13 May ascends the heights above Lewes

14 May battle of Lewes

Evesham campaign 1265

8 May Montfort and the court in Hereford.
12 May William de Valence lands with a force in Pembroke
28 May Edward escapes, joined by Valence, Mortimer and Clare in Ludlow
1 June Simon V leaves Pevensey for Odiham
14 June royalists take Gloucester
15 June Simon V arrives in Dover with his mother Eleanor
19 June Montfort concludes treaty with Llywelyn in Glasbury
24 June Montfort moves to Monmouth
Late June Simon V reaches London
4 July Montfortians reach Newport
Royalists destroy the ships of Bristol Channel
10 July Montfortians abandon Newport, return to Hereford,
royalists return to Worcester
16 July Simon V plunders Winchester
31 July Simon V arrives in Kenilworth
2 August royalists attack relief army in Kenilworth,
return to Worcester
2 August Montfortians leave Hereford
4 August Montfortians arrive in Evesham shadowed by
the royalists

4 August battle of Evesham

Left: 27. Henry III enthroned, flanked by Westminster Abbey and church bells. A deeply devout man, the king had lots of time to contemplate rebuilding the abbey as the Montfortians took complete control of the realm.

Below: 28. The ruins of Odiham Castle in today's Hampshire. Given by Henry to his sister Eleanor, Simon left here on 1 April 1265 to deal with Gilbert de Clare. It was the last time he and Eleanor saw each other.

Above: 29. Greenhill in Evesham. Montfort's men made a desperate bid to break through the line Edward posted on the hill and nearly succeeded. They were forced back, hemmed in around this spot, and cut down.

Right: 30. This miniature of Louis' brother Charles of Anjou in action, perhaps with Guy de Montfort close by, could be any medieval battle in terms of terror and chaos. Evesham, as one chronicler remarked, wasn't a battle, just murder.

31. Simon turned Kenilworth Castle into a nearly impregnable fortress after Henry gave it to him and Eleanor in the 1240s. It held out after Evesham until December 1266, when the Dictum of Kenilworth began the process of reabsorbing the Montfortian survivors.

32. Robin Hood, if he lived at all, most likely appeared during Henry's reign. Certainly the outlaws that hid in the woods after Evesham wreaked havoc on royal officials. Interestingly, Robin is first mentioned in print together with Simon's former patron Ranulf of Chester.

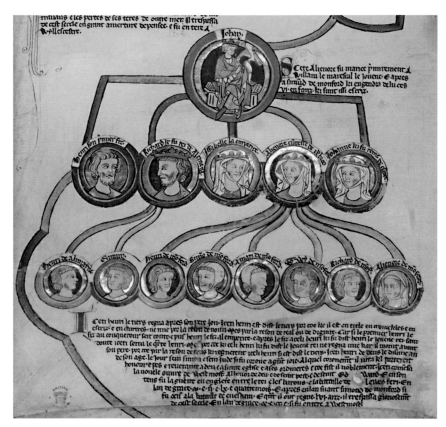

Above: 33. The roll of the genealogical line here shows the children of John and Isabella of Angoulême in the second row: Henry III; Richard of Cornwall; Isabella, married to Frederick II of the Holy Roman Empire; Eleanor de Montfort, who was probably the youngest; and Joan, married to Alexander II of Scotland. From left to right in the bottom row are Henry of Almain, Richard's son with Isabel Marshal, and Edmund, his son with Sanchia of Provence. The other six are Eleanor's children with Simon: Henry, Simon, Amaury, Guy, Richard and Eleanor, wife of Llywelyn, the last Welsh Prince of Wales. *Below left:* 34. In this little church in Viterbo, Italy, Guy de Montfort slew Henry of Almain in front of a congregation of worshippers in March 1271. The murder scandalised all Europe and was mentioned in Dante's *Inferno. Below right:* 35. The ruins of Hailes Abbey in Gloucestershire. Built by Richard of Cornwall in thanks for having survived a difficult sea voyage, he was buried here next to his son Henry of Almain and wife Sanchia of Provence. The minions of Henry VIII destroyed the abbey in the sixteenth century.

Above left: 36. Henry III's greatest achievement was the rebuilding of Westminster Abbey. Enough of the work was completed in his lifetime to have the remains of his idol Edward the Confessor translated there in 1269. Henry himself was put in the Confessor's old resting place until his own tomb could be finished. *Below:* 37. The memorial to Montfort marks where his remains were interred at Evesham Abbey. The plaque was raised in 1965 to commemorate the 700th anniversary of his famous parliament and the final reconciliation between Montfort and the Crown.

the trip did a poor job, for Alexander was unrelenting. Henry was ordered to make peace with France and appear in Sicily with an army by March 1259.

Peace was possible, and here Simon was playing an ever more active role. Henry knew that Montfort's reputation in France was key to gaining leverage in the final treaty. None of the magnates were as intimately familiar with Louis as he was, nor could any of them, with the exception of Peter of Savoy, match his breadth of experience in European affairs. Eager to have Simon return to his council, especially now that Richard was gone, the little favours started coming his and Eleanor's way again, like pardons for dependents, rights to markets and fairs, and so forth. He even authorised him to pursue whatever claims his side of the Montfort family might still have in France. While this might look like a conflict of interest to modern eyes, these claims would have to be settled sooner or later as part of the final deal, and Henry had to offer him something as an incentive to take on the task.

Whether this was enough to get Simon to agree to act is another question. The negotiations would give him a major role to play in England and France and the chance to look after his family's interest in the process. But he also knew that Henry would go off and blame him the minute there was something he didn't like in the treaty. By this stage in their relationship, however, he probably didn't care. He had no fear of the king and made the truth of that abundantly clear when he was confronted one day by William de Valence in front of Henry and other members of the nobility.

Like his brothers, Valence went wherever he pleased and took whatever he wanted, knowing as he did that Henry would never move against him. One of his raids included the Leicester estates, and when Simon's steward successfully retrieved the stolen goods, Valence grew angry and heaped all sorts of abuse on Montfort. It was when he accused him of treachery that Simon had enough and rushed at him. Henry had to throw himself in front of his brother-in-law to keep him from killing his brother. There's no telling if Simon would have, but the message he sent was clear enough. The Lusignans were going to have to physically hide behind the king the next time they crossed him.

For Henry, it must have been one more reminder of how things were spinning out of control. The situation with Sicily and Wales, with the rains that were ruining the crops and now one of his barons threatening his brothers, put an incredible strain on him. In May 1257 the death of his four-year-old daughter Katherine, the girl born to the queen during her regency, must have driven home the vulnerability of his own family at a time when many in England were suffering under his rule. Broken-hearted, the queen took to her bed at Windsor, the king to his in London.

While he teetered on collapse, the Welsh put aside their differences and united against their English neighbours. Their new leader, Llywelyn, warned them that if the King of England freely impoverished and debased his own natural subjects, heaven knew what kind of extermination he had in store for them. Thus rallying his people, he cut off and obliterated another troop sent by Edward to deal with them, including several illustrious knights.

His son having failed him totally, Henry had no choice but to rouse himself from bed and lead an army there himself. The feudal host was called out and left Chester in August 1257. His heart was never really in it, and he gave up after a month when provisions ran low. He was back in London in time for the feast of St Edward. The lack of campaigning didn't stop him from levying a scutage for this latest inglorious retreat, naturally leading to suspicions that he never intended to march on Wales, rather used it as an excuse to raise more money for his other problems.

As the year drew to a close, Henry had to wonder when it was all going to end. Some of the misery, of course, wasn't his fault. He had given his people relative peace and prosperity up until that point, but this had created a population boom. With so many people outstripping the land's ability to feed them all, the country was especially susceptible to the weather. The rains and blight that ruined herds and harvests alike that year brought the onset of a famine that would continue well into the next. The scarcity of food caused the price of basic goods to skyrocket, which only exacerbated the poverty that befell the nation as a result of so much money being siphoned out of the economy.

Not an innately cruel man like his father John or son Edward, Henry could be moved by suffering to perform acts of mercy that not even a pious soul like Louis would dare, like kissing the feet of lepers. In this case, however, he was in another world, and spent Christmas, as usual, in regal splendour. Perhaps nothing is more telling of his state of mind during that period, of his incredible detachment from his people and reality, as one other project he embarked on that year.

Through all the madness of the Sicilian business, the king had been quietly collecting gold to mint a coin patterned after the Italian florin, presumably for use in Sicily someday. As with his war banner, he spent long hours working on the design and waited until the business-savvy Richard, who would surely scoff at the idea, departed for Germany before giving the order to strike the first coin. He was in Chester at the time, no doubt still poring over the sketch when he should have been planning his campaign against the Welsh.

The end result had all the hallmarks of Henry's personal touch, being a thing of beauty and a total flop. Valued at twenty silver pennies, it was of no use to farmers and labourers barely eking out a hand-to-mouth existence. Henry was almost offended that nobody liked his gold coin and refused to withdraw it from circulation until 1270. By then, the fiasco was complete and the coins couldn't be melted down fast enough. Out of 50,000 struck, only eight remain today.

8

1258

The papacy's diabolical obsession with unseating the Hohenstaufens was entering its twentieth year and Alexander decided that was long enough. He warned Henry in no uncertain terms that unless he fulfilled the terms of their agreement, he would excommunicate him and lay his entire kingdom under interdict. That same threat had been carried out against his father half a century earlier when he refused to accept the pope's choice for Archbishop of Canterbury. John responded by seizing more than £100,000 in Church revenue and property. It took four years for him to give in, but by then he was such good friends with the pope that he only had to give back less than half that amount.

John didn't really seem to care if there was a heaven or hell, but Henry sure did. When the pope threatened, he listened, so he sent him another few thousand pounds to tide him over until Parliament convened in spring and he could make another tiresome plea. It would have to be the performance of his life; no shabby theatre like the year before with his son Edmund in borrowed clothes, rather a cry of desperation to save his soul. Instead, he antagonised the assembly from the outset, ruining whatever chance he had of evoking sympathy. The result of this singular blunder was to make 1258, much like 1789 and 1917, the beginning of a political revolution that put power and privilege, long engrained in the social fabric, through the grinder of widespread dissatisfaction.

It started, inevitably, with one of the Lusignans. On 1 April of that year Aymer, the bishop-elect of Winchester, sent a group of men to attack a rival group connected to John Fitz-Geoffrey, killing one man in the process. When Parliament met on 9 April, Fitz-Geoffrey, the former justiciar of Ireland, demanded justice, but Henry brushed him off, suggesting they attend to more serious business. That was the proverbial final straw, and over the next couple of days a group of barons met outside of the proceedings to hatch out a plan.

Three days later, Fitz-Geoffrey entered a sworn confederation with six other nobles to stand together against the king and his hated brothers. Simon was one of them, as was the other de Montfort, Peter. Roger Bigod, the Earl of Norfolk, and his younger brother Hugh, a member of the council and sometime peace negotiator with the French, joined them. The appearance of Peter of Savoy in the confederation was an indication that the queen and Savoyards had decided that the time was right to move against the Lusignans. Their hold over Edward had reached alarming proportions, and he had begun mortgaging away his properties to them for loans.

The last, youngest and most surprising of the confederates was Richard de Clare, the Earl of Gloucester. In 1247 he was twenty-five and recently knighted by Henry when he challenged the newcomer Lusignans to a tournament near Dunstable. Henry forbade it, but two years later another tournament went forward at Brackley, and Clare, inexplicably, switched sides and helped the Lusignans defeat the English party. Branded a traitor, he was further drawn into their orbit after Henry gave him £3,500 to marry his son and heir Gilbert to Alice Lusignan, the daughter of his half-brother Hugh and granddaughter of Peter of Dreux.

The queen was disturbed by the proximity of this powerful baron to her enemies, and so, like her husband, she used marriage to woo him to the Savoyard camp. She offered him a kinsman, a marquis, for his eldest daughter, and together they arranged it at a secret meeting in 1257, one that took him away from the war in Wales. Clare's break with the Lusignans came out into the open during the April parliament when William de Valence accused him of being in cahoots with the Welsh. His disappearance from the front the year before had not gone unnoticed, nor the fact that the Welsh seemed to be raiding everyone's lands but his. William next snarled that Simon's lack of enthusiasm for a Welsh campaign was proof he was a traitor as well, even insinuating that his father had been a traitor to boot. Simon nearly killed him for running off at the mouth in similar fashion; now he gave him a measured reply.

'No, William, I am neither traitor nor traitor's son. My father wasn't like yours.'

That, of course, hurt, because Hugh Lusignan really was a traitor and everyone knew it. When William fumed and repeated his charge, it was the previous year all over again, with Simon ready to shut him up for good and Henry having to restrain him. Simon demanded that William be called to account, addressing not only Henry but the community at large. In this atmosphere, it's a wonder the king thought he would ever find his magnates in a charitable mood.

As the session was drawing to a close, Henry stood up and made his request for their help with Sicily. The barons told him they would give him their answer in three days' time. On 30 April, they did just that, this time with some theatre of their own. Appearing at his palace in Westminster in full chain mail and body armour, they left their swords at the door but otherwise marched in force to see the king. Henry understandably suspected that it was a coup and asked if he was their prisoner.

The earl who spoke for the barons was neither Montfort nor Clare, but Roger Bigod. He too had a personal quarrel with the Lusignans. Aymer, he claimed, had cheated him out of a wardship. While he didn't have Simon's oratory or Clare's ranking, he was considered something of a bruiser, and his honorary title of Marshal reminded audiences of the times when his uncles, the Marshal brothers, opposed the king. His response to Henry's question was a mix of diplomacy and hostility.

'No, my lord, but let the wretched and intolerable Lusignans and all aliens flee from your face and ours as from the face of a lion, and there will be glory to God in the heavens and in your land peace to men of goodwill.'

Bigod then demanded the establishment of a committee of twenty-four, half chosen by the king, half by the barons, to meet and discuss reforming the realm. The demonstration of power worked. Three days later Henry submitted and agreed to work out the details of their petition at a new assembly in June. The king's sincerity was immediately called into question because he included William, Aymer and Guy Lusignan among the twelve men named by him to the committee. Either he didn't pay any regard to Bigod's opening line or he was bereft of friends and support outside of his family. It could also have been his way of saying that he wasn't going to get rid of his aliens until the barons got rid of theirs.

Theirs technically included Peter of Savoy and Simon de Montfort, but the cases between these two men were entirely different. As far back as 1237, four years before Peter arrived on the scene, Simon was already being described as an Englishman. His wife, children and affinity were all English, and he made it clear on two occasions, when his relations with Henry were at their worst, that his allegiance was only to England.

The same could not be said of Peter. Like his brothers, he spent more time abroad than in England, and when he was at court, it was usually in the service of the queen and other Savoyards, not to mention himself. He generally did not alienate the English the way the Lusignans did, or Boniface for that matter, but like the queen, they were of no concern to him.

Henry might have been peeved by the Savoyards conspiring against his brothers, but he showed there were no hard feelings when Thomas of Savoy arrived that summer after more than three years of captivity in Turin. His ordeal left him in such a bad way that he had to be carried in a litter. Why he decided to make the arduous journey to England in poor health became clear the moment he asked for a handout. Henry scraped together £666 for him, which Thomas aimed to use to destroy Turin. He never managed it, nor did he ever return to England. He died the following year, allegedly poisoned like his older brother William.

Death was all around Henry that summer. Famine had claimed thousands of poor people in London alone until they 'lay about, swollen and rotting, on dunghills, and in the dirt of the streets, and there was scarcely anyone to bury them'. Richard tried to help by sending fifty large ships laden with wheat and corn from Germany, and various noble families set up bread kitchens. Feeding the poor had always been a pet project of Henry's, one lost amid the lunacy of his grander vision of himself. He generally fed 150 paupers a day when the queen was in residence, 100 when she wasn't. For special occasions, that number rose into the thousands, as in the 6,000 he fed at Westminster on 1 January 1244, the day of the Circumcision.

The famine robbed him of the chance to mention all those great feedings should the barons demand to know what good he had done for the realm.

Oxford was chosen as the venue for the next parliament because there was still the problem of Wales to deal with. The tenants-in-chief were ordered to muster there with their levees in early June in preparation for a new campaign. The knights and freeholders who arrived in their train, the ones suffering the most from Henry's exactions, were more eager to flex their muscle against the king than to march westward. This show of strength among all sections of landed society was probably intentional on the part of the magnates, who were worried that the Lusignans might try to bring in foreign troops to bolster their side. In and around the Dominican priory in Oxford, where Parliament convened, Henry found himself facing an armed gathering of his own making. He was handed a list of grievances that covered everything from castles, forests, wardships and escheats to arranged marriages, the sheriffs, Jewish bonds and judicial proceedings. In his isolation, Henry admitted that their demands were reasonable and he did not hinder work from going forward on a series of provisions to reform his government.

These Provisions of Oxford were never set down in the form of a constitution, rather they came together piecemeal through the work of the committee. Their reorganisation of the realm, however, was revolutionary. It included the election of a permanent council of fifteen invested with unheard-of executive powers. The council would oversee the appointment and behaviour of royal officials and approve all major royal patronage. Another provision called for Parliament to meet three times a year, at fixed intervals, to discuss the business of the realm. Henry was deeply upset by these infringements on his prerogative, but admitted he brought them on himself by his unwillingness to seek advice and consent beyond his circle of friends and family.

More important for the knights and lesser baronage were the provisions that affected them locally. They included resurrecting the office of justiciar, whose job it would be to go around the country and collect complaints against both the king and barons, and naming local officials as sheriffs to make them more accountable to their jurisdictions. To impede corruption, they were put on salary and given one-year appointments only.

While none of the provisions disqualified aliens from holding land or office, all alienated royal castles were to be returned to the Crown for future management under English castellans. Still officially an alien, Simon surrendered his two castles, Kenilworth and Odiham, but later regained both of them. The Lusignans knew they could forget about similar treatment. When it came time for everyone to swear an oath to abide by the Provisions, they swore 'never' instead. William de Valence started bullying and bellowing until Simon cut him off.

'You will either restore the king's castles or lose your head,' he warned him.

Evidently they took his threat seriously. During a lunch break, they stole away to Winchester, where they holed up in Aymer's castle residence. As soon as their flight was discovered, the barons broke up Parliament and took off in pursuit, followed by Henry and Edward. In the ensuing siege, the Lusignans and their Poitevin supporters agreed to go into exile and left for Boulogne. But even there they found no peace, because nineteen-year-old Henry de Montfort gathered up a force of friends and family on the Continent and began harassing them for the insults they levelled at his father. The king and queen of France were also hostile after hearing reports that the Lusignans blamed Queen Eleanor for their demise and were defaming her as a result. At first Louis refused them passage to their homeland of Angoulême, but eventually relented and the brothers retreated from the scene for the time being.

A pair of chroniclers reported that even Simon himself wavered before taking the oath and had to be nudged into joining the others at the ceremony in Oxford. It may have been an embellishment, aware as all the chroniclers were of Montfort's later frustration with the English habit of turning and running whenever the going got tough. The conclusion here was that he demurred from laying his soul on the line because he knew they would betray him sooner or later. He certainly took the inviolability of oaths seriously, as evident by his troubled conscience over Eleanor's vow of chastity. During the Albigensian Crusade, his father had been merciless with men who had broken their oaths to him. A third chronicler goes on to describe how Montfort, after solemnly declaring the Provisions to be 'holy and virtuous', began another extreme regime of prayer and abstinence. He was about fifty years old and the last phase of his life and career was set to begin.

One of the current complaints against the Lusignans was that they tried to keep Edward and his closest supporters from taking the oath, but the heir to the throne was just as unhappy with the Provisions, especially the part about reforming his household. He refused to take the oath on his own, as did his cousin Henry of Almain, who insisted he could swear to nothing without permission from his father Richard first. In the end, their oaths had to be wrung out of them.

The same was true of John de Warenne, the Earl of Surrey. The twenty-seven-year-old Warenne was a good example of why marriages and wardships were being taken out of Henry's hands. Often when doling them out, the king's toughest decision had always been whether to satisfy Savoyards or Lusignans, almost as if the native-born nobility didn't count anymore. The death of Warenne's father when he was nine gave Henry the opportunity to please both sides of the family, first by making him a ward of Peter of Savoy, then by marrying him to his half-sister Alice Lusignan. Evidently it had been a happy marriage, because Warenne, now a widower, was firmly in the Lusignan camp. Like Richard de Clare, that other pawn of the Savoyard–Lusignan tug-of-war, Warenne spent much of the reform period unsure of where he truly belonged.

Even with the Lusignans gone and Edward under restraint, the queen could not rest easily. The Provisions that arose out of her desire to get rid of her husband's relatives also gave the council control of her queen's gold, and these men were not so readily browbeaten like Henry. She already got a taste of what the future might hold when she tried to interfere in the estate of the dying Earl of Lincoln just as the Provisions were taking shape. He was married to one of her relatives, and since he was about to die childless, the queen was anxious for his Savoyard wife, and not his English mother, to get control of his property. Henry favoured his queen in the matter, naturally, but the council decided on a compromise for the benefit of both the wife and her mother-in-law. Clearly, however, the free rides enjoyed by the Savoyards for twenty years had just now got harder to come by.

Henry probably thought they got what they deserved, inasmuch as they helped launch the revolution he had on his hands. Boniface had certainly played his part earlier when, in August 1257, he defied the king and summoned a council to air complaints about all the extortion of his churchmen. The prelates drew up a set of articles on the liberties of the Church, which Henry saw as a provocative attempt to restrict his own rights. Still, there was no thought of abandoning any of them now, not as isolated as he was from the English baronage, and Boniface for one was in the perfect position to make amends. Although he led the oath to observe the Provisions, he could at some point later on read out a dispensation from the pope absolving the royal entourage of that oath.

As for why Henry took an oath that went against his entire notion of kingship, he realised that, similar to the rebellion of 1234, his personal rule had painted him into another corner. There was no way he could meet the terms imposed on him by the pope, nor was there any sense in doing so now that Manfred was on the verge of proclaiming himself King of Sicily. The only way for him to avoid being excommunicated was to play on what he thought had been the case when the barons marched into his palace of Westminster. He would become their prisoner after all. They were in control now. Alexander would have to deal with them.

Not that he was entirely keen on washing his hands of the affair. Like the Savoyards, he still wanted Sicily for Edmund and was working towards peace with France to achieve that end. But the pope's intransigence had been instrumental in bringing about the phantom *coup d'état*. Alexander would see that that had been a mistake, and once he moderated his demands and absolved the king of his oath Henry would be free to reclaim that which was rightfully his, a kingship free of restrictions, and that would enable him to prosecute the Sicilian business with renewed vigour.

Henry had every reason to feel confident. The barons complained that the Savoyards and Lusignans had done extremely well under him. Well, so had they. He let them get away with defaulting on their payments, infringing on his rights and being petty tyrants, and they also got a wardship here and there. Sicily was their big gripe, but little of that money was their own. Anyone could see that all this revolution business was coming from the people who did have to pay: the knights, abbots, freeholders and city dwellers. They were the ones fed up with the king coming down hard on them, but his barons were equally guilty. Their real interests were the same as his, in hunting and feasting and acting important, while the rest of the realm toiled in the fields and shops or else just plain starved. The barons were as much sitting ducks as he was but were making him the scapegoat of all that was going wrong. Well, let them play clerks for a while, let them grapple with the machinery of government that in the end would straitjacket them all, then they would quit all this reform nonsense and resume the good life.

Nowhere, apparently, was this self-interest more evident than in his brother-in-law Simon de Montfort. The committee of twenty-four had only recently been established when Henry agreed to allow it to settle Simon and Eleanor's claims against him. All the barons had grievances, but those of the Montforts went further back and were more personally involved. They were all young adults when Eleanor's dower first became an issue; now they were in an advanced age for that time, with still no modern sense of closure in sight. Henry had never tried to buy off his sister the way he did Richard, and the only time he had seriously addressed her claims was when his mother-in-law shamed him into doing so fifteen years before. Then he only made it worse by giving William de Valence land Eleanor felt rightfully belonged to her, favouring their half-brother over her. This perceived slight no doubt figured into Simon's emotions when he threatened to chop Valence's head off.

Henry was being disingenuous by making the Montforts, like Sicily, the barons' problem now. He had so little land left to give that someone, probably on the baronial side of the committee, was going to have to disgorge to make way for them and that would inevitably lead to cracks in the movement. Unlike the vast majority of the population, however, the Montforts weren't doing badly in 1258, so if Simon's principal motivation was something other than personal gain and satisfaction, then Henry had to know he was playing a dangerous game. Montfort's military skill notwithstanding, he had a tenacious intensity of purpose that made him a host in himself. Like Robert Grosseteste, he was the type fired up by causes, one who set out to finish whatever he took in hand. The man who cast his burning taper down on the floor and said 'Amen' when he swore to observe the Provisions of Oxford would definitely take it amiss if the others at that solemn ceremony went on to cast their oaths aside – particularly the king.

And so Henry had to be feeling uncomfortable as the summer wore on and Simon's role in the reform movement grew ever stronger. There was no more telling sign of it than the appearance of so many of his friends and adherents as councillors and castellans. These men weren't about to disappear from the scene no matter what the outcome of his claims against the king was. Montfort was clearly organising a political party and had the prestige and qualities to make it a force to be reckoned with. Whether it could be called 'baronial' remained to be seen, but the idea of his brother-in-law at the head of any opposition to his personal rule had to be unsettling to Henry. He had wanted the barons' help in rescuing him from an impossible situation with the papacy, but like the queen's moves against the Lusignans, he was now faced with an unintended, and unpleasant, consequence. Thrust into the forefront of the reform movement was the one man he feared the most, even more than nature itself.

The other confederates were just as busy that summer, but one of them, Richard de Clare, was temporarily sidelined when, in late July, right around the time Henry was trembling before Simon at their riverfront meeting, he and his brother William sat down to have breakfast with Edward in Winchester. Edward was extremely perturbed by the treatment of his uncles and registered his displeasure by making land grants to Guy Lusignan and appointing Geoffrey Lusignan his seneschal in Gascony. The committee forced him to revoke both acts immediately.

The point of the meeting was for Edward to show he was finally on board, but the result couldn't have been worse. Both Clare brothers fell extremely ill afterwards, with William dying and Richard losing all his hair, teeth, and fingernails. It was certainly food poisoning, but whether it was intentional or accidental, Edward wasn't affected. Clare's steward was accused of being in the pay of the Lusignans and fled the scene. He was caught and protested his innocence all the way to the gallows. Edward escaped suspicion, but since the steward was his tenant, he got to keep all the income from the executed man's lands.

Clare's last contribution before becoming incapacitated was to help draft a letter to the pope explaining the situation in England. In it, the barons declared they were ready to bring the matter of Sicily to a happy conclusion if the king agreed to cooperate with them in reforming the realm and if the pope would ease the burden of the conditions. The king was cooperating. Now it was up to the pope.

Alexander glumly replied that since Henry had not fulfilled his obligations, he had the right to offer the crown to someone else. He might as well have given up at that point, because Manfred crowned himself in Palermo in August 1258. Since it made no sense to excommunicate Henry under these conditions, the pope suspended all penalties 'with our accustomed kindness, special grace and during pleasure'.

Beneath the gloss, he vented his frustration by sabotaging another item dear to the reform movement, namely keeping Aymer de Valence out of the country for good. A thief and a thug to the barons, he was still the bishop-elect of Winchester in the eyes of Rome. The letter of the barons dealt more with him than with the wretched Sicilian business, spelling out the crimes of the Lusignans and warning of all kinds of evils that would visit England if he returned. The pope answered by saying he was troubled by the matter but deferred from taking action until Aymer had his say. That said, he would show those presumptuous barons and do everything in his power to return Aymer to his diocese.

One churchman whose counsels were welcomed at home was Walter de Cantilupe, the Bishop of Worcester. There was little in his early career, which went all the way back to John's reign, to suggest a reforming spirit. He came from a Norman family closely tied to royal service and patronage. He resisted attempts to restrict pluralism, the practice of occupying more than one benefice, because he said that such income was necessary for the Church to perform good works. Like Montfort, he became fired up when he met Robert Grosseteste.

The late Bishop of Lincoln had been keen to introduce Aristotle to the medieval mind, and in one of his tracts he dwelt on the nature of kingship when it became more take than give, which is what Henry's rule had come down to. Cantilupe, who was probably introduced to Simon through his nephew, Peter de Montfort, stood by Boniface's attempts to protect the liberties of the Church and did not assume the mantle of spiritual guide until later, when Boniface had enough of reform and fled the country.

Boniface's name, followed by those of Walter and Simon, led the witnesses to the proclamation of the Provisions of Oxford that was read aloud at a public gathering in Westminster on 18 October 1258. In the presence of the king, it was declared that Henry would abide by the statutes of his councillors 'for the honour of God' and commanded his subjects to obey and defend them. The importance of this document cannot be underestimated, for it was distributed in Latin, French, and English: Latin for the record, French for the nobility and English for the working stiff. Its appearance in English, making it the first known state paper preserved in that language, shows that it was meant to be read out locally, that the events in Oxford touched upon the entire realm, and that whatever course Henry decided to take in the future, he would have to answer to all the people, and not just to his barons and councillors.

Of course, the reformers would have to come up with more than just a proclamation to show that change really was in the offing. It had started almost immediately when the office of justiciar was revived after a quarter of a century and Hugh Bigod was named to the post. His appointment was certainly political, for he had no training in the law and had not served in any judicial capacity, and the first case he heard was that of his brother-in-law John Fitz-Geoffrey against Aymer. He was chosen not because the barons were looking for expertise in this field, rather because they wanted someone with clout, who would enforce the law and was willing to endure what was going to be a long, grinding process. Since Hugh was the most junior member of the confederates, and probably a bruiser like his brother Roger, he was given the task and sent on his way.

His first circuit, or eyre, dealt with cases already pending, like the sheriff of Northampton and his predecessor, two beastly individuals who had robbed and extorted the local peasantry at will. By the time Bigod's second eyre got underway, four commissioners for each county had been appointed and were collecting complaints. As expected, he found himself besieged by plaintiffs, a far cry from the not too distant past when the arrival of an eyre would send people scurrying into the woods for cover. Not all the complaints were about the sheriffs and their henchmen extorting money, however. There were business partners and neighbours quarrelling with each other, village bullies to deal with, and the occasional case of somebody coming after somebody else with an axe. The difference this time was the hope that justice would take precedence over fundraising.

Henry probably didn't keep close tabs on these events. Important for him now was to keep the pope from giving Sicily to another candidate and find a way to reinstate his brothers. One piece of business he was able to conclude under these circumstances was the peace treaty with France. A preliminary version had been drawn up in May of that year, but the only other progress allowed by the barons after Oxford was to send an envoy to Louis asking him not to interfere with events in England. Pulling what might aptly be called 'a Henry', Louis used the extraordinary situation across the water to beg his own barons for money.

Finally, in November, a conference was scheduled in Cambrai, where Louis, Henry and Richard, the King of Germany no matter what Alfonso said, would ratify the peace treaty. The barons, however, were worried that Henry might try to cause mischief while abroad and refused to let him leave the country. They sent a formal delegation instead, under chief negotiator Simon, but Louis felt insulted at being asked to deal with underlings and not principals and refused to attend.

But since he had come this far, Richard decided to keep going and return to England after an absence of nearly two years. He had been the leading magnate when he left the country, a man of such wealth and power that 'all business of the realm hung on his nod'. The barons might not have got as far as they did with the reform process had he contented himself with being a mere noble and never left. Now he was returning a king, but he was about to discover that he had no more influence or prestige than that other king, his brother.

9

For and Against the Common Enterprise 1259–1260

It was a nervous group of barons that met Richard at the seashore at the end of January 1259. They were worried he might be accompanied by one or more of the Lusignans, who were after all his brothers too, and so refused to allow him to enter Dover Castle. Even after none of them appeared, he was ordered to proceed to Canterbury and take the oath to observe the Provisions before commencing with any other business. Richard must have been aghast that they were bossing him around like this, but he had only himself to thank for it. When he was asked to take the oath while he was still on the Continent, he had sniffed that he had no peer in England. He was the son of the late king and brother of the current one. Only Henry could order him to take the oath. So Henry did, at the insistence of the council, and the humiliation continued when the oath was administered to Richard as the Earl of Cornwall and not by the title he gave himself, the Latin equivalent of 'By the grace of god King of the Romans, always august'.

To drive home the point that he was indeed surrounded by peers, the oath was administered by his stepson, Richard de Clare, who had sufficiently recovered from his food poisoning to take a leading role again among the barons. From their ranks could be heard grumbling over the absence of the one peer who should have been there, whose soldierly reputation was a mainstay of the movement. Simon de Montfort was lingering on the Continent, reportedly to the wonder and amazement of all, and this gave rise to fears about some hidden conspiracy in the works.

After the peace conference failed to materialise in Cambrai, Simon delayed his return in order to attend his private affairs, which included drafting his will. He was with his two older sons at the time, and Henry de Montfort, educated by Grosseteste, wrote it out in his own hand. His role in drafting his father's will reflects the intensely personal nature of medieval testaments and the importance given to the deceased's peace of mind rather than to his property.

In Montfort's case, he was clearly in need of it. He wanted his family to be freed of all the debts he had incurred and was even willing to admit claims there might be uncertainty about. He had recently taken a step in this direction by making arrangements with the executors of Peter of Dreux to settle those debts after almost thirty years.

He was also troubled by the burdens he had inflicted on his peasants, the 'poor people of my land' as he called them, and wanted them compensated before his family came into their inheritance. It was possible he was trying to spare his children future legal problems, but the appearance of the will in January 1259, six months after the excitement of the previous summer, and dictated in a language laced with introspection and remorse, suggests that, for Montfort, the issue of reform no longer addressed the king and his barons but the community as a whole. By the time he arrived for the February parliament, it had become, in his words, the 'common enterprise'. Having his son draft his will and naming Eleanor as one of the executors also indicates that he intended it to be a family enterprise as well.

On the other hand, Clare's enthusiasm was starting to wane as the reform work became evermore intrusive. Not the grind of administrative work, for nearly all of that had been done by judges and clerks by the time Parliament convened. Rather, he was disturbed by reports that Hugh Bigod was receiving complaints not just directed at Henry and the sheriffs but at magnates like him. Such complaints might somehow infringe his rights, he announced, but his fears fell on deaf ears, and Parliament went on to adopt an ordinance that gave tenants more say in disputes with their lords.

The five-week delay between its adoption and formal issue was a sign that Clare had tried his best to obstruct it. Disgusted by his behaviour, Simon turned on him in a fury.

'I do not care to live with people so deceitful. For we have promised and sworn to carry out these plans we are discussing. And as for you, my lord Earl of Gloucester, the higher your position is above us all, so much the more are you bound to carry these wholesome statutes into effect.'

Simon left England again, this time on more treaty business, but a group of barons attributed his departure to Clare's intransigence and advised the Earl of Gloucester to make good on his oath and reform his own administration. This he did with all due haste, but he was already making plans to strike back. In March of that year, he entered into a formal alliance with Edward, where they promised to help each other and their supporters.

Parliament had sought to curb this practice of lords extending protection to someone who wasn't their man since it blurred feudal obligations. The alliance between Edward and Clare was a repudiation of this effort and something of a surprise, given they were feuding over a castle in Bristol at the time. But in practical terms it made sense. Clare probably presumed that Edward was still opposed to the reforms being carried out, and Edward saw Clare's obstructionist tendencies as vital in preventing the forthcoming ratification of the peace treaty with France.

Edward had a big problem with the treaty because he rightly suspected his overseas lands would be affected by the agreement. His opinion hardly mattered anymore, because after years of negotiation, the treaty was ready to be sealed and not even the Earl of Gloucester, one of the final proctors, could prevent it from going forward. What nobody had stopped to consider was whether the Earl of Leicester could, or to be more exact, whether his wife could.

In addition to Henry renouncing his rights to Normandy and other lands in France, the treaty called for his sons Edward and Edmund, and his siblings Eleanor and Richard, as the other surviving children of King John, to do so as well. There didn't seem to be anything out of the ordinary with such a provision until Eleanor sideswiped Henry by saying she would renounce as soon as he made good her financial claims. It was an unexpected impasse, one that exasperated Henry and led him to assert that the insertion of this clause was Simon's work.

Henry's weak justification was that other members of the royal family, like Richard's youngest son, had not been asked to do the same. Seen in this light, the Montforts were alleged to have planned this little surprise all along in order to get Henry to finally take their claims seriously. Of course, it also raises the question of how Henry and his advisers, particularly the astute John Mansel, did not see it coming through all the years and toil on the treaty. However it came to pass, ratification came to a halt as Eleanor, it might be said, insisted on her day in court.

First, it had been a quarter of a century since she was forced to take an unfair dower settlement over the Marshal estate. In that time she had to put up with endless defaults and watch other widows get more favourable treatment. Next, she wanted her brother to assign her the land he promised in place of their £400 fee six years earlier. Henry had done as much for their half-brother William de Valence, whose £350 fee had long been completely converted. Finally, she wanted him to pay the money he owed her husband that was still outstanding from their arrangement over Gascony. Once he fulfilled these obligations, she was ready to renounce.

There was nothing for it except to try and satisfy them. The last point proved the easiest despite Henry's poverty and he paid up in early May. The second was trickier, because although Henry authorised the transfer of nine manors to Eleanor within a fortnight, they were probably part of the royal demesne and therefore could not be alienated from the Crown. Moreover, as part of his councillor's oath, Simon had sworn not to accept any grants from the demesne. When Henry later accused him of violating his oath in this manner, without explaining why he granted the lands if he had known this to be the case, Simon skirted the issue by saying they were given to his wife. Certain members of the council agreed with the king that the transfer was ethically problematic, including Peter of Savoy, but his reservations were more concerned with the Savoyards who were dispossessed on account of it.

The issue of the dower, however, was going to require arbitration, and medieval arbitration was, if nothing else, a notoriously slow and unreliable process. Often nothing ever came of it because the arbitrators, who could be almost anyone, didn't want the job, or one of the parties pulled out at the last second, or the case dragged on for too long. By this point, Eleanor's case was already twenty-five years old and it would be another twenty-five before it was off the books, long after all the principals were dead.

This particular arbitration had no chance from the beginning anyway. The Montforts were claiming arrears of £24,000, more than twice the £10,000 to which they were probably entitled. Far from overplaying their hand, the higher figure was a good way to browbeat Henry with what they considered his blatant favouritism for the queen's relations. Of the 170 Savoyards who came to England after Henry's marriage, thirty-nine of them had received land from him and the others got generous payments. So little property was left by the time the Lusignan wave arrived a decade later that only twenty-eight of them were similarly endowed, but that was twenty-eight ahead of Eleanor in the king's disposition of the land he inherited from their father.

What's more, Simon knew the king's poverty was about to be relieved by a windfall from the treaty. He was to receive enough money to maintain a force of 500 knights, ultimately worth £33,500. If he never got around to using these knights, meaning they never made it to Sicily, he was required to use the money with the advice of the 'good men of the land'. It would have been better for Henry and the realm to use that money to satisfy his sister or at least for rebuilding Westminster Abbey. Instead, much of it would eventually go to hiring mercenaries.

Another reason why the arbitration was doomed from the start was because the earls of Hereford and Norfolk sat on the panel. They were heirs to the Marshal fortune and so stood to lose out from any settlement in Eleanor's favour. The third arbitrator was Philip Basset, the brother of the recently deceased Bishop of London. Philip had revolted with his family against Henry back in 1234, when their own interests were at stake, but since that time he was squarely behind the king. The panel was supposed to make its award by November. For reasons unknown, they never declared it. Henry later accused Montfort of learning that the award had gone against him and so had it quashed, but it's difficult to see how

Simon could have exerted that much influence over these heads of three of the most prominent families in England.

In fact, Henry may have been reckoning with a no-decision all along, for he had a version of the treaty drawn up without his sister's renunciation in time for the parliament of October 1259. Upon learning of it, Simon hit back by telling the French envoys in attendance that Eleanor, in this instance, would press her claim to Normandy after all. Finally, Louis stepped in to end all the bickering by declaring that he would withhold £10,000 of the money due Henry under the treaty until he settled his sister's claims, to be done within the next two years. He also made a gift of £110 in annual rent to the Montforts, a form of inducement which Henry never seems to have considered. Out of respect for Louis and his negotiator Eudes Rigaud, the Archbishop of Rouen, who was also a good friend, Eleanor acquiesced and made her formal renunciation the day after Eudes read the treaty aloud in an orchard of the king's palace on 4 December.

For Clare, Eleanor's refusal to renounce was his chance to get back at Montfort when they went to France as proctors earlier that spring. He berated Simon in a quarrel so violent that the French got a good laugh out of watching the English side almost coming to blows. Clare couldn't care less about the treaty. His own family claims in France were sure to come to nothing, and as one of the major beneficiaries of the Marshal partition, he knew he stood to lose over any accommodation for Eleanor. The recent reforms, moreover, had made him realise just how conservative he was at heart. He marked his gradual drift back to Henry by becoming a booster for the treaty and rallying the baronage to also look askance at Montfort's stance. That got the attention of Edward, who had unwillingly renounced his rights. He now saw Simon as his last hope of scuttling the treaty.

The background for this shift was the parliament of October 1259 and a protest lodged by a group calling itself 'the bachelors of England', probably the knights in attendance at this session. They appealed to Edward and Clare to make good the legislation from the previous spring and force the magnates to submit to reform. If these two were approached on account of their alliance, then the bachelors had not heard that Edward had come to despise

Clare and his unreliability. Two days after the October parliament opened, Edward ditched Clare for good and made a new alliance with Montfort. With his uncle behind him, Edward took up the cause of the bachelors and helped to push through the final major provisions in the reform movement, subsequently enacted at Westminster. They offered redress for even the lowest rungs of feudal society and further tightened the screws on the royal family by taking firm control of wardships and queen's gold.

The king and queen were naturally indignant at their son's behaviour, but were determined to enjoy their trip to France. They left in November with a retinue that included their son Edmund, daughter Beatrice, Richard de Clare, Peter of Savoy, John Mansel and about eighty knights and clerks. Their party met up with the Montforts and even then the treaty was held up by another eight days in the final gruelling hours towards Eleanor's renunciation. In all probability, both sides preferred the company of their French hosts to each other as they gathered in the freezing orchard to witness Henry doing homage to Louis for Gascony. The King of France made sure there was nothing unbecoming about the King of England kneeling before him, although to his own barons, who could not understand why he just didn't finish with the English on the Continent, he all but bragged about Henry becoming his man.

Eager to show Louis that the reforms had not impinged on his dignity, Henry insisted on paying his way. To that end he brought bags full of his glorious gold pennies, 20,000 of which were eventually melted down in Paris. That enabled him to live large as he was accustomed to and also to stage another of his great feedings, this time providing for 1,500 of France's poor in a single day.

He had a chance to seal the loyalty of the French royal family when their fifteen-year-old son Louis died and Henry shouldered the boy's coffin for part of the funeral procession on 14 January 1260. The event that should have taken place on that day was the wedding of his daughter Beatrice to John, the son of the Duke of Brittany. The postponement of the wedding, and the terms of the wedding itself, would be the next source of contention between Simon and Henry, and showed that if there ever had been a friendly understanding between Montfort and the Savoyards, it was gone now.

The marriage was the idea of Queen Margaret, who struggled to enjoy the same influence with her husband as her sister Eleanor had with Henry. The problem of the match for Henry was that the Duke of Brittany had an ancestral claim to the honour of Richmond, which his father Peter of Dreux had forfeited when he did homage to Louis in 1235. The duke saw the marriage of his son as the chance to get Richmond back in the family and so suggested it would make a nice marriage portion for Beatrice. This put Henry in a tight spot, because he had already given Richmond to Peter of Savoy, lock, stock and barrel, and Peter wasn't about to vacate his ownership for anyone.

The English proctors offered the young couple a financial equivalent from other rents in France until something could be worked out, only this looked suspiciously like the king was protecting Peter's interests. Since he was a Savoyard and therefore an alien, it was sure to be an act the council would frown upon. When Simon informed the Duke of Brittany that the king could only proceed in this matter with the council's approval, Henry and his queen were livid.

Simon was also determined that they respect the reforming provision that called for Parliament to be summoned three times a year, starting with the one commonly known as Candlemas, in February. The English entourage had originally planned to return by Christmas, but the adulation of the crowds, the architecture, the funeral and the wedding all set them back by a month. They could still make it, but Simon felt that the king was deliberately stalling as a way of undermining the Provisions. He registered his protest by departing without taking leave of Henry, a bit of anti-protocol the king found offensive.

Henry was probably thankful he left, as he could now enjoy the rest of his visit in the company of councillors ready to support him, including Richard de Clare. He might have thought differently had he had any inkling that Simon would try to convene Parliament in his absence. When that alarm reached him, he immediately ordered the justiciar to make sure it didn't meet until he arrived home, whenever that would be. Three months later, it turned out.

The justiciar, Hugh Bigod, realised more than ever what a

thankless position reform had put him into. After hearing 268 complaints in one year, he had given up any hope of hearing what were likely to be thousands more waiting for him throughout the country. He was acutely aware that the reformers had set an enormous task before him, and that he perhaps wasn't up to it. Now, when Simon showed up with Peter de Montfort, Walter de Cantilupe and other councillors to summon Parliament, he sheepishly told them that the king had forbade it.

Montfort wasn't having any of it and told the justiciar that at the least he should not honour Henry's request for money, because he would only use it to hire mercenaries to keep Parliament from meeting. It was all too much for Hugh and, like Clare before him, he began his eventual defection back to the king. In fact, it had probably begun earlier, before the king went to France, when Henry granted a wardship to a Savoyard, and Hugh, together with John Mansel, authorised the transaction without the council's approval.

Of the seven confederates, only the two de Montforts were still committed to reform as the spring of 1260 approached. John Fitz-Geoffrey had died in November 1258. Reform seemed good to Roger Bigod when there were less militant and adamant people like Simon and Edward in control. Like his brother, his allegiance to the king took precedence over the Provisions. Clare, Hugh and Peter of Savoy all stood by Henry now, although there had never been any real defection on Peter's part. He was sneaky by nature, always dealing and trying to play the diplomat, and his departure for Savoy at the end of January gave him an excuse to avoid taking sides in the issue over Parliament. When he lost his position on the council as a result, Henry pinned that action on Simon as well.

The loss in confederates was made up for by Edward, who at a youthful twenty years of age was spoiling for a fight. His parents had barely crossed the Channel for France when he threw out the handlers imposed on him and seized control of his castles. He made his base in Bristol, where he hoped Clare would finally get the message to stay away if he knew what was good for him. He could afford to act tough from his proximity to Marcher country and his new friends, which included many of the lords of that violent region. He wasn't just out to assert his independence, however. His meeting with the bachelors had stoked what was a growing awareness that he had an obligation to do justice to all men. The days of hooliganism were over, presumably.

Edward joined his uncle in insisting that Parliament be convened and brought in a troop of young warrior knights to bolster their demand. And yet by late February he was already backtracking. Learning that his father had reached the coast, and had heard certain rumours, he wrote him a conciliatory letter. Henry's reply showed he was no fool. He told Edward how greatly pleased and rejoiced he was to hear from him, but that he would nevertheless send someone to ascertain whether his 'deeds matched words'.

That someone was Clare, a choice calculated to put the burden of proof on Edward, and in this situation he had no chance. The Earl of Gloucester took one look at all the armed men and assumed that Edward and Simon were planning to seize the throne. He snitched this information back to Henry and began raising troops for the king.

Despite the tension, Henry continued to linger across the Channel. He finally roused himself after Louis visited him at the end of March and shamed him into returning. It was meant to be a private rebuke, but Henry could never give up the habit of airing his humiliations in public. Louis nudged him along by giving him nearly £6,000 as the first instalment of his treaty money, which was probably the true reason behind the king's delay.

Before crossing, Henry tried to discredit Simon in Louis' eyes by claiming he had used a safe-conduct pass from the French king to import arms and warhorses into England. In the same breath he added that his Lusignan brothers were planning, against his will, to enter England by force, as if to suggest they were now in league with Montfort. 'By this you can clearly deduce for yourself the way in which the earl's mind works,' he told him.

April 1260 saw both sides descend on London with their armed retainers. Simon was determined to hold Parliament and Clare was equally determined to stop him. Richard of Cornwall had been warned by his brother of the trouble brewing and hurried to the city to convince the mayor and aldermen to lock the gates and set a watch. Henry had summoned Parliament in the meantime, carefully excluding Simon and his supporters from the list he sent ahead of him.

The king finally arrived on 23 April, backed by a force of up to 300 foreign knights. When Clare was invited inside the city walls and Edward wasn't, the young prince cracked and begged for a chance to explain himself, but Henry let him sweat it out for two weeks. He was finally admitted to a gathering at St Paul's, where he was forced to swear before his family and a select group of magnates that he never meant any disobedience. He threw himself at his father's mercy and did him proud by proclaiming that only a king could judge him. The queen, however, only welcomed him back under condition that she again have the authority to pick and choose his friends and advisers, and the first of the bad influences she wanted rid of was Montfort.

With his son back in the fold and Simon seemingly isolated, Henry felt emboldened to move against his adversary. He decided to put him on trial again, much like in 1252, only now he could be sure the magnates would not support him as they had during that earlier process. His confidence was misplaced, for Louis got wind of Henry's intentions and sent two Normans, one of them Archbishop Rigaud, to monitor the preliminary investigation.

Knowing of Rigaud's closeness to Simon, Henry and the queen made an effort to curry his favour, but as usual Simon was a step ahead of them both. Rigaud and his fellow envoy had business to transact in England and Montfort facilitated it for them. The archbishop then returned the favour by offering a benefice to his son Amaury in Rouen. But so deep was Henry's anger at his brother-in-law by this point that he didn't care if Louis himself was there, he would still ruin him.

The pre-trial hearing consisted of questions put to Montfort that were meant to get him to admit that his behaviour had been treasonous and seditious. There were thirty-nine in all, mostly carping over the peace treaty, the arbitration award and the attempt to hold Parliament. Simon's replies show he was more than a match for whatever Henry and his advisers threw at him. He either denied the charges outright or referred his actions to the authority of the Provisions and council. What must have really had Henry gnawing at his beard was Simon's dismissive attitude towards the king's feigned sense of outrage. From the transcript:

> The king says that he was forced to return to England with a large following, and that in bringing these men he incurred great expense. The earl says that he had done nothing which would have justified the king in bringing armed men into England, and that his incurring the expense was his own affair, for there never was any need for it.
>
> The king says that the earl was thinking of giving such a welcome to these men from overseas that others would have no great desire to follow them. The earl says that he said many things for the honour and profit of the king to dissuade him from bringing such a following, for he knew it would be harmful and dishonourable both to the king and the country.

When Simon was asked if the king decreed that no one should come to Parliament with horses and arms, he said that he wasn't there when the decree was made, but that it was a good decision. So then when asked if he came to Parliament with horses and arms, he replied that he came in the way he usually travelled around the country.

One charge that may have been the work of the Savoyards was Simon's alleged reconciliation with the Lusignans. It had to do with the county of Bigorre again, the ownership of which had passed to Simon in lieu of the debts his nephew Esquivat, the nominal Lord of Bigorre, owed him. Simon then ceded the county to Henry, but he too failed to pay up. In the spring of 1260, Esquivat forgot all of Gaston de Bearn's bullying and teamed up with him to take the county back.

Given the geographical remoteness, the only person who could help Simon exert his authority there was Edward, the Lord of Gascony. He was still on friendly terms with his uncle despite recent events and so asked his other uncles, Guy, Geoffrey, and William, to secure Montfort's hold on the county. Simon refuted the charge of collaborating with the Lusignans by saying he had only patched up his personal quarrel with William and in no way did that affect the 'common enterprise'. He even implicated the king by saying he had begged him to make up with them before he left England, thus exposing Henry's continued protestations against his brothers as a sham.

The trial itself seems to have been interrupted at the urging of Clare, who was afraid his attempt to turn Henry against his son would come out into the open. It was further postponed in July when the Welsh overran and destroyed the castle of Builth on the very day the castellan, Roger Mortimer, arrived at court. Edward was enraged, not least because Mortimer was allied to Clare, and he joined other barons in accusing Mortimer of deserting his post. Henry tried to restore unity by calling out the feudal host, with one army to be led by Clare and the other by Simon. The king entrusting command to a person he had lately accused of plotting against him generated comment at the time that it was a win-win situation for him. Simon would either be victorious in the field or prefer death to defeat. The Welsh pre-empted that option by agreeing to a truce before any troops set out.

Dying around the time of the muster for Wales was Walter Kirkland, the Bishop of Durham, whose home on the Thames was the scene of Henry's panic attack when he met Simon. The king and queen saw his death as an opportunity to reward John Mansel for years of able and loyal service by having him installed as the new bishop. In an almost childish intrigue, the royal pair even planned it so that as soon as the representatives of the bishopric had been wined and dined by Henry, a message would arrive from the queen asking the king to press for the election of Mansel, thereby allowing an unseen party to bring up his candidacy with the monks.

In early September, after both Henry and Eleanor wrote letters to the chapter lobbying for Mansel, Edward wrote one of his own, wherein he urged the monks to stand firm against that scoundrel Mansel and choose Walter de Cantilupe's nephew Hugh instead. He justified the choice by declaring that Hugh would be for the 'whole people' and not just for the king and queen.

The monks played it safe by electing one of their own, and Henry almost seemed resigned to it being a done deal when the bishop-elect showed up at Parliament in October 1260. Montfort was there too, with his two older sons, and Edward underscored their alliance by knighting his cousins during the St Edward's Day festivities. Another cousin, Henry of Almain, was deputised by the council to perform the duties of steward for the occasion, which Simon had been accustomed to doing as the Earl of Leicester. This time he asked the council to let Almain do it, another bit of anti-protocol Henry found hurtful, probably because he couldn't bring himself to wait on the king any more than was absolutely necessary.

Under Clare's direction, Parliament set out to circumvent the reforms aimed at major landlords like him. The magnates were given full discretionary power to correct abuses on their estates, and the special eyre meant to weed out these abuses was replaced by a general eyre. Henry charged that the new sheriffs appointed under the Provisions had been too timid to stand up to the magnates, and it was precisely for this reason that Parliament, controlled by the magnates, decided to keep them past their one-year tenure. Had he been allowed to appoint the sheriffs himself, as in the past, tenants would be enjoying better protection from their landlords. Of course, if that were truly the case, there wouldn't have been any Provisions in the first place.

Montfort probably closed his eyes to this watery version of the Provisions as a means of finishing off his trial and gaining reinstatement in government. Whatever the sanctity of the Provisions, they were worthless without power to back them, and in this regard he gave Clare what he wanted in exchange for an agreement to change the top Crown officials. This in itself was a reminder that reform was here to stay, for Henry bitterly resented the council appointing his officials for him. The removal of Hugh Bigod as justiciar was certainly a blow. Henry hadn't wanted him, but his waxen loyalty had so far worked to his advantage. The man who replaced him now, Hugh Despenser, was a friend of Simon's, but he was also Philip Basset's son-in-law. Any doubts about which side of the debate he was on were removed when he undertook an eyre that targeted royalists such as Peter of Savoy, Richard of Cornwall and John de Warenne.

Peeved though he was by these appointments, Henry already had a plan in place to gut the Provisions, and if all worked out, the new appointees would soon be sent packing. The first step called for Edward and his entourage, which included Henry of Almain, John of Brittany and the Montfort boys, to go overseas and cool their heels on the tournament circuit for a while. Peter of Savoy returned shortly after they left, perhaps timed so that he wouldn't have to face John of Brittany, and was quickly readmitted to the council. He wasn't there for long, because the next step was to disband the council itself.

Henry decided he didn't need a council, only to surround himself with a royalist faction consisting of Richard (who had given up all hope of ever being anything more than a titular king), Peter of Savoy, John Mansel, Robert Walerand and Hugh Bigod. Clare, whose unreliability both camps were finding irksome, was ignored. Simon wasn't even considered, but he had gone abroad anyway. With these two and Edward removed from the scene, Henry felt strong enough to plot his next move as 1260 drew to a close.

It would involve the connivance of the pope, and Alexander had already shown his readiness to help Henry out of his difficult situation. In 1259 the pope had sent one of his chaplains to England to plead for Aymer's return to his diocese. Henry never sought the council's approval for the visit. He waited till the keeper of the great seal was absent to issue a safe-conduct pass and then despatched it to Dover. That bit of intrigue ensured the chaplain got a frosty reception when he reached London. Undaunted, the pope officially consecrated Aymer as the Bishop of Winchester just to spite the barons. It was in vain, however, because Aymer died that December in Paris, without ever seeing England again.

10

Royalist Resurgence
1261–1262

Almost three years into the reform of the realm and Henry had laid the groundwork for completely undoing it. The barons had been divided and dispersed, Louis was now a good friend and source of funds, and the council had been mothballed. All he needed before he could take all power back into his hands was a papal absolution from his oath to uphold the Provisions, and for that he despatched the nephew of John Mansel to Rome in January 1261. Since he wouldn't be back until late spring, Henry would have to play for time, but Mansel and the other court fixers already had that figured out.

The king would attack the barons during the upcoming parliament and keep them on the defensive, all the while professing to stand by his oath. There was no telling how they might react, especially with that firebrand Montfort always insisting they hold him to account. Taking no chances, Henry left Windsor on 9 February and moved to the safety of the Tower for the next three months. The magnates were summoned to appear at Parliament a fortnight later, but a week before that Henry sent a private message to two dozen lesser barons to precede them and, more importantly, come armed. Simon must have wondered what happened to the decree forbidding such action. Henry, however, was in no mood to quibble. In what had to be a masterful performance, he gave the magnates a dressing down that summed up his belief that their little experiment had failed.

Because of them, the King of England was a laughing stock in the eyes of the world. His nobility treated him as a child and refused him the use of his seal. They named his officials, kept him impoverished and allowed the business of the realm to suffer as a result. They used the pretext of reform to enrich themselves while doing nothing for the profit of the king and his people. If this was kingship, they were all on the wrong page.

Had he stopped there, Henry might have made a more lasting impression. Instead he reverted to form and let petulance and immaturity tack on more mundane charges. It was because of them, he cried, that his baggage had been waylaid and his living quarters were going to ruin. Still, he had shrewdly avoided attacking the whole concept of the council and Provisions, and the fact that they were even holding Parliament was an indication of his willingness to abide by the latter. Forming a newly resurrected council on the spot, the barons replied there was no help for any of it. The king had gotten himself into this mess and begged them to extricate him from it. He had only himself to thank if he felt bridled by his own subjects.

The charges and replies were actually part of an arbitration process that Henry clearly had no intention of respecting. It was a ruse to keep the barons occupied until his plan to subvert the Provisions went into action. Confusing matters even further, he juggled it with a second arbitration meant to resolve his dispute with his sister and brother-in-law. This one he would have to respect, because Louis, Queen Margaret and French minister Peter le Chamberlain were the arbitrators.

It had been over a year since Henry agreed to settle their claims and still nothing had come of it. Simon turned to Louis because the families of the two Frenchmen went way back. The French monarchy owed their gains in the south to the crusade of Simon's father, and his brother Amaury had been the constable of France before his own crusade did him in. Louis and Simon had also been on crusade, as Henry had not, and their austere piety stood in contrast to Henry's habit of wearing his religion on his sleeve. No less important was Louis and Margaret's own grievance that they too had never received an adequate dower for her. On the other hand, Margaret was connected to the Savoyards, now the hardened enemies of the Montforts, and their influence on her, and she on her husband, could prove decisive.

Simon and Eleanor had asked the French royal couple to intervene while they were abroad on more litigation, this time against her Lusignan brothers. Her mother Isabella, who abandoned her when she was three, had made no disposition for her in her will, more proof that Eleanor had a greater right than most to be aggrieved by the way her family treated her. This particular case would drag on for ten years before being settled by the French *parlement* in Eleanor's favour. Simon was dead by that time, and the judgement went a long way towards securing her future in exile.

One of the brothers who missed the suit was William de Valence. In April 1261 he returned to England in the company of Edward. It was a sign of Henry's confidence that he was able to invite him and other members of the Lusignan party to come back and pick up where they left off some three years earlier. It also brought a new alliance out into the open, certain to be the most dangerous one facing the reform movement.

After spending years sniping and clawing at each other for Henry's favour, the Lusignans and Savoyards realised that their only hope of enjoying the bounty of England under the current climate was to get along with each other. The two French factions would have to put aside their mutual disgust before the Anglo-French faction, in the person of Simon de Montfort, ran them out of the country for good. But first, the queen laid down the condition that Valence had to swear to her sister Margaret that he would forgo any more slanderous attacks against her. As for the barons, they were only willing to let him return on his oath to abide by the Provisions. He swore on both accounts, most likely with no great feeling of endearment in either case.

Henry finally emerged from the Tower at the end of April and headed for Dover. It was essential for young Mansel to arrive from Rome without being searched by a baronial sympathiser, who might discover the papal absolution and rip it to shreds. He was also there to secure the passage of eighty foreign knights he hired for protection for when the big moment was at hand. The castellan of Dover was Hugh Bigod, and as much as the former justiciar had been obedient for the past year, Henry still wasn't taking any chances. He unceremoniously ejected Hugh from the castle and replaced him with his steadfast clerk Robert Walerand.

The papal bulls arrived at the end of May. They included

instructions for the Archbishop of Canterbury to excommunicate anyone who defied Henry in his resumption of power. Boniface was an energetic reformer and not easily cowed, but he was a Savoyard first and foremost and realised that his own survival now depended on closing ranks around the king.

Worried his moves might be detected in London, and always inclined to make a show of things, Henry decided to resurrect his kingship in his birthplace of Winchester. There, on 14 June 1261, he announced that the pope had absolved him of his oath. He would henceforth disregard the Provisions and the council and rule as he saw fit. One of his first acts was to dismiss Hugh Despenser as justiciar and replace him with Despenser's father-in-law Philip Basset. Henry really didn't have anything against Despenser or the chancellor, whom he also replaced, but he had to make it clear that he would pick and choose his own officials free of any restraint.

At Mansel's urging, Henry sent his costly contingent of foreign knights home and scurried back to the Tower. He got there just in time, for this lowest of all his underhanded tricks had united the barons in a show of boldness not seen since the heyday of 1258. Roger Bigod reappeared on the scene to join Clare and Montfort in denouncing Henry's actions, and the baronial ranks were swelled with the unlikely figures of John de Warenne and Roger Mortimer.

The one conspicuous absentee, the only reformer who like Simon was militant enough to force the king to back down, was Edward, but he was not the same idealist who had left for the Continent six months before. His relationship with his mother had improved drastically thanks to her grudging acceptance of his Lusignan uncles, and it helped that her son had come back from abroad preferring the company of foreigners to his English friends. But more importantly, he was broke. He had spent enormous sums of money on his bachelor sojourn, and Henry only agreed to bail him out at the price of his total submission. His pride more than his politics would suffer if he caved, but he donned a dutiful mantel and never again challenged his parents. Since there was no saving face, he decided not to show his, least of all to his uncle Simon, and slunk out of the country in July just as things were heating up.

Louis thought that war could be averted if the personal quarrel between Simon and Henry could be patched up. When his previous arbitration failed to reach a conclusion, he instigated a new panel involving Philip Basset and John Mansel for the king and Walter de Cantilupe and Peter de Montfort for Simon, with Peter le Chamberlain and the Duke of Burgundy mediating for the French king. As usual, the two sides got nowhere, probably because Henry was never sincere about reaching an agreement. It would work to his advantage if Simon were seen as an irascible, irreconcilable disturber of the peace whose only interests were war and enrichment. He was the chief threat, the only baron who came from a warlike background, who kept clamouring for money as much as he did for the holy Provisions. The others would fall in line once they got past their indignation and realised that Montfort was shouldering them with a burden they neither wanted nor were prepared for.

Until such time the barons took their cue from Simon and appealed to Louis to arbitrate for them, too, to help them ward off 'the desolation, destruction and irreparable loss which threaten the whole land'. Louis' ultimate failure to act, together with Edward's desertion, left the barons bereft of royal allies. It might have been the end of their movement then and there had they not received unexpected support from another source of discontent. Freeholders, burgesses and clerics were also furious at the king's duplicity and turned his standoff with the barons into a national front.

Local society had known something was afoot in Westminster since the Provisions were published in the counties in the autumn of 1258. One year later the bachelors marched on Parliament to protest the lack of progress on reforms that affected common folk. The year after that saw no resumption of the special eyre or any change in sheriffs as promised by the new legislation. When the change finally came in 1261, it wasn't the work of the council, rather the king, as telling a sign as any that the bad days were at hand again.

Henry knew he was poking a hornet's nest and tried to be reassuring in a proclamation that insisted no evil intent was meant. He recalled his long reign, where peace and justice had always prevailed. He had given in to the barons' experiment and the result was calamity. Now he was stepping in to restore order, albeit with foreign mercenaries where necessary, and putting men he could trust into positions of power.

These new sheriffs were also given control of royal castles, a move clearly designed to deal with any resistance. Among the barons tossed out from their perches were both Bigod brothers. For Hugh, it was his second ejection in as many months. He had tried to show the king he was again his loyal servant, but had been humiliated at every turn. All he had left was his oath to the Provisions, but even that wasn't enough to arouse him or Roger into action. They had Montfort for that.

Under Simon's leadership, the response of the barons was to install their own sheriffs, or 'keepers of the peace', in the counties to contest the king's sheriffs. Henry struck back, demanding that the baronial sheriffs cease and desist and ordering his foreign mercenaries, whom he referred to as his friends, to be ready to sail at the end of August. For a while it looked as if both sides had finally reached the brink, but the only notable confrontation between the rival groups took place in Gloucester.

There, Henry's man was Mathias Bezill. Originally from Touraine, he preceded the Savoyards in England, but was eventually absorbed into the queen's circle. When he heard that William de Tracy, the baronial keeper, was attempting to hold a session of the county court, Bezill and his men broke into the proceedings, grabbed Tracy and dragged him through the mud on the way to prison. It was a clear example of an Englishman being trampled underfoot by an alien, and yet the king, who said he was proud of his Englishness, openly stood by the brute from abroad.

The division in the country came to a head in September when Montfort, Cantilupe and Clare decided to hold their own parliament without the king. Through their baronial keepers, they summoned three elected knights from every county to appear for an assembly in St Albans to treat on matters of state. It was a revolutionary move, the first time Parliament would meet without the king's approval or participation.

Henry naturally saw it as more provocation and immediately sent out an order to his sheriffs to make sure those knights did not come to St Albans, but to Windsor, where he would receive them. Confused, the knights apparently took the safe course and never left for either venue. That was just fine with Henry, who was already making plans for the regularly scheduled parliament in October.

Expecting trouble, he ordered 150 tenants-in-chief to come armed and made sure to weed out as many disaffected barons as possible. Clare was one of the latter, and this probably proved too much for him. By mid-October he was asking Henry for a truce. With that, the united front disintegrated and other barons like the Bigod brothers crossed over as well. As far as Hugh Bigod was concerned, the Provisions were a dead letter.

The Earl of Gloucester's second bout of treachery was ascribed at the time to 'promises or favours of the queen'. While her personal history with Clare did go as far back as winning him over from the Lusignans, he could never stomach what he saw as Simon's radicalism. The summoning of the knightly class to Parliament against the king's wishes may have been the tipping point. Whatever the case, Clare and Hugh Bigod would never stray again. Peter of Savoy, of course, was solidly behind the king. Roger Bigod was still a reformer at heart, but preferred mediation to confrontation. That left only Simon and Peter de Montfort as the last of the original seven confederates who refused to capitulate.

And then, at the end of October, Peter de Montfort and his uncle Walter de Cantilupe agreed to arbitration with Henry, and Simon realised it had all been in vain. The English had turned tail again. He scorned any thought of life under such an unfettered king and took his family to live in France, declaring that he would rather 'die without a country than desert the truth'.

Of course, it was easy for him to say that. He came from France, still had lots of powerful family there, and enjoyed Louis' esteem and respect in a way he never got from Henry. Louis, moreover, had instituted his own reforms in the mid-1250s to root out corruption and oppression, to see to it that justice was served to all. They were meant to atone for his failed crusade, but the initiative had all been his. In England, similar concerns for ordinary folk always had to be imposed on Henry.

But even if Simon's friends also found Louis' kingship more to their liking, they didn't have the choice to uproot their station in life and resettle abroad. England was and had always been their home, Henry their king. He had outwitted them and there was nothing they could do about it except try to get the best possible deal. Taking the moral high ground was not a viable option at this time.

What should also be considered is whether Simon left England in a huff as this famous quote of his suggests. The portrayal of him at this point as a defeated and disappointed man hardly squares with the later coolheaded and daring leader who shrugged off adversity. It seems almost certain that the decision to go into exile was taken in consultation with the rump baronial leadership, or at the least with his affinity. Henry had won this round, it was true, but if there was to be another then the place for Montfort to be was in France, where he could organise troops and, perhaps more dangerous for Henry, win Louis over to their cause. Henry himself saw things this way and planned to deal with him there once he mopped up his gains at home.

Arbitrating for the king at Kingston-on-Thames in November 1261 was John Mansel, the solidly royalist Bishop of Salisbury, and Peter d'Aigueblanche, who had lain low for most of the reform period, reportedly due to a skin disease. The barons were represented by Roger Bigod, Peter de Montfort and Robert Marsh, the brother of Adam Marsh, who had died in 1259. The main issue was the appointment of sheriffs and here the resultant treaty allowed the king to choose from any of four knights offered by each shire for the post. This was only provisional, however, a bone tossed to the barons. It would be up to yet another arbitration committee to decide on the long-term method for their appointment, and in the event they were unable to reach an agreement, Richard of Cornwall would step in to decide.

Supposedly he was chosen because he had a reputation for being a fair and skilful mediator, neither of which was in evidence when he broke the expected deadlock by coming out totally on his brother's side. The king alone had the right to name the sheriffs, he declared. The only real surprise about this foregone conclusion was that it took Richard four months to come up with it, and it might have taken him even longer had he not been forced to return to Germany.

Henry did have one setback when, at the start of his offensive,

Pope Alexander IV died, barely a month after issuing the bull absolving the king of his oath to the Provisions and before it was actually published. Fearing the validity of the bull may be questioned, Henry solicited the new pope, Urban IV, for a reissue, and it was here that he understood how much influence Montfort was able to exert abroad. The royal proctors reported back that another English clerk had already procured new papal letters, only these affirmed the king's obligation to observe the Provisions. Urban, it seemed, was genuinely confused about what was going on in England. Somehow or other Henry's proctors were able to straighten the matter out and secured another absolution in February 1262. Where Urban refused to be obliging, however, was in regards to Sicily.

Now that Henry felt he was a king again, he presumed to ask the new pope to renew the grant to his son Edmund, as clear an indication as any that this man was simply incapable of learning from his previous mistakes. He even had the effrontery to claim that Edmund was ready to come in person at the head of an army, despite the fact that he himself had needed mercenaries just to safely publish the original absolution. Urban, who probably knew that Henry's other promises had come to naught, curtly informed him that that ship had sailed.

While Henry was subduing the nobility, his queen was preparing an assault of her own. Her greatest distress during these years had been Edward's irresponsibility and disobedience. Now she was determined to make a full sweep of the bad influences on him, especially the men of the lordships whose borders, like his, edged up against the Welsh principality. The violent tendencies of these Marchers, as they were known, appealed to Edward much the way the Lusignans had. Chief among them were Roger Leybourne, his brother-in-law Roger Clifford and the improbably named Hamo Lestrange. Leybourne actually came from Kent and was twice Edward's age, but he managed to insinuate himself into the young man's ranks in part because he was conducting his own feud with Clare.

At a tilting in 1252, Leybourne killed the same knight who had broken his leg in an earlier contest. It was all an accident, Leybourne insisted. Clare oversaw what passed for an inquest on the field and discovered that Leybourne had failed to blunt the point of his lance, which in modern terms was like using live ammo. Still, he escaped punishment after he swore on the spot to go on crusade, which of course he never did. As Edward's steward, he repulsed a raid by some of Clare's men in their ongoing clashes and had the ones he captured summarily hanged. He got away with that bit of vigilantism as well.

At her urging, Edward had thrown him and the other Marchers over before he went abroad in the summer of 1262. The queen and Clare finally saw their chance to ruin them. Edward's accounts were audited and Leybourne was found guilty of embezzling nearly £2,000. He claimed he was being framed and tried to stash his goods to keep them from being seized by the sheriff. When Clifford offered him protection, Henry called in his debts and those of their friends. Edward, meanwhile, did nothing to help any of them. While the Marchers knew it was the Savoyard-dominated court behind their downfall, they seethed at their former patron for being weak and callous.

They probably wouldn't have felt any better knowing that Edward was getting a raw deal himself. In June 1262 Peter of Savoy exchanged a group of menial manors he held in the honour of Richmond for Edward's more lucrative Hastings honour. If it was meant to keep Edward from squandering his prime real estate, as he was wont to do in the past, Peter was also making contingency plans for the day when John of Brittany got back Richmond and somebody other than him would be the loser.

In addition, Edward was put on a fixed allowance with money from the Jewish exchequer, and the queen got what was left of the English-born court, now only Mansel, Basset and Walerand, to stand surety for another major loan to him. At twenty-three years of age, Edward was completely in the grips of his mother. He didn't seem to care, as long as he had enough money for the tournament circuit. Reportedly he was badly injured in one, but was able to meet up with his parents in Paris that summer.

By now, the unease throughout the country had grown so bad that Henry declared anyone preaching against his resumption of power to be an outlaw. His treasury was practically empty, with receipts this year only half their level the year before. Withal, he decided to go abroad. Louis still owed him treaty money and there was also the £10,000 he was withholding until the quarrel with the Montforts was settled. It's a wonder Henry ever thought he was going to see any of that money, for although Queen Margaret had agreed to arbitrate their case, Henry was determined to expose Simon as an interloper and, in the process, replace him in the esteem and affection of the French king.

As might be expected, Henry got things off on the wrong foot by arriving late the first day. He had been summoned to attend *parlement* as the Duke of Aquitaine (Gascony), but in his absence no work could be done. He excused himself by saying he simply couldn't resist stopping to hear Mass at all the churches he passed along the way. When he showed up late again the next day, for the exact same reason, Louis felt compelled to order all the churches shut up along Henry's route so they could finally get something done. Henry was aghast and feared that France had suddenly come under interdict.

Louis no doubt found such simplicity quaint, but couldn't hide his annoyance over Henry's tardiness and asked why he enjoyed hearing so many Masses, usually three times a day back in England. Henry deflected the obvious rebuke by asking Louis why he enjoyed hearing so many sermons, as was commonly known.

'It seems to me exceedingly delightful and healthy to hear very often about my creator,' replied the French king.

Sharp as ever, Henry said that he preferred to see his creator than just hear about him, and for that he needed Mass.

Henry's feisty mood grew nasty when it came time for the arbitration. He had a dossier prepared to show all the good things he had done for Simon, like restoring his inheritance and giving him his sister in marriage, whereas all he got in return were insults and contempt. Montfort had nearly lost Gascony on account of his brutal rule there, and there would have been no Treaty of Paris to speak of had he gotten his way. Perhaps worst of all, he was fomenting rebellion among Henry's subjects. Margaret didn't even have to take Henry at his word. He had prepared witnesses, from as far away as Gascony, to testify to the truth of his charges.

Simon's replies merely showed that there were two sides to every argument. Henry had restored his inheritance, but it was as much his right as was Henry's right to the throne, and the king forgot about all the years of loyal service he got in return. Henry had given him his sister in marriage, but it was what she wanted, and his failure to provide her with a proper marriage portion was the chief reason why they were even in arbitration. As for Gascony, Henry wouldn't be at the French court as the Duke of Aquitaine if he hadn't put down the rebellion there. Finally, he was doing nothing more in his defence of the Provisions of Oxford than what was required of him by his oath.

What Margaret thought about what had evidently become a personal feud will never be known. An epidemic struck the English court in September 1262 and the hearings were broken off after Henry fell deathly ill. How ill can be seen in an arrangement made that again shows sister Eleanor totally supplanted by Queen Eleanor in Henry's thoughts and concerns. Should Henry die, his queen was to receive a dower of £4,000, a remarkable improvement over the original £1,000 fixed on her at the time of their marriage. This provision was not merely a deathbed stroke, rather a carefully planned distribution of royal income engineered by who else but Peter and the Savoyards. The English flunkies Mansel and Walerand put their seals to the deal, as did Edward, though doubtless he was not amused that the extra £3,000 was going to come out of his inheritance.

Henry survived, but the epidemic claimed more than sixty members of his court. The new Bishop of London had come specifically to Henry to obtain confirmation of his election and ended up dying of the disease as well. Instead of returning to England after regaining his strength, and despite the breakdown in negotiations with Montfort, Henry decided to make a pilgrimage to Rheims. But he was clearly worried. In early October he wrote to Basset to warn him that Simon was 'unpacified' and planning to return to England to sow discord. Just days later Simon did in fact show up for the convening of Parliament and, disregarding Basset's order, he published the papal letters obtained by his agents from Urban IV that confirmed the Provisions and revoked Henry's absolution. And like that he disappeared, going back to France and leaving the English baronage to discuss the meaning of his lightning strike.

If Henry knew he had the letters, he was apparently untroubled by it, for he took his time on pilgrimage. Not until December, almost five months after he left, did he come back to England, and found he had quite a mess on his hands. It had started after he landed in France, when Richard de Clare died in July 1262. He had been missing from court since his latest defection, suggesting the illness that killed him had also incapacitated him before the end. But because he was only forty at the time, and had been poisoned four years previously, there were rumours that something had been slipped into his food again.

Peter of Savoy was identified as the culprit, probably for no other reason than because his brother Boniface immediately moved in to seize some of the Clare property in Kent. This was the challenge now facing Henry, how to prevent a mad scramble in the wake of the death of a major landowner. Clare had an heir, eighteen-year-old Gilbert, who could normally expect his inheritance on the payment of a relief. Henry, however, was reluctant to confirm him until a careful study had been made of all the Gloucester holdings. He suspected that the elder Clare had used his ascendancy after 1258 to usurp royal rights and so placed his dominions in temporary custody for the time being. Henry was totally within his authority, but Gilbert had a keen sense of his own importance and followed the king to France to demand his inheritance. Rebuffed but not denied, he returned in a temper and swore revenge.

The death of Richard de Clare also coincided with the end of the two-year truce with Wales. According to Llywelyn, a new outbreak of war had been brewing for some time due to the oppression of Welsh tenants by English lords like Roger Mortimer. By the end of November, they rebelled and seized Cefnllys. Mortimer was trapped and surrendered when invited to, further tainting him with rumours of collusion. The situation became dire enough for Henry to reproach his son for delaying abroad while his lands were under attack.

'This is no time for laziness and boyish wantonness,' he wrote him. 'I am getting old and you are in the flower of early manhood.'

It would be another two months before Edward returned.

The uprising marked a disastrous end to what had started off as an optimistic year. To make matters worse, Henry's favourite palace of Westminster burned to the ground and the winter was so cold that the Thames froze over. There had been evil forebodings about his trip to France and all he had to show for it was a near-death experience. The poor English response to the Welsh incursions indicated a lack of willingness by the Marcher lords to do anything about it. Their disaffection, and that of their neighbour Gilbert de Clare, could spell trouble if they were able to concentrate their grievances into one united action.

Luckily for Henry, none of them had the charisma or experience necessary for national leadership. What they needed was somebody who was tried and tested in warfare, politically astute, and above all not afraid of the king. He had to have prestige at home and abroad and an air about him that commanded respect, devotion and, when necessary, fear. In short, he had to be a legend, and he was just across the water.

11

The Return of the Alien
1263

Nobody was more familiar with Henry's weaknesses than his brother Richard. He too had been exasperated by the king's servility to favourites and the cravenness that made him resort to duplicity. He knew that now more than ever Henry needed to put these tendencies aside and focus on his true priorities. While he may have sympathised with Henry's desire to discredit their sister and her husband, all the magnates had been brought back into line except Montfort, and placating him, whether it was justified or not, was key to consolidating his recovery of power. And so, before going back to Germany in the spring of 1262, he advised Henry that whatever decision was reached in the arbitration, he should respect it. That was his way of warning him to act in good faith and not let petulance sabotage what was the country's best hope for peace.

Of course, petulance won the day and perhaps no one realised what a mistake that had been more than Henry. On his way back to England, he met Louis in Compiegne and implored him to find a way to mollify Montfort. He then despatched two trusted hands at the beginning of 1263 with a new proposal, but interestingly ordered them to see Margaret first. The Queen of France, intrigued by what she heard, asked them to delay their petition to her husband until she returned to court and could offer her own advice. When they finally got to see Louis, presumably with Margaret casting a long shadow over their audience, the envoys were told to wait while the King of France took up the matter with Simon.

They ended up waiting four days, and the news brought back

by Louis was not good. According to him, Simon believed that Henry meant him well, but that some of his councillors kept him from acting on that impulse. Although these councillors were not identified, Margaret's insistence on participating in the discussions, and the presence of a Savoyard knight as one of the two envoys, strongly suggests Queen Eleanor and Peter of Savoy were not prepared to let Henry go too far in any reconciliation.

The intervention of the Savoyards probably made no difference in any case. The years of strife had turned Montfort's property claims into political demands, and any buyout or victory on principles would have been hollow unless the Provisions were secured as well. Simon could not make an honourable peace while his enemies intrigued against him and, as he saw it, the community of the realm. Since the queen wasn't about to get rid of the Savoyards, and Henry wasn't about to get rid of his queen, conflict was now inevitable.

Louis finally understood that what he was dealing with here was not just some squabble over a few manors but a constitutional crisis. At Simon's request, he withdrew from the negotiations because there was little he could do about that. Not yet, anyway.

Henry next tried to assure Simon and the other malcontents of his good faith by publishing a series of 'constitutions', which were basically a reissue of the Provisions of Westminster. He was doing so, he declared, on his own free will, as if to show that he too was a reformer at last. He was being disingenuous, because he never had a problem with the reforming legislation that dealt principally with the magnates and their conduct. It had always been Henry's contention that they were the biggest oppressors throughout the land, not him.

This apparently desperate bid for popular support fell flat, however, thanks to his one insurmountable problem: nobody trusted him. Time and again he had gone back on his word – a trait his son would frightfully call his own soon enough – and expected all to be forgiven and forgotten. As long as the barons were afraid to hold him to account, all was secure. The failure to hold the Welsh in check was an indication that this was about to change.

Edward's lands and castles had been particularly vulnerable to Llywelyn, but only Roger Mortimer, stung by the shame of his surrender, was eager to counter-attack. The other Marchers were still fuming over the way they had been treated and refused to come to Edward's aid. They were half-expecting him to come crawling back to them first, only when he showed up at the end of February, he completely ignored them. He had with him a company of foreign knights, and it was these he threw against the Welsh.

As with his earlier drive, this one also ended dismally, and yet he didn't disband his foreign mercenaries and send them home. Instead, they formed his new retinue and enjoyed the positions and trust previously held by the Marchers. For Leybourne and Clifford, this was the final straw. They sent word overseas that if Montfort would return and lead them in open rebellion, they would supply the shock troops.

It wasn't exactly the moment Simon had been waiting for, and there was something decidedly mediocre about this new crowd compared to the one he marched with on Westminster almost five years earlier. But he was in his mid-fifties now and couldn't wait forever for the English to rise up and reclaim the realm for themselves. And so he returned on 25 April 1263, never to see France again except for a couple of days in the autumn.

The venue was Oxford, chosen for its symbolic value, and the men who greeted Montfort joined him in renewing their oaths to the Provisions or else they took it for the first time. The one provision that stood out, later identified by Henry as the source of all the problems, was number five, which called for making anyone opposed to the Provisions a mortal enemy, save for the king and his family. The idea was to show that they meant business, but the presence of so many disgruntled middling lords with axes to grind fuelled fears that it would give them licence to commit all kinds of heinous acts.

Indeed, Simon probably wouldn't have bothered with the violence-prone ex-Edwardians if they were all he had to depend on, but the gathering also included the more reputable likes of his nephew Henry of Almain and John de Warenne. One was a member of the royal family, the other an earl, and both were also nursing grudges against the queen because they had been purged on account of their Lusignan association. Far and away the biggest coup, however, was Almain's father, Richard of Cornwall.

Richard had returned from Germany around the same time as Edward. Most likely he had been informed about the meeting by his son, and his attendance there led to all kinds of speculations. It was said that, having been frustrated in his attempts to become the undisputed king of the Germans, he came home to be crowned king of the English in place of his convalescing brother and self-absorbed nephew. Rumours that the king had in fact expired led one chronicle to write a premature obituary of him on 23 March 1263. Henry himself must have heard them, because he ordered all and sundry to swear their fealty to Edward wherever he may appear. One who refused to was Gilbert de Clare, who was still stewing over Henry making him wait to receive his earldom. Gloucester would make him second only to Richard in terms of wealth and rank once the king finally got around to confirming his inheritance.

Richard was angry too, in his case at Henry for failing to follow his advice and make peace with Montfort. Perhaps he was at the meeting because he decided to do it himself. Doubtless he thought he had a good chance. Like Henry, he was Simon's brother-in-law. They had been on crusade together, where Richard secured the freedom of Amaury de Montfort, and he stood by Simon at his trial over Gascony. Surely he owed him one. Only the movement wasn't, and never was, just about Simon de Montfort.

Since they were first enacted, the Provisions of Oxford had become something of a sacred cause throughout the land, and the return of their most ardent defender had galvanised young idealists to rally behind him. This was thanks in part to the preaching of friars who, like Montfort, had been imbued with the teachings of Grosseteste and his ideas about just government. The previous year John Mansel was in Sussex and noticed lots of preachers working the countryside on behalf of the barons. If only the king could boast the same, he lamented.

This mobilisation of peasants and freeholders under a charismatic leader, supported by faithful lieutenants like Peter de Montfort and Hugh Despenser, and blessed by Walter de Cantilupe and other leading churchmen, created what was in effect the first political movement in English history. Writing years later, the chronicler Thomas Wykes was unimpressed and saw something sinister in their motives. These 'boys', as he called them, were soft as wax and followed Montfort 'not from any love of justice but from greediness of gain'.

Whether moved by greed or justice, or some equal parts of both, they were ready to strike. They launched their campaign by sending a letter under Clifford's seal to the king demanding that he abide by the Provisions of Oxford or risk the enforcement of provision number five. Even if the letter was only meant to justify the ensuing violence, as they hardly expected Henry to agree out of hand to everything that was anathema to his idea of kingship, the choice was nevertheless his in the end. Still beholden to his alien-dominated court, he refused, and the Montfortians set out in June 1263 to bring him to heel.

The plan called for a two-pronged assault. The Marchers would take aim at all the Savoyards that had been set up in their neck of the woods, most specifically at Peter d'Aigueblanche, the Bishop of Hereford. His role in the Sicilian fiasco had made him roundly detested, so much so that he had once tried in vain to get the friars to say some nice things about him in their sermons. The most visibly marked of the Savoyards, he was quickly seized in his cathedral and imprisoned in one of Clifford's castles.

After looting his lands, the rebels moved on to besiege the infamous Sheriff Mathias Bezill, who had ingloriously tossed his English counterpart into the mud. Bezill put up a good fight, but was eventually overpowered and packed off to join d'Aigueblanche. The uprising then spread to other counties, suggesting that Simon was at the helm, in Oxford or Kenilworth, applying the professional touch of a command post. Henry's response was to appoint captains to administer local loyalty oaths, but as one of them reported, he would no sooner deem a man loyal than he was converted to the rebellion by one of Montfort's 'runners'.

By the middle of the month, Simon had taken to the field and was leading a small force towards London. Richard sent word to him that he would like to parley, but for Simon, the time of talking was long past. He was intent on reaching his objective, which wasn't in fact London but the Channel ports. His plan was to cut off Henry's links to the Continent, thereby depriving him of reinforcements or funds from abroad.

He also moved to isolate him politically by sending a letter to London asking the city aldermen for their support of the Provisions. He knew from 1258 that he could rely on the city, but was shrewdly counting on Henry buckling under any demands put to him by the aldermen in person. On 24 June a delegation of leading citizens went to the Tower to inform Henry that it was their intention to welcome Montfort in 'the interest of the king and the benefit of the realm'.

They showed him Simon's letter together with a petition from the barons that included good news and bad. While demanding the king's 'inviolable observance' of the Provisions, the baronial party, as it was still at this stage, offered to remove anything found prejudicial to the king and make other adjustments as necessary. For example, provision number five could be expunged and a power-sharing agreement reached that took into account Henry's concern for his dignity. That was the good news, because this willingness to compromise on the Provisions indicates that Simon and his compatriots were after a peaceful settlement.

The bad news was the demand at the end of the petition calling for the realm to be governed by native-born men only. It was language similar to that used five years earlier to oust the Lusignans, only this time they were after the Savoyards. Five days later this demand was embodied in an official 'form of peace' sent to Henry by the bishops. The leading primate Boniface didn't even wait to see if the king would accept the condition or not. He fled to France that very day, followed by John Mansel. The flight of these two ex-warriors is an indication of the terror that must have gripped the court. The queen committed several foreign ladies to Mansel for safekeeping until he reached the Continent, with her son Edmund accompanying them as far as Dover. Why Edmund and not Edward is clear from what happened next.

Richard was with Henry at the Tower of London and urged him to treat for peace. Edward, however, was in a fighting mood and had been so since the outbreak of hostilities. Now, with the rebel army closing in and the royal family out of money, Edward got it into his head to rob a bank. It was arguably the first high-profile heist of its kind in English history and predated the Great Train Robbery by seven centuries.

On 29 June 1263 Edward gathered up Robert Walerand and

some of his foreign knights and rode off to the New Temple, just west of the city walls. These headquarters of the Templar crusading order were used by the oligarchs and merchant class of London as a depository for their valuables. Finding the place locked up, Edward gained admission from the custodian by claiming he wanted to see his mother's jewels. When the coast was clear, he and his men produced the hammers they had concealed and began smashing open the chests and stealing the treasure inside. The gang made off with at least £1,000 worth of private deposits and headed for Windsor. There they proceeded to raid the countryside and plunder riverboats making their way downstream to the city.

With this singular criminal act, Edward ensured that London would remain behind Montfort to the bitter end. Already heartily sick of his mercenaries, the citizens drew the most natural conclusion from the heist. Their future king had robbed them to pay his alien soldiers. Riots erupted as word of the robbery spread. The mayor, Thomas Fitz-Thomas, broke away from the oligarchs ruling the city and declared for the Montfortians.

Henry could never have imagined that his subversion of reform would come to this. Unnerved by the upheaval, he capitulated on 16 July. It was a spectacular victory. The king had been forced to submit with next to no bloodshed. Worse for Henry, an emotionally needy man, he had to face the music all alone.

Mansel, Boniface and Peter of Savoy were in France. Richard had retreated to one of his castles outside the city. Edward and Walerand were in Windsor and Edmund in Dover. The queen was still in London, but not by his side. Three days earlier she had attempted to flee the unrest for the safety of Windsor and Edward's gang. The people, however, had got wind of her plans and gathered in force on London Bridge to show what they really thought of their queen.

They had first welcomed her twenty-seven years earlier as a young girl from a strange land, escorting her to Westminster in a dazzling display of ceremony and hospitality. Now she was a woman of about forty and still from a strange land for all they knew of her. She had chosen to live an isolated existence among them, which might have been tolerable had she not insisted on importing hundreds of freeloaders to enjoy the rewards of their labours. She was the alien *numero uno* in their eyes, and they were going to let her know it.

The craft, similar in shape to a longboat, carried a dozen or so oarsmen. The queen sat behind them with her ladies-in-waiting while guards and attendants stood on the aftcastle at the rear. As the boat neared the bridge, the crowd began shouting 'whore' at her and other bits of invective typically popular when a woman is the centre of mass animosity. Since they were uttered in English, which there is no record of the queen ever having learned, she could probably ignore the insults. It's when the people took to throwing objects at her barge and dumping whatever putrid contents were on hand that the crew gave up any attempt to run the gauntlet.

The boat turned around and headed back to Tower Wharf, only to discover that Henry would not allow it to dock. Whether this was out of spite at the queen for deserting him or because he was afraid it might draw in the crowd to besiege the Tower, the boat was forced to put ashore elsewhere. By this time Mayor Fitz-Thomas, who was a patrician despite his Montfortian politics, had intervened and had a guard ready to escort the queen to safety.

Never again would a Queen of England be subject to such public abuse by her subjects. Similar to when Eleanor de Montfort had Henry in her power over the Treaty of France, this spontaneous outburst of vehemence occurred because the people had the queen in their power for this one brief moment. There is no evidence that she was in any real physical danger, no record of lethal objects being hurled at her or medieval ninjas attempting to board the craft. She was scared witless to be sure, and the incident at London Bridge played a major role in her later decision to stay abroad, for over two years as it turned out. For Edward, the action of the Londoners was unforgiveable. He would take his revenge on them when the time came, but it would be yet another blunder that cost his parents dearly.

In the meantime, his next move had been to slip away to Bristol with his mercenaries in an attempt to make a stand there. As in London, the townspeople rose up and prepared to besiege them. Edward pleaded with Walter de Cantilupe to come to his rescue, promising he would go straight to London and put his seal to the peace agreement. The bishop obliged, but Edward and his force were no sooner free than they went back to Windsor to carry out their guerrilla tactics.

This bit of treachery forever marked the heir to the throne as a loose cannon, even less trustworthy than his father. In response, the Montfortians marched on Windsor to force its surrender, with Henry accompanying them in almost a repeat of the barons pursuing the Lusignans to Winchester in 1258. Henry's presence probably ensured the castle was given up peacefully, which occurred on 1 August, and the mercenaries were escorted out of the country with no violence.

Deeply embittered by the experience, Edward went off and sulked rather than take leave of his knights. It was up to the queen to express her thanks and make gifts to them, not just a sign that she had recovered emotionally from the bridge incident, but that she was determined to have them ready to come over again to stamp out their rebellious English subjects.

One of the mundane terms of the provisional peace agreement called for the release of Henry of Almain. Richard's son had taken off after John Mansel, either to thwart his influence abroad or bring him back in irons, but he was overtaken and imprisoned himself by a loyal Savoyard after landing on the Continent. Richard demanded his freedom at once and insisted that both the king and queen procure it. The order went out on 10 July, perhaps the last point of agreement between the royal couple before her attempt to flee to Windsor three days later.

While thanking Henry for his intervention, Richard was still ambiguous about where he stood in the conflict. He never had any love for the Savoyards. They had prevented Henry from giving him Gascony and Chester, and while he personally liked Peter of Savoy and allowed him to do business for him, he would only lend him money, whereas Henry unloaded it freely on him and his brothers. Despite being the leading magnate and a king to boot, he was merely a bystander when the formal peace was sealed. When Montfort and his men entered London, on 22 July, they camped out at Richard's park in Isleworth. Henry betrayed his brother's vague sympathies in a letter to the pope, inciting Urban to denounce Richard for allowing, even promoting, the 'boisterous fluctuation of the storm that shakes the solid foundations of the kingdom of England'.

The council resurrected to rule the land was far different from the last one dismissed by Henry in 1260. Richard de Clare and others were dead, the Savoyards and Mansel exiled, and the other great nobles like the Bigod brothers were either hostile or held aloof. Simon was virtually the prime minister, but since that term was centuries into the future, he sought to legitimise his role under the title of steward, taking what was essentially the honorary title of the Earl of Leicester and giving it political significance.

The agenda pushed forward by him and the council mainly involved reforming the king's household and installing wardens to serve alongside the sheriffs in the counties. Both cases reflect the new ideological support for the Montfortian party now embedded in the peace agreement. Controversially, that agreement included a statute that not only enacted the baronial call for government by native-born men, but now stipulated that all aliens leave the kingdom 'never to return'. This radicalisation of their platform occurred after the movement against the Savoyards revealed mass antipathy towards foreigners in general. Henry's entire reign had always been marked by anti-alien feelings, due in large part to his misguided favouritism, but only the barons had found some satisfaction for this grievance with the expulsion of the Lusignans in 1258.

Now the local gentry and townsfolk, fed up with Italian priests they couldn't understand and French moneylenders charging them usurious rates, wanted their turn. To call it xenophobia would be to confuse it with the racism and cultural bigotry associated with the modern connotation of the word. Here language was generally the only immediate distinction. Roving bands of Marcher henchmen would utter a few words of Anglo-Saxon to determine a person's Englishness. If the person failed to understand or responded in a way deemed unsuitable, they were likely to be robbed, roughed up or imprisoned.

These indiscriminate attacks grew to take in wide swaths of society, including foreign merchants and ordinary clerks with no connection to the Savoyards. The Jews were targeted as well despite having lived in England for two centuries. They bore the added burden of religious intolerance during times of disturbance, and since they were officially under the king's protection, they had the most to fear from any abrogation of his power.

The proposed banishment of all aliens from the kingdom was

clearly a propaganda ploy. Montfort himself was an alien the same as the Savoyard Archbishop of Canterbury. Walter de Cantilupe and the bishops could hardly condone Boniface's expulsion or that of other foreign clergy appointed by the papacy. The statute was added both to harvest this unexpected political capital and also to put a lid on it. As long as aliens were seen to have free run of the realm, the attacks on them would surely continue. Montfort's government had to demonstrate that the days of foreign favouritism, of the king squandering the wealth of the nation on spongers from abroad, were over.

An escape clause was needed, however, to prevent senseless mass deportations that would inevitably include the steward as well. Aliens who were found to be accepted 'in common' were therefore permitted to stay. This was another way of saying that only truly despised aliens like the Savoyards were susceptible to exile, and even then it was rarely applied. There was no better example than Boniface. His rival and most hated of the Lusignans, the now deceased Aymer, had actually been well liked around his diocese of Winchester compared to the loathing felt for Boniface in Kent. Although he had to be accepted because he was the archbishop, the statute was promulgated with future policy in mind, to prevent others like him from becoming prelates who knew 'neither the manners nor the language of the country'.

Even a bruiser like Mathias Bezill was not expelled upon his release from custody. Like Montfort, he had been in England for three decades and had an English wife. He might have even been retained as sheriff had Clifford not angled for the job. The Montfortians were in fact keen to keep Henry's sheriffs in office as the quickest way to return to normalcy. The only change was now they had less to do. They were told to continue collecting rents and revenue, but newly appointed wardens were given the task of maintaining order, protecting people and property, and returning unlawful seizures.

Another man released at the same time as Bezill was the most notorious alien in the land, Peter d'Aigueblanche. As the Bishop of Hereford, he too was untouchable, but, conscious of how hated he was, he wisely took the next boat to join the other émigrés in France. It was to this group that the king and queen looked for deliverance from their status as figureheads of Westminster. Together they contrived to have Louis summon Henry to France as his vassal to explain what was happening in his kingdom. Simon was not inclined to let them go. He had seen how much trouble the king made the last time he left while under constitutional restraint. Two separate delegations were despatched to excuse Henry, but neither found much favour at the French court. The matter was taken up at the first parliament of the new government, held on 9 September in St Paul's.

The gathering was fraught with discord from the outset. The magnates were irked at Simon for playing the statesman when they felt that restitution for all the destruction and seizures should be the order of the day. It was eventually agreed that the king and his family could go to France upon their oaths to return by an assigned date. It was also decided that Simon should go to represent the council, assisted by Walter de Cantilupe and Peter de Montfort. His closeness to the King of France would ensure they received a fair hearing, perhaps even some legitimacy in Louis' eyes. Far from being displeased, Henry welcomed his adversary's presence. He even admonished him in a letter not to be absent from the meeting set for 23 September in Boulogne 'as you love our honour and yours'.

Henry wanted him there because he would again try to ruin him politically as in the previous year during Margaret's arbitration. He was confident this time around because Margaret was now a bitter enemy, having heard all the wails and lamentations of her Savoyard relatives in exile. When her sister showed up and relayed the horrors of London Bridge, Margaret and their mother Beatrice could only gasp and demand that Louis restore her honour.

He obliged in so far as the conference he set up included many leading French nobles, as if he were arraigning the English council on charges of rebelling against their king. Simon dismissed the notion, declaring they could only be judged by the peers of England. Otherwise, he made a good impression, for Louis voiced his approval of the Provisions, as Henry had done, and agreed that a country should be ruled by natives and not aliens. Montfort's perceptive and persuasive way of speaking, together with his friendship with Louis and his brothers, apparently carried the day, but it wasn't a total defeat for the Savoyards.

Although Henry returned to England in time, the queen and their son Edmund disregarded their oaths and stayed behind. The plan was for the two Provencal queens, Eleanor and Margaret, to enlist funds and military support abroad while Henry and Edward took the offensive on the home front. If that had been the objective all along, it brings into question what was going through the queen's head when, before departing, she swore an oath she had no intention of keeping. Nothing is quite so frustrating about this one particular royal family – Henry III, Eleanor of Provence, and Edward I – than the ease with which they flouted their oaths and promises.

Another equally important reason for the queen to remain on the Continent had to do with Edward's plan to whittle away at support for Montfort's government. His foreign knights had barely departed when his former Marcher friends began sending him feelers. They had been given a fair shake under Simon, whether appointed as castellans or in Leybourne's case as a sub-steward, but their wish all along had been to be reinstated in Edward's confidence, to be 'his friends in all his affairs'. Nothing was standing in the way of a rapprochement now that his foreign knights had been sent packing.

It's also possible they were worried about Simon's overtures to Llywelyn. Peace with Wales was vital to the new government, but the Marchers were suspicious of any alliance with a man they considered their natural enemy. Since their grievances with Edward and the queen were as raw as ever, deserting Montfort would have to come at a price. With Henry of Almain and John de Warenne acting as emissaries, and giving signals they were ready to become Edwardians again as well, promises and grants started going out left and right. It was agreed. They would wait until the next parliament, summoned for October, to strike.

This had to be the bitterest pill of all for the queen to swallow. It had been only three months since the Marchers unleashed their wave of terror against her and her family, culminating in her humiliation at London Bridge. Now, they were not only to be forgiven but rewarded. By contrast it took three years for the Lusignans to be readmitted to the court, and all they had done was defame her. It didn't matter what arguments she and the Savoyards put forward, however. Edward was putting his foot down. Leybourne, Clifford, and Lestrange were in, and if his relatives couldn't stomach them, they were better off in France until victory was theirs.

The parliament that resumed in October had no chance from the start. Accusations went back and forth about restitution for the despoiled, and Henry undermined the arbitration over the terms of the Provisions by insisting on his right to appoint his own household. It was a matter of dignity for him and the realm, whether a king was in fact a king if he was not allowed to choose his own servants, but the council argued that it could be a backdoor for the Savoyards to get their hands again on royal patronage.

As the bickering intensified, Edward announced that he wanted to be excused so he could go visit his wife. It goes without saying it was another lie. He set out immediately for Windsor and seized the castle, thereby declaring himself in open revolt against the government. Henry followed him the next day, and together they laid down the gauntlet to the barons assembled in Parliament. They would have to choose between the king or steward. Only one could rule. Sitting on the fence was no longer an option.

Given the feudal nature of England at that time, the choice was actually quite easy for most of them. Henry was the king, regardless of whether he was a good one or bad one. All of them held their land from him. None of them had had to work for their great estates the same as Henry never had to work for his throne. They had all been born into the power and privileges that ensured they never starved in times of famine.

On the other hand, the Provisions, admirably conceived though they were, were still an experiment, and judging by the disorders over the summer, an experiment that would have failed long ago had it not been for one man. And it was this one man they were coming to look upon as the source of all the trouble in the land. Well, of course. He too was an alien, he too owed everything to Henry, no more or less than the Savoyards and Lusignans. He was just another haughty, self-righteous Frenchman angry at the king because he didn't get his fair share and now he was running roughshod over the country in a high temper and claiming he was doing it all on behalf of some oath. His oath! Real Englishmen didn't bother with such niceties.

Most of the magnates, including the reclusive Roger Bigod, joined the royal party at Windsor. Bribed by Edward and pardoned by Henry, the Marchers then deserted, although one of their number, John Giffard, yet another former ward of the queen, had an unexpected change of heart and returned his gift of land. Henry of Almain kept his and defected, but he seems to have similarly wrestled with a guilty conscience. He went to Simon and explained that he simply could no longer fight against his father and the king. Still enamoured of his uncle, however, he asked for his leave to depart, assuring him that he would never take up arms against him. Simon greeted the news with cheerful indifference.

'Lord Henry, I grieve not for your arms, but your lack of constancy. You can go and return with your arms, they are of no concern to me.'

Despite the brave front, there was no denying Simon's disappointment. The young man had not only let him down, but seemed indicative of a land where commitment mattered nothing among the people to whom it should have mattered the most.

'I have been in many lands and among many nations, pagan and Christian,' he is said to have remarked, 'but nowhere have I found such infidelity and deceit as I have met in England.'

As Almain indicated, his father Richard of Cornwall had preceded him to Henry's side, but as usual he got something in return, in this case a wardship. Richard was nevertheless anxious for peace and worked out a truce in preparation for Louis to arbitrate their dispute. Knowing he could count on London, Simon withdrew to Kenilworth to warily watch developments from the Midlands. There was little he could do as Henry went about reclaiming the machinery of government, including the chancery and exchequer. It was when he made a stab at the Channel ports that it became clear that the royalists were preparing for war.

If they could secure Dover, that would pave the way for mercenaries to arrive. The Marchers probably would have scrupled to welcome them as long as Edward didn't play favourites again, but in the event the garrison of Dover was manned by Montfortians and they refused to hand over the keys. Not willing to so flagrantly violate the truce with a military assault, Henry entrusted Leybourne with starving them out.

Seeing what Henry was up to, Simon assembled what men and arms he could at short notice and headed back to London. That drew an angry response from the king, who demanded that the city expel them at once. In fact, London was never enthusiastic about quartering any army and made the Montfortians camp across the river in Southwark. A group of oligarchs went one step further by barring the gates on London Bridge and informing the king about it. With Henry in Croydon and Edward in Merton, they could trap Simon's forces in a pincer movement if they moved fast enough. They immediately set out and got close enough on 11 December to call on Simon to surrender, but he refused, saying he would never surrender to 'perjurers and apostates'. Then, in a classic moment of deliverance, the people of London discovered the plot, broke open the gates, and swarmed en masse across the river to escort the tiny army inside the city.

It was a terrible setback for Henry. More than anything, he wanted to capture Simon so as to limit his involvement in the arbitration in France. As far as Henry was concerned, the Provisions lived or died with this one man. Montfort had persuaded Louis of their legitimacy in Boulogne and could easily do so again at the panel scheduled for January 1264 in Amiens. And so Henry sank to the diabolical depths of his father by conceiving a plan to at least occupy Simon until then, maybe even keep him from attending at all.

He was still fuming over the nine manors he had been forced to give his sister back in 1259. Three of them were located in Herefordshire, not far from the Mortimer estates. Roger Mortimer had been openly accused of colluding with the Welsh and was in a long-running dispute with Richard of Cornwall over a manor he felt rightfully belonged to him. He had no great enthusiasm for the Provisions, but seemed to like them better whenever he made no progress with Henry in his quarrel with Richard. Now, in an unscrupulous stroke, Henry told Mortimer to let Richard have the manor. He could have the three Montfort properties instead, providing he could take them. Mortimer thereafter became a solid royalist and went right to work.

Henry's action has long been interpreted as a shrewd move, with the claim that the king knew better than anyone that Simon de

Montfort was first and foremost a man wedded to personal gain and materialism. The moment he heard of Mortimer's attack, he would drop everything, even defence of the Provisions, just to go and save his property. Nothing of the kind happened. He could always tend to Mortimer later, and this blatant breach of the truce by Henry made a nice addition to the arguments his team was putting together for Louis. For historians looking for another example of Simon putting his private interests before idealism, all they got here instead was another chapter in the royal family's legendary malice and perfidy.

Another major baron not so easily bought off was Gilbert de Clare. He had finally received his earldom in August, during Montfort's tenure at the helm, but wasn't quite ready to throw in his lot with either side. If age had been a factor, the royalists were definitely not for the twenty-one-year-old Earl of Gloucester. The earls of Cornwall, Norfolk, and Hereford were all over fifty, the Earl of Surrey and the Marchers were at least ten years older. Edward was the closet in age, only four years older, but Gilbert had inherited his father's feud with him.

The Montfortians by contrast were the party of youth. Aside from top leaders Simon, Walter, Peter de Montfort and Hugh Despenser, most were in their twenties. Interestingly, several, like Baldwin Wake, Henry Hastings and John Vescy, were former wards of either Lusignans or Savoyards.

So was Robert de Ferrers, Earl of Derby, another example of the king's decadent family business. He had been a minor when his father died and, although the same age as Edward, Henry made him a ward of his son. When Edward fell short of cash, he sold the wardship to his mother and Peter of Savoy. Henry retained his own clutches on the boy by marrying him at the age of nine to Mary, one of his Lusignan nieces and sister of Gilbert's wife Alice. Forever embittered by the experience, Ferrers took advantage of the summer offensive to seize three of Edward's castles, but like the Marchers, he was only in it for himself. He and his men had accompanied Simon to Southwark, but that was as far as he was prepared to go.

Gilbert had been spared the indignity of being an English ward to a French nobody, but his marriage to a Lusignan was a miserable failure. Dowdy Queen Margaret had an inkling of something wrong when she noticed Alice's flirtatious behaviour with her uncle Henry during their visit in 1262 and took exception to it. Like the other resentful young men, Gilbert was inclined to rule under the Provisions and a system that took wardships and marriages out of the hands of a small family coterie. The one obstacle that kept him from joining the Montfortians, however, was Montfort himself.

The bits of propaganda being disseminated at this time included a circular in the Tewkesbury annals, which were nominally connected to the Clare family. It claimed that Montfort had been unfair in expelling some aliens while protecting others, and that he had given Mansel's confiscated lands to his son Simon. Lastly, he was old like all those earls on the other side. What the reform party needed was a new, young, vigorous leader. Gilbert, knowing his father Richard de Clare had often been considered the leader of the reformists despite his betrayals, no doubt thought he was the most suitable candidate to replace Simon.

All the charges against Montfort were true. The one about aliens alludes to his bringing in mercenaries as late as May of that year, just before the offensive began, when the king sent a message to Dover declaring his surprise that men and horses had landed there without being arrested. 'Do not let it happen again,' he warned the garrison.

As for Mansel's lands, Simon committed them to the care of his second son while he was serving as steward of the realm, and he installed his third son, Amaury, in a prebend in London. These latter actions generated allegations, both then and today, that Montfort was out to use the movement to enrich his family, even though his two other adult sons got nothing from what can be determined.

There is no denying that Simon and Eleanor had for years been consistently frustrated in their attempts to provide for their sons. Henry failed to turn their fee into land and not once did he step into the role of matchmaker for his nephews despite the efforts he made for other leading noble families. Declining to make amends when he was in position to do so might have left Montfort's contemporaries wondering what kind of man neglected his own family in pursuit of the country's welfare. Henry certainly wasn't that type.

Where the Tewkesbury's circular got back to the issue of the king's misrule was in warning of the coming of a papal legate. Louis had apparently begun to think better of his pronouncement in Boulogne about the validity of the Provisions, doubtless with a little prodding from his wife Margaret. Together they wrote to the pope asking him to assist Henry in his troubles, and Urban replied on 22 November 1263 by appointing Cardinal Guy Foulquois, the Bishop of Sabina, as his legate for England.

Guy was well known to the French royal family. He was a former administrator who had helped Alphonse of Poitiers solidify his control over Toulouse, the irony being that the process had been begun by Simon's father during the Albigensian Crusade. Urban gave him extensive power to interfere in the affairs of England, all spelled out in a letter addressed to Henry, the nobility and the 'chief disturber of the realm', Simon de Montfort.

The two queens meanwhile were busy on another front in trying to get Alphonse to supply ships for ferrying over mercenaries, which had been the whole object of Henry trying to take Dover. Louis' brother, however, maintained a neutral stance tinged with a bit of annoyance at Margaret's frequent entreaties. She had even asked him to pardon Gaston de Bearn for his latest aggression so he could come to the aide of his nominal overlord Edward. Alphonse was adamant that Gaston was at fault and left it at that.

For now, all eyes were on Louis. Just two days after Henry's attempt to ensnare Simon and his party at Southwark, the Montfortians sealed their letters of agreement to arbitration before the King of France. Three days later, on 16 December, the royalists sealed theirs. Henry's group of supporters was by far more impressive in terms of the baronage, but he knew he remained weak in the towns and counties. He tried to head off any unrest while he was away by publicly declaring that his move to take Dover had been a misunderstanding. He was trying to prevent mercenaries from coming in, not the other way around. As for the Provisions, he was committed to them as always. Of the brief he planned to present to Louis, wherein he demanded that the Provisions be quashed in their entirety, he said nothing.

Leaving Richard in charge, Henry crossed over on 28 December. There he met a small party of Montfortians led by Peter de

Montfort and his cousin Thomas de Cantilupe. Simon wasn't there, nor was he coming. On his way to catch the boat to France, he had turned off towards Catesby to visit an abbey and was injured when his horse tumbled. With a fractured thighbone, and no doubt in great pain, he was brought back to Kenilworth to await the news from Amiens. He received it sometime after 23 January 1264, when Louis issued his award.

The Provisions of Oxford, declared the King of France, were null, void and no law. The King of England was free to rule his subjects as he pleased.

12

Lewes and the Days of May 1264/I

Nearly all the English chroniclers were stunned by Louis' decision and accused him of bad faith for reversing the opinion he gave in Boulogne. He was 'unmindful of his own honour' said one. He went from 'good to bad to worse' said another. His point-blank dismissal of the constitutional crisis that had been gripping the country for five years was bad enough, but what had to be particularly galling for the losing side was his verdict that the Provisions were responsible for all the ills and strife besetting the realm. Not a word was said about the wasteful and capricious rule that led to their enactment in the first place. And so, with the wave of a hand, he declared that his fellow monarch had the right to name his own officials and household, appoint all the sheriffs and castellans throughout the kingdom, give land and offices to all the aliens he wanted, and basically go back to ruling as he did before 1258.

Where the chroniclers got it wrong in their critique of Louis was their claim that he had overstepped the bounds of his authority. In the letters empowering him to act, both sides promised to observe whatever he decreed 'high and low' in their dispute. This has often been judged as a singular miscalculation on the part of the Montfortians. For all his reputation for justice, Louis had been under constant assault by the Savoyards, led by his wife, and by a papal lobby reminding him that the Provisions had been nullified by two different pontiffs. Both groups wanted Henry reinstalled on his throne without any qualifications.

The Montfortians surely had to have taken this into account

before making their submission to Louis, so it would seem that their readiness to allow one king to rule on the rights of another was a mark of either desperation or overconfidence, perhaps both. On the one hand, they were made desperate by the royalist revival and so were hoping to buy time and legitimacy through arbitration. As for overconfidence, that could be traced to the leader of their party and the fact that he had already convinced Louis of the legitimacy of the Provisions only several months earlier. They were counting on Simon pulling off the same feat at Amiens, only no one counted on his horse buckling beneath him on their road to salvation.

In fact, it's doubtful whether even Simon could have succeeded now that the cause had become increasingly identified with revolution, but his replacement in Amiens, the learned Thomas de Cantilupe, was certainly a capable man, probably more distinguished than anyone in the king's party. He was the chancellor of Oxford and, importantly, had known Louis during his student days in Paris.

Cantilupe's brief, while overly long and inclined to nitpicking, reiterated that the Provisions were made because the king was 'bound to give justice to everyone'. Cleverly, he argued that they were the result of the king's violation of Magna Carta. Had Henry ruled in accordance with that charter, as he had sworn to do on no less than three occasions, there would be no Provisions of Oxford. The Provisions were but a piece in the evolution of government since Henry took the throne. No one, not the pope or any king, could invalidate them without invalidating the statutes that gave rise to them in the first place. While rejecting that assertion, Louis did try to hedge by insisting, in addition to a pointed reference to the papal nullifications, that his ruling had nothing to do with Magna Carta. That could stay, but the other one had to go.

This raises the question of what Louis was trying to accomplish with his award. During the peace agreement reached during the summer, it was agreed that the Provisions could be amended until they were acceptable to both parties. Apparently this was what the Montfortians had in mind by preparing an elaborate defence, much more so than the king's case. They wanted Louis to adjudicate on the individual points of the dispute, including the spoliations that occurred during the disorders, and to offer a compromise.

It's likely he would have declined the commission had they included each such article in their submission, thereby limiting the sweep of his powers. But he could not have failed to miss that what the Montfortians were really asking was for him to pass judgement on the spirit of their dispute. Quashing that spirit outright, by a person lauded for his fairness, integrity, and humanity, was perhaps the most mind-boggling episode of the entire reform period. Even the royalist chronicler Wykes felt that Louis had acted 'with less wisdom and foresight than was necessary'.

Today his decision is known as the Mise of Amiens, but then it was called 'The re-establishment of peace between Henry, King of England, and the barons of his realm'. If Louis had truly seen that as the intention of his arbitration, then he failed in it miserably.

The only thing Henry was compelled to do by the award was to pardon the other side and welcome them back to his peace. This he was more than willing to do, but the Montfortians dismissed the almost crass overture. Refusing to abide by the award itself, which they had sworn to do no matter what the outcome, was more complicated and left them open to charges of perjury, of the kind they so often, and accurately, hurled at Henry and Edward. Their only defence was the link between Magna Carta and the Provisions of Oxford. Any verdict that said they could have one but not the other was simply ridiculous, and bad law to boot.

It probably wouldn't have mattered in any event. The struggle had gone well beyond the king being at odds with his leading nobility and churchmen. Montfort and the others could have observed the award and dropped out, but London and the localities had not signed on to the arbitration and immediately rejected the ruling from the Continent. Henry found that out when he returned to England on 15 February and Dover Castle refused to admit him. Since London was equally hostile, he made his way to Oxford, which forever seemed like the crossroads of this turbulent era, and there summoned the feudal host to muster for an assault against Llywelyn.

Again, it was Henry at his duplicitous worst. He had no intentions of moving against Wales and everyone knew it. He was planning to strike directly at Northampton and the Montfortian strongholds in the Midlands. Meanwhile, he wanted Roger Leybourne to pacify his native Kent, but to make that happen Henry had to intervene between him and the Savoyards.

They were understandably aggrieved to see him and his Marcher accomplices rewarded without making restitution for the damages they had caused them. Henry agreed that they should, but now that war was about to break out, he correctly saw the need for the queen and Savoyards to compartmentalise their hatred for these men and allow him to answer for their depredations. Only after he was assured of the king's clemency did Leybourne apply himself against the Montfortian pockets in Kent with the same vigour he had shown against the Savoyards.

Montfort, still laid up at Kenilworth with a broken leg, was doubtless dismayed by Louis' injudiciousness, but wasted no time in seeking an alliance with Llywelyn and despatching his two oldest sons with an army to punish Mortimer. By now an almost famed escape artist, Mortimer slipped away, leaving his wife Maud to deal with the Montforts. Edward had raced back ahead of his father and, finding Mortimer at loose ends, joined him in taking castles belonging to Humphrey de Bohun, the son of the Earl of Hereford. Bohun had refused to follow his father back into the graces of the king, but his fight with Mortimer was personal. Both men were married to sisters, Marshal granddaughters, and had been waging their own long-standing feud over that infernal estate.

All these raids and counter-raids finally came to a head in Gloucester, where the Montfortians, together with Robert de Ferrers, the Earl of Derby, succeeded in bottling up Edward in the castle. Once again Edward asked Walter de Cantilupe to intercede for him, promising he would retreat from the town without committing any harm. The bishop got Henry de Montfort to agree to withdraw his forces to Kenilworth, but the moment the coast was clear Edward reverted to type, robbing the inhabitants of the town and stealing away to Oxford to join his father. Ferrers was enraged. He longed to get his hands on Edward and blamed the Montforts for allowing him to escape.

Henry de Montfort has often been ridiculed for trusting the one man not to be trusted under any circumstances, but growing up with Edward and spending time with him as adults probably led him to believe that his cousin wouldn't betray him. He was sorely mistaken and got the full measure of his father's wrath on that account. And yet the Bishop of Worcester should have known better than to try to make a deal with Edward that would stick, especially after the young man treacherously broke the one he brokered for him, also at Gloucester, during the previous summer.

Simon, however, was not about to alienate Walter with any harsh words. More than ever, the sanctity of his movement depended on the bishops, whose numbers among the Montfortians included Richard Gravesend of Lincoln, John Gervais of Winchester and Stephen Berksted of Chichester. These men were wholly unlike the bishops who followed his father around during the Albigensian Crusade and encouraged a swath of destruction. The English bishops were much influenced by Grosseteste and followed in the tradition espoused by Stephen Langton in the creation of Magna Carta. Militant as they were in their support of the Provisions, they worked tirelessly for peace and now tried to engage the king in reopening negotiations.

The king could be expected to agree. He never ceased to be proud of the fact that the people of his realm had known peace for as long as they had known him on the throne, and that was well over forty years, an eternity in medieval terms. It's true that neither he nor his brother Richard had any warlike skills to begin with, and it may be added that of all John's children, Eleanor would have made the best general. There was also what Henry said back in France, that there were no hard feelings. He was ready to take all into his peace.

In truth, he didn't think there was much to negotiate since Louis' judgement was final, but he sent proctors to Simon at Kenilworth to arrange a conference in nearby Brackley. Louis, seemingly surprised that his decision had brought the country to the eve of war, sent one of his own men to serve as the go-between.

The Montfortian side came ready to give ground, even going as far as to accept the nullification of the Provisions on one condition: that the king would agree to rule through his native-born subjects and not aliens. This was not such a spectacular turnaround as it might seem, since the implication here was that Henry was not the problem. It was the aliens, the Lusignans and Savoyards, who had corrupted the kingdom. Henry, decent but simple, had violated Magna Carta to satisfy the lawlessness of the Lusignans and the greed of the Savoyards. The Provisions of Oxford were meant to protect a king like him from the scurrilous likes of them.

Everything Henry hated about the Provisions, especially the choosing of his household, would vanish just by allowing England to be run by the English. The bishops were even willing to make an exception in Boniface's case, who was after all their primate, but of course he would be bound by certain conditions. Henry's response was profound irritation that the conference took place at all. He ordered the bishops to be gone and never return unless he summoned them. They could tell their party that he intended to use all his power to enforce the judgement of the French king on his English subjects.

As troops began to pour into Oxford, Henry ordered the student population to leave, not because of their pro-Montfortian sympathies or tendency to riot in the spring but to protect them, he said, from the 'fierce and untamed chieftains' of Scotland who were coming to assist him under his son-in-law King Alexander III. The students certainly found no such protection in the countryside around the town, where William de Valence was going about pillaging farms and hamlets at will.

Meanwhile in London, the bells of St Paul's provided the signal for mobs of Londoners to follow Hugh Despenser in sacking royalist properties throughout the city. Richard's house in Westminster and estate at Isleworth were among those gutted, with the hooligans even destroying his fishpond. That gratuitous act of violence alone ensured Richard's eternal hostility to the Montfortians, for nothing upset him more than the destruction of his property.

At this time Simon was getting about in a coach especially built for his injured leg. He had gone to London, hoping to draw Henry's attention there, but the king moved instead against Northampton. With his red dragon banner flapping in the wind, he stormed the fortress on 5 April, rather with ease thanks to the local monks weakening one of the defensive walls for his benefit.

This first official engagement of the civil war was a huge royalist victory. Young Simon de Montfort was captured and reportedly saved from a frightful mauling by Edward. Peter de Montfort and eighty other barons and knights also fell into captivity, some of them signatories to the arbitration in Amiens. Henry was outraged when he learned that the haul of prisoners included some of the students he had expelled from Oxford. He would have put them all to death were he not reminded that many of them came from powerful families.

With the Montfortian Midlands now at the king's mercy, the royalists decided to do some punishing of their own. Edward went north to take his vengeance out on Ferrers while Henry marched into Leicester and allowed his men to ransack Simon's earldom. In the words of one chronicler, 'there was no peace in the realm; all things were wiped out with slaughter, burnings, rapine, and plunder; everywhere there was wild crying and lamentation and horror'.

Things were just as bad in London, as gangs roamed about, plundering whatever they could find, attacking others indiscriminately, regardless of whose side they were on. The revolution had unleashed an urban frenzy, and in one horrendous act of terror, on 9 and 10 April, the Jewish community was set upon by a horde that spared neither age nor sex, but slew all who were not able to buy their freedom or refused to undergo a ritual baptism amid the shrieks and horror. Looting and a sadistic sort of free-for-all were the primary motives, but not even money could save Kok, the most eminent Jew in the city, from being murdered by John Fitz-John, the son of John Fitz-Geoffrey, one of the seven confederates.

The chronicle of the mayors and sheriffs of London puts the number of victims at more than 500. It suggests that some warning was in the air, for the survivors had found shelter in the Tower before the slaughter took place. The keeper of the Tower was Hugh Despenser, who was both Fitz-John's brother-in-law and Simon's right-hand man. The Dunstable annalist says it was Simon himself who instigated the attack because the Jews had made keys to the city gates and, failing to betray it, planned to set it on fire. None of those claims are mentioned by Wykes, who gives the most in-depth account. He implicates Montfort only by his order to Fitz-John to turn over most of his plunder.

Simon's whereabouts during this singular tragedy of the civil war are unknown. He had gone north to try and relieve Northampton, but had turned back in St Albans after learning of its fall. It's improbable he would have condoned, much less unleashed, such a fearful massacre. The war was being lost and London was his main bastion of support. If anything, he needed to restore order there. There was no evidence the Jews, unlike the Christian oligarchs, were actively working against the city, and Simon would have also risked estranging the bishops by perpetrating such an atrocity. As for his culpability, the leader of any popular movement must inevitably answer for whatever ensues as a result of it. That said, much of the class warfare on the streets of London, like the unrest throughout the land, had their roots in the monarchy's exploitation of Jewish finance and everything that was wrong with Henry's reign in general.

After sitting on the fence for a whole year, Gilbert de Clare finally chose sides, but by all appearances it was the losing side. The Montfortians held London and Dover and not much else, but he was reportedly pushed into their camp by his mother, the daughter of John de Lacy, Simon's friend and fellow councillor from the 1230s. Gilbert was at his castle in Tonbridge at the time, the same one Boniface had tried to seize after Richard de Clare died, and his first move, also according to the Dunstable annalist, was to carry out his own attack on the Jews of Canterbury.

Whatever Simon thought about the younger man's true principles, he was now in a position to help him strike at the royalist city of Rochester. Not only did it guard the road to Dover, but Montfort needed to get his unruly urban irregulars out of London before they took the place apart. Also, if he could draw Henry south, that would allow Ferrers and Henry de Montfort to bring their forces from the Midlands to London.

Rochester stood firm, but on 18 April, Simon breached its defences using an assault by fireboat, a tactic unheard of up to that point in the British Isles. Their attempt to take the great keep, however, ended in failure and the irregulars were reduced to pillaging and defiling the town. As hoped, news of the siege got Henry moving and by 26 April, he was advancing towards Rochester via Croydon. Unable to swallow up the rest of the town, Simon grudgingly withdrew his army to London.

Two days later the royalists retook Rochester. The men left behind by Montfort to maintain the semblance of a siege were captured and, in a grossly inhumane act, were restrained while their hands and feet were chopped off. For Henry, it was all about mopping up now. He seized Gilbert's castle of Tonbridge with ease and took aim at the Channel ports. His plan was to use their fleets against Dover and London and then import an army of mercenaries being gathered by Queen Eleanor from as far away as Gascony. Gaston de Bearn himself had volunteered to come to the king's aid, but lacked the means to get himself and his men there. The queen asked Alphonse of Poitiers to seize the English ships in his ports for this purpose, but he recoiled from such blatant interference.

The path to the sea took a toll on the royal army as enemy archers lurked in the trees and picked off stragglers and those unprotected by armour. On 2 May, the king's cook, Thomas, was slain riding out at the head of the column. In his fury Henry demanded that 315 archers who had given themselves up appear before him in a village called Flimwell. Together with Richard, he ordered all the men to be beheaded as a reprisal and warning that the king's patience with the rebellion had run its course. To show what sterner stuff he was now made of, he even sat and watched the grisly scene unfold, apparently unmoved by the pleas and shrieks of the unfortunate men as they were dragged to the chopping blocks and one axe after another fell with the king's justice.

Since the outbreak of hostilities, Simon had done little to justify his reputation as a great military commander. While that may have been due to his broken leg keeping him from taking an active role in the field, the fact remained he had a huge problem now. He was cornered in London with a piteously small army. Ferrers failed to show up, preferring to keep the war a private affair between him and Edward. Henry de Montfort arrived, but even with these reinforcements, the Montfortians were vastly outnumbered. Now more than ever, it was time for him to rise to the occasion and seize the initiative.

Perhaps he might have been encouraged by a fleeting memory from his early boyhood, when his father faced a similar circumstance at Muret. Confronted by a much larger army, the elder Montfort risked everything on facing the enemy out in the field and was rewarded with a victory said to have been divinely inspired. There was only one way to find out if a similar fate awaited the

Montfortians, and so, on 6 May, Simon de Montfort led his army out of London to seek out the king 'with all for all'.

As Muret had shown, medieval battles were rare events because they were so unpredictable. No matter how big the army, there were always unseen forces at work that could tip the balance. It also came down to the nerves and discipline of the army commanders and here Henry was no match for his brother-in-law. Had he not resorted to pillaging after his victory in Northampton, had he kept Edward on a tighter leash, Henry might have had Simon penned in soon enough. Instead he was on the loose somewhere, and the king's first response to the report of his advance was to keep his armour on and gather his forces around Lewes, home to John de Warenne, the mutilator of Rochester. There the royalists would be safe while they tracked the enemy through their scouts and spies.

On 11 May, Montfort's army encamped in and around his manor at Fletching, about eleven miles north of Lewes. The next day he sent a party to the top of today's Mount Harry, the highest point of the South Downs, to reconnoitre the king's position to the east. There they were spotted by royalists from the town, who despatched a contingent of soldiers to chase them off. From that height, these soldiers spied the Montfortian army in the valley below next to a wooded area. They fell back towards the town and reported the sighting, but no other action was taken.

Sometime later the bishops arrived in Lewes to make yet another stab for peace. One party led by the Bishop of Chichester again reiterated to Henry that the Provisions of Oxford could be amended, but there was simply no going back on their oaths to observe them. The bishops of London and Worcester also conducted their own mission, promising compensation for the royalists in the amount of £30,000. Apparently this offer had Richard's grievance over the destruction of his property in mind, hoping it would be an inducement to his pride as a peacemaker.

Henry was inclined to accept, but Richard and Edward banded together to avert any settlement. Whether or not he was motivated by revenge for the loss of his fishpond, Richard saw that the Provisions of Oxford in any form represented a restriction on the king's privileges and authority. And he was a king, too, after all. Edward was of the same mind, but he also detected weakness in the offer and preyed upon it. He let the Montfortians know in a letter that, as far as he was concerned, they could only have peace if they presented themselves before him with halters around their necks, ready for hanging and drawing. While it sounded like more of his usual swagger, as king he would show he wasn't joking.

This episode too recalls Muret a half-century earlier. In spite of their militancy, the French bishops were scared of the numbers opposing them and attempted to negotiate with Peter of Aragon. The elder Montfort rightly suspected they would only be spurned and so broke off further talks. His son may have thought the chances for peace were better at Lewes. Peter was a famed warrior, itching for a fight. Henry clearly wasn't, and Montfort's decision to seek him out only reinforced the king's fear of him.

Henry was also a notorious softie, his brutality at Flimwell notwithstanding, and Simon long believed that most of the belligerence came from the people around him. He knew that one of the two men urging him to fight could always be bought off and had to wonder if he had underestimated Richard's greed when the bishops returned empty-handed. The other one they had no chance of persuading. As his letter had shown, Edward was a boastful, temperamental hothead, and if he would do something stupid in battle tomorrow, as Peter had done at Muret, then Henry was going to rue the day he didn't stick up for himself and choose peace over war.

With his offer rejected, Montfort inched his army closer to Lewes and sent Henry a letter assuring him of his fidelity and that of his men, but also of their equal determination to attack 'our enemies who are also yours'. Henry was having none of it and responded with a letter that defied him and all the other Montfortians. They were no longer his subjects, he declared, only his enemies. Not to be outdone, Richard and Edward added their own letter, trumpeting that they would do everything in their power to injure their persons and properties.

After reading these letters, Simon and his men went through the formal process of withdrawing their homage and fealty to Henry. He was no longer their king, only their enemy. It was war for real now.

Lewes was guarded to the east by the River Ouse. The west bank running north offered only a narrow corridor of marshland, and

Montfort's earlier feint towards Lewes may have been meant to lure the royalists into this boggy trap. When that didn't happen, he figured the only other way the terrain could work to their advantage was by descending on the town from the heights to the northwest. Sometime during the night of 13 May, he got his men on the move. They made a convoluted ascent so as to avoid detection and, once on top, they found that the royalists had posted all of one sentry on Mount Harry, and he was asleep. As they came within sight of the silhouette of the town, they stretched out into formation along the ridge.

Since many of the young nobles had yet to be knighted, Simon took out his sword and did the honours for them, including Gilbert, Robert de Vere the Earl of Oxford, and Hubert de Burgh's grandson John. Then began the final preparation of the troops, which revealed the religious fervour they were to take into the battle below. The men threw themselves to the ground in the shape of a crucifix and said their prayers while the bishops of Worcester and Chichester absolved them. They got up, put the white cross of crusaders on their garments, both as a sign of devotion and to recognise one other, and listened as Simon de Montfort addressed them.

'Today we fight for the sake of the realm of England, to the honour of God and to maintain our oath. Let us pray that he may grant us strength and aid to overcome the malice of our foes.'

Sometime before dawn on the morning of 14 May 1264, they began their march on the town.

Foragers from Lewes were out and about around 4.00 a.m. They saw the rebel army advancing from the South Downs and immediately raced back to sound the alarm. The royalists may not have been partying all night as one friar suggested, but they were clearly asleep at the time. Rousing themselves, Henry and Richard emerged from the priory, Edward from the castle sometime later. They would have been greeted by an awe-inspiring sight, three divisions of the Montfortian army gleaming in the first rays of light from the sun coming up behind them.

A quick council of war decided that Henry would lead the royalist left wing, facing his nephews Henry and Guy de Montfort. The Earl of Hereford was with him, but Humphrey de Bohun, his son and heir, was opposite with the Montfort brothers. Richard and his son Henry of Almain took command of the centre. Opposing them was Gilbert de Clare, who was Almain's nephew. Edward was on the right together with his uncles William de Valence and Guy Lusignan. Leading the Montfortians at this end of the field was Henry Hastings, who had been a ward of the tyrannical Guy.

The contemporary claim that there were 100,000 men on the field was surely an exaggeration common in ancient sources. It would not be unreasonable to assume that the actual figure was just over one-eighth that size, with 150 Montfortian knights, 4,000 foot soldiers and 500 cavalry, arrayed against 500 royalist knights, 7,000 foot and 1,500 horsemen.

Edward started things off with a smashing charge against the Montfortian left, capturing Marcher lord John Giffard and chasing off the other knights. Many of them tried to escape by crossing the Ouse and were drowned in the process. The foot soldiers behind them were next. They were composed mainly of London irregulars, many of them barely armed, carrying no more than a stick or sling, and therefore easy prey for the royalist knights. While some of them had probably taken part in the massacre of the Jews and in the outrages in Rochester, it was said that Edward took special delight in this slaughter on account of the way his mother had been treated at London Bridge. He and his fully armoured gang, including former justiciar and reformer Hugh Bigod, ran the terrified Londoners down with their chargers, crushing their skulls and spines with hoof and mace alike.

They hunted them down in this fashion for four miles, well out of eyeshot of the battle. Finally, one of them noticed the Montfortian standard at the top of the hill. They reared their beasts to the left and in no time had fallen on Simon's rearguard, headed by his faithful knight William de Blund. They slew him and the rest of his men and surrounded the coach they had been protecting. Assuming it to be the same one that Simon had been using to get around, they broke into it, hoping to find the 'devil' inside.

All they got instead was a couple of elderly citizens who had been trying to rally London for the king. Simon had been worried that these men might destabilise the city while he was away and so imprisoned them in the coach, using it as a mobile jail. Unfortunately for them, they were killed before they got a chance to make their case.

It was sometime during that action that Edward turned his sights to the town 430 feet below and realised what a terrible mistake he had made. After he took off, Richard and Henry slowly began advancing their troops uphill. Once they were in range, the Montfortian slingers began pummelling them with stones and scrap, an effective barrage in the absence of archery regiments on either side. The infantrymen then hurled themselves in a rolling phalanx towards the royalist lines and pushed them back towards the city walls.

Montfort had kept a fourth division in reserve, and after seeing Edward disappear from the field he threw these men towards the centre. This second frontal assault added just enough pressure to break and scatter Richard's line. With the right wing gone and no centre to speak of, Henry took it in the flank, causing his line to crumble as well. Although it was the first time the king had ever fought in real combat, his courage did not fail him, even after two horses were killed underneath him.

The battle was clearly lost and Henry's attendants now worked towards getting him safely back inside the priory. The Montfortians followed, combing through the city passages and converging on the king's holdout. By this time Edward and his men had returned to the battlefield. With at least 500 horsemen, they were ready to storm the city until the Montfortian knights came out to face them mace to mace. Sometime during this next engagement, Valence, Warenne and Bigod spurred their horses around and fled for the coast, while Edward, Mortimer and Leybourne managed to fight their way into the priory.

Up to 2,000 men fell on that day, with the Londoners accounting for most of the dead. The Montfortians had won the battle, but knew a full-scale assault against the priory was not in their interest. The king and his son had to be coaxed out, and to make that happen they were offered terms that would at least allow Henry to save something of his dignity.

Known as the Mise of Lewes, Henry would have to agree to observe the Provisions, remove all the traitors from his council, and pardon those who took up arms against him. The Provisions could always be amended, as the Montfortians insisted all along, and a complicated arbitration would be set up for that purpose. It would once again involve the French, this time in the expectation that Louis would reconsider his ill-advised award and work for a permanent peace.

By offering Henry what he could have had before the battle, Simon was making a concession to whatever semblance of authority the king still thought he had. Edward also got something, the release of his Marcher friends. Simon probably balked at this demand, inasmuch as they were stamped with treachery and he and Mortimer were now deadly enemies, but it was equally important to get Edward to come out quietly. While later events might suggest this was a mistake, the Marchers by themselves would prove only a nuisance for the year Edward was in captivity.

Unlike other battles, Lewes stands out for certain features that give it an almost mythical quality. There was the exchange of letters between both camps, the smaller army challenging the larger one to come out and fight, Edward's vengeful blunder, the coach at the top of the hill. And then there was the windmill.

In his flight from the battlefield, Richard had found refuge in a nearby windmill. The Montfortian soldiers quickly tracked him down and began shouting at the king of the Germans to come out, poking fun at his contemptuous dismissal of the £30,000 he was offered for peace. Their jeering led to the composition of a song, presumed to be the first political paean written in English. The first stanza gets right to the heart of the matter, that it was money that led Richard to his inglorious state:

Sitteth alle stille ant herkneth to me!	Sit all still and listen to me
The Kyn of Alemaigne, bi mi leauté,	the King of Alamein, by my loyalty
Thritti thousent pound askede he	Thirty thousand pounds he asked
For te make the pees in the countré,	to make peace in the country
ant so he dude more.	And so he did more
Richard, thah thou be ever trichard,	Richard, though thou art ever a traitor
tricchen shalt thou never more.	A traitor you shall be never more.

Another poem, much longer and more serious, also appeared after the triumph. The *Song of Lewes* was written anonymously, most likely by a friar in the entourage of the Bishop of Chichester, Stephen Berksted. Its length and composition in Latin most likely prevented it from gaining wide acceptance, although today's student could probably pick out more recognisable words than from *Beowulf* in Old English.

'Now England breathes again,' exults the author. He praises the victory and the Montfortian programme, admonishing Henry and all other kings that they are not above the law. They should rule through natives and not strangers, otherwise discord is the outcome. The king who would do so anyway may think his councillors mad if they did not obey him, but in fact they would be if they did.

There are only two main characters represented in the work, Edward and Simon. Edward is called a leopard. He's a leo, or lion, thanks to his fierceness and bravery, but equally a pardus, or panther, because he's sneaky and sly. He will tell you everything you want to hear, only to go back on his promises the first chance he gets.

Simon also deserves circumspection, because the author knows he is considered a 'seducer and deceiver' in some quarters. It was his devotion to the cause, however, that made victory possible. He 'squeezed out the red juice' because 'truth compelled him to fight'. The peace of all England depends on the 'faith and fidelity of Simon alone'.

They were heady words that couldn't mask the problems ahead. The enforcement of the Provisions in this manner, with Richard, his sons and Edward as hostages for Henry's compliance, meant a captive monarchy, a seemingly unnatural state of affairs bound to be viewed with hostility both at home and abroad. England was a mess after one year of tension and disorder, but rather than work to reunite the country, the elements at work against it would take every opportunity to pounce.

Simon's cause may have been doomed to frustration, as one historian put it, but 'a sense of beauty lingers over those days in May'. For whatever else it achieved, this cause had brought the people of the realm together in defence of principles that touched and united them all in the will and courage to die for them. When Simon was addressing his troops, he might have added that where Moses had climbed the mountain alone, they did it together. They needn't fear the momentous clash before them below, for victory was already theirs.

13

The Rise of the Montfortian State 1264/II

It was the Victorian era that ushered in and nurtured the legend of Simon de Montfort as the founder of Parliament. To be sure, his brief government did as much as any to enhance the prestige of Parliament, but its origins went at least as far back as the Conquest two centuries earlier. The feudal system implanted by the Normans required the tenants-in-chief to provide the king not only with military service in return for their lands, but also with counsel whenever he required it. By Henry's reign, these councils had grown to include churchmen and middling lords as his ever urgent need for taxation forced him to seek a broader band of support. In 1236 the word parliament appeared for the first time to distinguish these larger assemblies from the king's other council, his inner circle of advisers that at one time counted Montfort among its numbers.

That must have seemed like ages ago as the former favourite took custody of the king in Lewes. Since coming of age, Henry had loathed sharing power. Now he emerged from the priory an old man with none to speak of. Twice the Provisions had been imposed upon him, in 1258 and 1263, and each time he secretly and successfully worked to overthrow them. There would be no more of that. Henceforth, he would be kept in close confinement, enjoying the privileges and comfort of a king but not much else. He was taken on a circuitous route to London (the surrounding countryside had been stripped bare during the campaign) and lodged in St Paul's.

Edicts immediately started going out in his name, proclaiming the peace and appointing wardens for this purpose to serve alongside the sheriffs. Pockets of resistance still held out, and not all the castles were surrendered. The touchy problem of prisoners and ransoming them still had to be addressed, but more important was the main problem facing the Montfortians in the aftermath of Lewes: what argument to use for keeping the king under their tutelage.

The easiest argument was the victory itself and the feeling of divine vindication that underscored it, and yet it was no secret that Simon's generalship and Edward's imprudence had each played an equal part in this particular miracle. A more prosaic sense of legitimacy was preferred, but that was only possible if Louis were persuaded to act on the terms of the Mise of Lewes. His dignity, however, was as much at stake here as Henry's and in the end that would prove more important to him. The last option was to let Parliament decide, and this act, it might be said, proved to be the occasion where that institution finally came into its own.

The process had started in 1258 with the provision that called for Parliament to meet three times a year at fixed intervals. This was implicit recognition that Parliament was the forum for discussing 'the common business of the realm'. The first test case of whether it would meet as prescribed by law, as opposed to the will of the king, came in 1260 at Montfort's insistence that the law took precedence.

Similarly significant was the role Parliament began playing in the drafting of reform legislation, in particular laws that concerned local interests. Ironically, it was Henry who turned the localities into a national constituency when he summoned elected knights to Parliament in 1254. Montfort revived this precedent seven years later when he summoned three knights from each county to his rogue parliament in St Albans. Now he wanted them again, and in June 1264 invited all the counties to elect four knights each, 140 altogether, and even if not all of them made it to the assembly, it certainly had to be the most impressive display of representative government yet seen on the island.

The major point of issue was the endorsement of a new constitution. The knights did not come just to rubberstamp Montfort's initiatives, however. They wanted and got something, too, namely the right to appoint their own sheriffs. Henry, forced to attend as the sovereign head of state, must have looked on glumly as that most cherished of his prerogatives slipped from his grasp. He couldn't have been happy about the constitution that was drawn up, either.

It called for three electors to choose a council of nine, three of whom would always be in attendance on him. The council was given authority over everything, from appointing state officials and the king's household to controlling his castles. Since the three electors consisted of Simon, Berksted and Gilbert, and the councillors were mostly Montfortian stalwarts, it was definitely a packed court. Parliament didn't have a problem with that and approved what became England's first constitutional monarchy. The text says that Henry also gave his consent, but one chronicler is probably more correct to say that his only other option was to face being deposed.

Officially called an ordinance, this constitution was meant to serve as a provisional government until the terms of the Mise of Lewes were implemented. Montfort was accused in his own time and ours of having no intention of fulfilling the Mise, only agreeing to it to get his hands on Henry and Edward. Now that he had them, he was content to let the Ordinance be the law of the land and he at the head of it.

Seen in another light, the Mise was preferable because, even if the Provisions came out of arbitration in diluted form, it would still give the regime legitimacy from the outside. Indeed, Henry's first letter to Louis after Lewes asked him to act on the Mise and offered to pursue a shorter way to peace if one could be found. The ball was in France's court, and Henry's subsequent letters took on an urgent tone, even warning that the lives of the hostages were at stake. That, of course, was the biggest joke in town. Edward was only a hostage in so far as to keep him from making trouble. The queen certainly would have ceased putting an invasion force together had she believed his life was in any real danger, and never once did Edward appear before the Montfortians with a halter around his neck as a way of getting her to stand down.

It was the threat of this invasion that kept the situation unsettled throughout the summer of 1264. The queen and the exiles heard of the royalist defeat from Valence, Warenne and Bigod, three men who were not normally to her liking and whose escape from the field, while her husband and son fought on, could not have rehabilitated them in her eyes. Her natural steeliness allowed her to overcome her grief and take charge of the situation.

First, she went to the court in Paris and collected an instalment of the money due under the Treaty of Paris. She got more by pawning the Crown jewels and selling Henry's rights in three French bishoprics to Louis. Despite her husband's predicament, she knew he would not be happy about her pawning away his rights and so she had wisely included a redemption clause for him to use later on, which he most eagerly did. The money went towards putting together an army of mercenaries from all over the Continent, from Germany and Flanders to Burgundy and Gascony, to be led by the indefatigable Peter of Savoy.

Across the Channel, an equally impressive army was being raised in the king's name to repel the queen. Men gathered along the coast from all around to defend what they saw as a great cause. It was an army amassed amid months of uncertainty while the harvest beckoned. Not all were volunteers. Most weren't even Montfortians per se. They were just ordinary folk whose common threads were the language they spoke and a newfound awareness that they were part of a political community. This was perhaps the one triumph that could never be taken away from Montfort, and the reason he was revered across all levels of society years after he was gone. The English nation had truly arisen under his leadership.

He himself wasn't there. Almost in collusion with events in France, the Marchers ignored the summons to Parliament and went on a tear through the Severn Valley. Simon and Gilbert were forced to march west to deal with this insurgency, but even with Llywelyn's help, they could manage little more than force them to terms with the threat of an invasion looming. Mortimer turned over one of his sons as a hostage, but as with Edward, it belied how useless and outdated this form of enforced diplomacy had become.

A more immediate threat came in the form of the papal legate, who was expecting to mediate the dispute despite his partiality. He was informed that his admission to the kingdom ultimately depended on both the king and the community's permission, and that had not been given. The legate was astounded by the ingratitude of the English. He reminded them that it was a legate like him who had saved England from being conquered by Louis' father, by which he meant saved Henry's throne. Montfort himself was unmoved by the legate's entreaties. He had already written to him to protest the connivance between Louis and the queen in using the treaty money to fund an invasion force when it should be going for the benefit of England. He was also of the opinion that the legate should work on disbanding that force before assuming the role of peacemaker.

The legate insisted he was trying to keep the invasion from gathering and was candid to admit he had failed there. As for the money, that was long gone. He moved on to Boulogne, where he expected to meet a delegation of Montfortian envoys. When they didn't arrive, he ordered Simon and his 'accomplices' to admit him by 1 September or face excommunication. He added that as far as the Mise of Lewes was concerned, none of the proposed commissioners had even received it. Louis, it turned out, had taken no heed of it and wouldn't stoop to give an answer one way or another.

By this time the English court was in Canterbury, and it was there that the Montfortians drew up a second proposal known as the Peace of Canterbury. It reiterated the rule of the Three and the Nine with restraints on the king's will, but added conciliatory gestures on restitution for the Church and leniency for aliens, who would be allowed to come and go in peace but were still not to hold royal offices. The caveat was that the Peace of Canterbury was to remain in force for however long it took to implement the Mise, even if that meant for the rest of Henry's reign and going into Edward's.

The point was to get Louis to quit acting petulant and take an interest in Henry regaining some semblance of power and freedom. The King of France was outraged. They were not only asking him to overturn his judgement at Amiens, but to approve an idea of kingship that was no kingship at all in his mind. The legate reported that he told him he would rather toil in the fields behind a plough than rule with such restrictions. The future Saint Louis was making it clear that come Judgement Day, he would make his case as an anointed king and not some insignificant farmer.

By now the bishops were feeling the strain. They had been putting off appearing before the legate as commanded for fear he would let them have it. In an attempt to show their deference and sincerity, they offered to submit the Peace of Canterbury for modification by a joint committee. In another act of conciliation, they would send one of the hostages, Henry of Almain, to promote it in person, agreeing to stand surety for his return to the whopping tune of £13,500. There was lots of haggling on both sides about who the arbitrators should be and how much control the council should have over the king, whether they should be English or not, and who should name them. Even Simon's old disputes with Henry over Eleanor's dower entered the negotiations at one point.

Finally, the bishops bowed to the inevitable and met the legate in Boulogne. Cardinal Foulquois was understandably aggrieved at being made to wait so long, but took an active part in the negotiations. He wanted to hear it from the bishops themselves that they were really advocating these Montfortian restraints on royal power. The intimidation proved too much for the Bishop of Winchester, who broke down on the spot and asked for forgiveness. The rest conceded certain points in the plan, such as the council's control over appointments. All this went back and forth until the legate had enough and sent the bishops on their way on 3 October. They were bearing bulls of excommunication and interdict, which he ordered them to publish if the Montfortians remained obstinate after fifteen days.

The only way they could get out of these ecclesiastical penalties was by giving the legate full authority to determine the outcome of the negotiations. He also wanted Dover Castle and the hostages in return for a French castle and Edward's brother Edmund. It was a lame trade all around, but then the legate threw in one more proviso: the settlement of Simon's private quarrel with Henry. Presumably he thought, or had been told, that Montfort would step aside once his claims had been settled, paving the way for the legate to enfeeble the Provisions and return Henry to undisputed rule. He evidently thought he could succeed where two kings had failed over the years.

When the bishops returned to England, they were searched and dispossessed of the legate's bulls, which were torn to shreds and tossed into the sea. On 11 October, the legate got his answer when an English knight approached the French coast near Wissant and dropped a chest into the sea. Contained therein were letters of rejection, the Peace of Canterbury and the Ordinance. It was as clear a statement as any that the community of the realm intended to rule through their revolutionary government with or without outside approval.

Doubtless beside himself, the legate published the bulls himself in Flanders, but the effect on Montfort's regime was nil. The cardinal's commission soon came to an end at any rate. Pope Urban IV died that same month, and he had to return to Rome, where he was elected the new pope. As Clement IV, he never forgave Simon for the failure to reach an agreement. He would write to the new legate appointed in his place that he was not to 'admit a treaty of false peace until the pestilent man with all his progeny be plucked out of the realm of England'.

With the departure of the legate, the invasion force began melting away. Apparently it had been of such size and ferocity that it would have easily brushed the peasant army aside after landing. The handiest explanation for what had to be the biggest bust of the year was again the hand of the Almighty. As he had ordained the victory at Lewes, so he made sure the Channel winds were adverse the whole four months' time the mercenaries were waiting for the signal. The legate didn't bother himself with such rubbish. He had been determined to succeed on the diplomatic front and probably had a few choice words with the queen and Peter of Savoy about not getting too impatient. By the time his options were exhausted, so were their funds and they simply could not afford the invasion anymore. It was a terrible blow to the queen, but undoubtedly there were people at the French court who were relieved the ships never sailed. They knew very well that the last time a foreign fleet left for England, it was completely destroyed by the sailors of the Channel ports, and it was precisely these men who were the most eager for the aliens to just try and land.

Stymied on the invasion front, the queen turned to the royalist insurgents at home to free Edward from his detention at Wallingford

Castle. She got a message through to Robert Walerand, her long-time confidant holding out at Bristol, and assured him that Wallingford was lightly defended should he and a few other knights make a bid to rescue him. There's no telling where she got her information, but a group of them did ride out that way and managed to breach the outer walls before the garrison warned them that they could have Edward all right, just as soon as a mangonel was ready for launching him. Edward was even produced on the ramparts to beseech them to desist, probably with a little help from his captors cranking the machine.

The knights withdrew, but a more serious uprising broke out again in the Marches. After moving Edward and the other captives to the more secure environs of Kenilworth, Simon marched again on Mortimer and the other Rogers, Leybourne and Clifford, in December and forced them to submit to even more stringent terms. They were ordered to turn their lands over for temporary custody while they took a year off in Ireland. The Rogers were brought to Edward to hear it out of his own mouth.

Simon knew that the alliance between Edward and these men would always pose a risk to his government. He needed to eliminate this threat if Edward was ever going to be released, and the most effective means for that was to remove him from the Marches. He therefore worked out a deal to swap his nephew's holdings in Cheshire for some of his own lands elsewhere. It was hardly a fair exchange. Edward's properties were probably worth three times more, and they were to come to Montfort in fee, meaning his son Henry would inherit them someday. The deal has been cited to this day as evidence that Simon tried to enrich his family at Edward's expense, even if under the guise of security claims. What is definitely true is that it wasn't the first time Edward got fleeced. He had been forced into a similar swap by the king and queen for no other purpose than to enrich Peter of Savoy.

What Henry thought about this wasn't taken into account. After Lewes, he lost control over everything: his seal, household, kingdom. He didn't, however, just mope around and refuse to take part in public affairs. His own voice comes through in some of his letters, and the Montfortians were keen for him to be seen as a king still in charge. The only change now was he had faithful councillors at his side, giving him sound and reasonable advice. The Three and the Nine for sure were Montfortians, as were most top officials like Despenser, again serving as justiciar, but otherwise no sweeping purge took place. The general policy was to project an image of business as usual. Royalist John Chishull was retained as chancellor and even a diehard and alien like Mathias Bezill was courted with moderate success to support the new regime.

Care was also taken to ensure the king enjoyed the same lifestyle he had before the war. The expenditures by the king's wardrobe actually increased after Lewes for luxuries like spices, jewellery and garments made out of fur and otter skin. Not just for Henry, but Richard too, who was being detained with his two sons, Henry of Almain and Edmund, together with Edward. Eleanor de Montfort saw to it that her brothers dined in the regal fashion they were accustomed to and sent them foodstuffs like ginger, cloves, raisins, almonds and barrels of sturgeon and whale meat.

There were, of course, immense problems behind the façade of continuity. The country was reeling from the devastation wrought by the war. The poor had been especially affected, losing everything down to the straw for their bedding. Simon's threat to chop off the head of anyone caught ransacking churches and cemeteries proved no deterrent. The government teetered on bankruptcy. The exchequer was closed for most of the year, with payments from sheriffs during that time totalling only £139, not even a tenth of the previous year's take.

Local trade was disrupted by bandits lurking about, and the projected invasion seriously hampered the overseas market for English wool. Normally the wool was sent to Flanders, where the queen was then collecting her troops, but exports were brought to a halt by the seizure of Flemish merchant vessels for coastal defences. The Countess of Flanders, the sister of the Joanna courted by Simon nearly thirty years earlier, responded by restraining English goods in her territory. The ensuing war of words between the two sides has Simon supposedly saying that the English 'could live comfortably without foreign trade' and the people expressing their solidarity by wearing plain white cloth, which was ordinarily dyed in Flanders, as if to show their willingness to live without creature comforts. Since Montfort's government was striving to restore normal commercial relations with the world, any public announcement along these lines was probably intended to offer reassurance in the face of the hardships ahead, which would make it one of the earliest references to an English leader telling the people to keep a stiff upper lip.

Re-establishing the Jewish communities in peace was admittedly a more arduous task. Whether the violence directed at them had more to do with indebtedness or deep-rooted anti-Semitism, the destruction was appalling. The chests (*archae*) that contained the records of their loans proved to be tinderboxes throughout the conflict. Pardoning the debts owed by their Christian borrowers might not necessarily offer them more security, but it would gain the Montfortians more adherents, and so, in a clear bid for popularity, the slates were wiped clean for various members of the gentry and knightly class. Henry deeply resented this action and would repeal the writs after being restored to power. Edward, however, took note of the precedent and employed it later when he needed similar political support.

It was with Edward in mind that writs were issued on 14 December 1264 for Parliament to convene in January. Theoretically, he could go on being a hostage forever since the Mise of Lewes had not been fulfilled, nor were the Marchers falling in line. Since holding him in custody was neither practical nor acceptable to the bishops or Gilbert de Clare, Montfort wanted Parliament's approval for the elaborate scheme he was drawing up for Edward's release.

This particular gathering of Parliament would be lauded as the first of its kind to summon representatives from towns and boroughs, and the act used to credit Montfort with creating the House of Commons. In a way, he had Henry to thank for it. The king inadvertently paved the way when he invited the knightly class to Parliament in what were the first official elections. The move wasn't meant to dilute the power of the baronage and clergy, he just needed money, and when the knights denied him the tax, mainly because they got nothing in return, he declined to repeat the experiment. Montfort had seen the value of their political support, of making local concerns a part of the national agenda, and so turned to them for the approval of his constitution. Now he was taking the initiative further by giving urban dwellers a voice in Parliament as well.

It was a bold move, even if the inclusion of the burgesses, as the town representatives were known, was inevitable some day. Henry certainly coveted the growing wealth of the towns, but perhaps out of concern for his dignity he couldn't bring himself to ask men of low birth for money. And that was, after all, what his parliaments were about. He probably had the same qualms about dealing with the knights and might not have ever summoned them again had Montfort's attempt to hold a rogue parliament not forced him to. But at least the knights carried an aura about them. They were the warrior class, men of morals, manners and muscle, all confirmed by an elaborate initiation ceremony.

The burgesses, on the other hand, were simple moneygrubbers, an incipient bourgeoisie with no pedigree to speak of. Of course, they didn't see themselves that way. The good life had made patricians out of them and they generally ruled their towns and cities with the same pretensions that prevailed among the landed elite. Royalists at heart, they were jealous of their power and privileges and treated the working stiff, whether plying a trade, engaged in crafts, or hustling on the streets, with open contempt. Indeed, Montfort would have lost London long before Lewes if the oligarchs had had their way. It would be centuries before any great democratic upheaval took place with these commoners sitting in Parliament, but a momentous step had been taken with the political mingling of the classes and governing England would never be the same again.

As Christmas 1264 drew near, the Montfortians no doubt reflected on how low their fortunes had sunk one year earlier, how they had been pinning their hopes on Louis when Simon tumbled from his horse. But the Almighty sets everything to right in the end, and England was now being ruled by a king who truly took the interests of his subjects to heart. The holiday for the Montfort family at Kenilworth was a magnificent occasion, if we can believe a chronicler's assertion that there were 140 household knights in attendance – far more than Henry ever had.

Not surprisingly, this same chronicler says that the king's Christmas at Woodstock was a much more solemn affair. Henry was well known as a family man, and to have to spend the holiday alone, with but a handful of attendants handpicked for him, must have evoked a lot of sympathy, perhaps even from a few who thought he had only himself to blame. The chronicler laments that the king, after fifty years on the throne, was now 'nothing but the shadow of a name'.

Another chronicler, the irascible Wykes, didn't mince words about the man he held responsible for it, who as far as he was concerned was worse than the devil himself:

> And just as the tutor is accustomed to lead his pupil, so Montfort ignobly led the king through all the counties of the kingdom, and with the natural as much as the legal order inverted, he was not ashamed to rule the king, to whom he should be rightly bound; and he acted above himself, it was as though the name of the earl completely overshadowed the royal highness. What shameless things of unheard evil, such that he exceeded the pride of arrogant Lucifer!

While Wykes never liked Simon de Montfort to begin with, he was undoubtedly not the only one to feel that the turn of events had inverted the natural and legal order. Everyone knew that the king was now a mere figurehead, that it was his brother-in-law running the country. Officially, Simon was the Earl of Leicester, one member of a triumvirate that included the Bishop of Chichester and the Earl of Gloucester. Stephen Berksted, however, busied himself with Church matters and Gilbert de Clare was nowhere to be found. The young earl had been rewarded with his place on the council of three in view of his support at Lewes and status as a leading peer, but he was nevertheless the odd man out.

At twenty-one years old, he was much younger than staunch Montfortians like Peter de Montfort and Hugh Despenser, who would have remembered the crack that went around Gilbert's circle about the party needing a younger leader. His decision to join up at the last possible minute certainly didn't endear him to the faithful. If they noticed him at all, it was for his red hair. Besides being touchy and resentful, he was the son of Richard de Clare, whose treachery had cost the barons their last big chance to present a united front to Henry. The elder Clare could never make up his mind where he belonged in the scheme of things, whether to side with the Lusignans or Savoyards, with the royalists or reformers, and the signs were there that Gilbert was plagued by the same muddled insecurity.

14

Darkness at Evesham
1265

By the beginning of 1265, the Montfortians had weathered the major threats confronting their truly provisional government. The legate, the queen and the Marchers had all been turned back, and the remnants of royalist resistance were beginning to come over. It was vindication for all they had set out to do, to have the king govern through a council of native-born subjects and fixed sessions of Parliament. The interests of the lower orders had now moved to the top of the national agenda, no more waiting for royal edicts to trickle down through an entrenched baronage. The community of the realm and rule of law, it would seem, had indeed triumphed. And yet within eight months Simon de Montfort was dead, his movement defeated and scattered, and Henry restored to full royal authority on a wave of vengeance and vindictiveness.

The events leading up to the Battle of Evesham in August began on 20 January with the opening of the parliament that made Montfort famous in later generations. It was beset by problems from the outset. Only eighteen barons were present, though not for a lack of trying. Roger Bigod had been won over, but most of the northern barons rejected the new regime. The knights from two counties held by the Marchers failed to show, indicating that the Rogers, far from going to Ireland as agreed, were disruptive as ever. They also continued to flout one of the terms for their release, namely to surrender the men they had captured before Lewes. It was this issue that finally brought Gilbert's dissatisfaction out into the open.

The exchange of highborn prisoners for ransom was a common

practice in the Middle Ages. After Lewes, Simon tried to head off the unsavoury business that surrounded it by declaring a clean sweep of all prisoners. When the Marchers refused to cooperate, that made it open season on the exchange for both sides. Gilbert staked a claim to his step-grandfather Richard of Cornwall, but Montfort, loath to lose so valuable a hostage, dismissed him with 'brevity and levity'. He also denied John Giffard two prisoners captured by one of his knights, William de Maltravers, on the grounds that Maltravers had let them go. This inexplicable action, combined with Giffard falling into enemy hands just after the battle commenced, gave rise to suspicions that the two of them were playing a double role. Giffard now turned to Gilbert for protection, who was only too glad to press his grievance along with his own about the inequality of the spoils system under Montfort's rule.

The other spoils included custody of the estates belonging to captured royalists. Here Gilbert received those of William de Valence and parts of John de Warenne's, but it irked him that Montfort took plenty more for himself, including all the baronies held by Richard. Even worse, Simon committed various lands and castles to his sons. The concentration of these strongholds in the eastern and western reaches of the southern coastline marks this move as a security measure, since it was hoped that he could at least trust his sons not to betray him, but others were bound to see it as more enrichment for his family.

It also didn't help that Gilbert was intensely jealous of Henry de Montfort and his brothers. They were older, had been knighted before him, and, for whatever it was worth anymore, were nephews of the king. He was the Earl of Gloucester, but as the makeup of Parliament was beginning to show, being a hereditary peer wasn't what it used to be. The Montfort brothers didn't care what his status was and needled him for one reason or another. It could have even been their work that got Gilbert stuck with the nickname 'Red'.

The only way to settle their differences like real knights was at a tournament, and for this the Montforts challenged Gilbert and his brother Thomas to meet them on the proving grounds of Dunstable. There each side would line up facing the other and charge, then turning (the origins of the word) after the initial crash to duel it out. Simon considered the presence of so many armed men with inflamed tempers to be dangerous given the still disordered state of the realm, particularly with Parliament sitting just thirty miles away, and had Henry ban the tournament. When Gilbert refused to obey, citing the expense that had gone into organising it, Simon led a squad of London militiamen to Dunstable to enforce the king's order.

Gilbert was incensed and let slip that he thought it was 'ridiculous that this foreigner should presume to put the whole realm under his yoke'. That got to the crux of what was really bothering him. Simon was an alien, and Gilbert claimed he even had alien knights working for him. The supreme leader of the land was making a mockery of the provision trumpeting the rule of Englishmen. It must have seemed like more of his tiresome complaining, because the anti-alien argument by that time had lost much of its appeal. Even Boniface was being wooed to come back and resume his post as Archbishop of Canterbury, but he and the other exiles were demanding nothing less than full restoration.

It probably wouldn't have made Gilbert any happier knowing that Montfort himself was displeased by the way his sons were acting. He couldn't believe their folly in organising a tournament at so sensitive a time and warned them not to try something like that again, else he would lock them away where they would enjoy the light of 'neither sun nor moon'. Still, he was as keen as ever to set them up while he had the chance to do so. When John Mansel died abroad in January of that year, he gave one of his many offices, that of treasurer of York, to his son Amaury. Guy and Richard also received lands if the official gifts of deer made to them by their uncle Henry are any indication.

Both older sons, Henry and Simon, were made constables at the Channel ports, and in this capacity they were accused of abetting in the piratical activities that flourished during the trade embargo. Wykes even disparaged Henry de Montfort as the 'wool merchant' for seizing all the wool at Dover. The young man justified his action by claiming he wanted to keep other people from seizing it. Montfort also had to reprimand his son Simon on one occasion for holding a merchant ship and ordered him to release it without having to be 'urged further in this matter'.

His namesake son received even more notoriety when he brought suit against William de Braose, a hardcore Marcher and royalist, for plundering one of the properties that came his way from Mansel. A kangaroo court that included his brother Henry and Hugh Despenser, the justiciar himself, saddled Braose with the impossible sum of £6,500 to pay in damages, and until he did his son would remain a hostage in the care of Eleanor de Montfort. It is in fact this hint of a family racket that has led to similarities being drawn between the Montforts and Lusignans. But since the Montforts were in business for just over a year, it is impossible to determine if they would have stooped to the beatings, robberies and gratuitous killings the Lusignans indulged in for a whole decade under the king's protection.

In Henry's mind, the chief threat to law and order at that time was not his nephews but Robert de Ferrers. The young Earl of Derby had taken advantage of Edward's captivity to carry on their feud with impunity. Henry was furious and wanted him arrested. Since Ferrers no longer had any affiliation with the Montfortians, his summons to Parliament could only have been meant for this purpose. Why he showed up nobody knows, but he was detained and packed off to the Tower. This suited Montfort just fine, because the release of Edward was tied to the transfer of his Cheshire holdings to him, and these included properties that had been part of the feud between the two young men.

As much as Ferrers was a menace to society and warranted confinement, Gilbert saw his arrest as Simon's way of eliminating potential rivals and was worried he would be next. He therefore excused himself from Parliament and went back to Gloucester. Simon had to know that spelt trouble, given that Edward pulled the same trick before the downfall of his first government, but Parliament was clamouring to wrap things up. It was time for the big show.

On 11 March 1265, Westminster Hall was the scene of an elaborate ceremony for officially reconciling the Plantagenets once and for all to their loss of absolute rule. In the presence of nine bishops, ready to excommunicate anyone who deviated from the agreement, Henry and Edward swore to abide by the provisional government, swore not to import aliens, swore to forgive their captors and swore not to seek absolution from what they were swearing to at that moment. Edward also agreed to his exclusion from the Marches by way of transferring Cheshire to Montfort, and the council was to retain hold of five of his castles for a probationary period of five years. The arrangements also called for all free men to renew their fealty to Henry. The mayor of London, Thomas Fitz-Thomas, was probably speaking for many of them when he qualified his oath to the king:

> Lord, as long as you will be a good king and lord to us, we will be your faithful and devoted men.

The final act was to release Edward and Henry of Almain, which entailed moving them from Kenilworth to the king's household. In this regard, the show was truly a show, because inasmuch as Henry was still a captive, so were they. It will never be known what Montfort's ultimate plans for Edward were, if he intended to disinherit him somewhere down the line and declare himself king, an implausible assumption that strangely finds backers today. The only thing that can be said for certain is that Edward and Henry survived their captivity in good health, and they would be the last Plantagenets so lucky until the dynasty disappeared in 1485.

With that formality out of the way, Montfort could now visit his wife at Odiham before attempting to appease the young Earl of Gloucester. He and Eleanor had stayed in regular contact in the time they were apart that spring, and he showed his thoughtfulness by sending her a porpoise for her table. Eleanor needed plenty more freshwater food when her nephews Edward and Almain, escorted by her son Henry, arrived in advance of Simon on 17 March. The size of their entourage can be seen in the over 1,000 herrings consumed on that first day alone. When Simon's entourage of 160 arrived two days later, attendants were sent to nearby ponds, where they fished continuously for eleven days to keep everybody fed. Judging by Eleanor's later actions, she and Simon worked out a contingency plan in the event fortune turned against them, as it soon did. On 1 April, he left for Northampton, where a tournament was scheduled in place of the one cancelled in Dunstable. It was the last time Simon and Eleanor saw each other.

Gilbert never did show up for the tournament, although Wykes acidly notes that the Montfort brothers were there 'abounding in money'. Simon realised the only way he could bring the difficult young man to terms was by marching on Gloucester. For this he brought the whole court with him, including Henry and Edward, the justiciar and several councillors. One who came and left was Thomas de Cantilupe. His appointment as chancellor had coincided with Gilbert's departure and provided a certain moral boost to Simon's government. Now he was leaving after just two months in the job, perhaps because he had become too fussy about sealing certain writs.

With the chancellor gone, Simon took the step of writing to his great-aunt Loretta, the widow of Robert de Beaumont, the last Earl of Leicester before Simon. He was looking for information about the 'rights and liberties' of the office of steward when Robert was earl, hoping they might enhance his authority in dealing with Gilbert. He might have spared himself the effort, because Loretta had spent the sixty years of her widowhood as a recluse, and if she wrote back, or could even remember that far back, her answer was lost.

Gilbert was unlikely to be swayed in any case. He and Giffard had already withdrawn their forces to the surrounding hills, lighting them up by campfire at night to boast of the strength they had at their disposal. As usual, the bishops insisted on mediation, but they too might not have bothered. In early May, William de Valence, John de Warenne and Hugh Bigod landed with a force of 120 armed men in Pembroke, which was under Gilbert's watch, thus confirming his collusion with the royalists.

Montfort's response was to move the court to Hereford to keep them from joining up with Mortimer. He tried to convince himself that everything would still end peacefully and ordered Parliament to meet at Westminster on 1 June. Incredibly, he continued to make concessions, like retaining the services of Gilbert's brother Thomas and allowing Clifford and Leybourne to visit Edward.

Thomas de Clare has the dubious distinction of being the last in a long line of nobles to betray Simon, and it came about on 28 May when he arranged for Edward to go off for a leisurely ride with an escort under Henry de Montfort. When a party of Mortimer's horsemen appeared out of the woods, Edward and Thomas bolted on their mounts in their direction and left the Montfortian knights behind. Mortimer took them to his castle in Wigmore, and from there on to Ludlow, where a meeting was set up with Gilbert. Edward's reputation for promising anything was already legendary, but Gilbert still felt it necessary to demand, in return for his support, that all the ancient laws would be followed and there would be no more aliens in government. Needless to say, Edward agreed and Gilbert came to bitterly regret he ever trusted him.

The shift in fortunes was dramatic. Now joined by Valence, Bigod and Warenne, Edward's army grew rapidly despite Simon's flurry of messages, sent out under Henry's name, condemning the uprising. Some veteran defenders of the Provisions like William de Tracy and John de Burgh were among those to switch sides. It had little to do with Montfort's government. These men knew that Edward would be king some day and that he would remember all those who helped him and those who didn't.

With armchair hindsight, Montfort should have headed east and attempted to deal with Edward from his natural bases of support in London and the Midlands. The strategy he chose instead was actually a good one. He would linger in the Marches with the aid of the Welsh until reinforcements arrived, then strike at Edward from both sides. Since Henry and Guy de Montfort were with him, along with his chief lieutenants, it was up to his son Simon to raise an army and head westwards. The younger man, however, spent two weeks helping his mother get to Dover, both to ensure its loyalty and to be ready to flee if all didn't turn out well. Finally gathering up a force in London, he detoured south to sack Winchester in order to pay his men before marching straight north to Oxford and Northampton. He reached Kenilworth on 31 July, two months after his father's urgent message went out.

Then there was Edward, who moved with lightning speed down the line of the Severn, breaking all the bridges and seizing the garrisons. Suddenly finding himself cut off in hostile territory, Simon made a hurried treaty with Llywelyn that invited scorn back in England but helped him with his next move, which was to cover his march south towards Newport. His plan was to cross the river there and join up with the troops he supposed were on their way. Gilbert, however, got there first and seized or destroyed the boats waiting to ferry them across. Forced back to Hereford, the Montfortian army arrived decimated by hunger and desertions.

Much as he would like to have struck just then, Edward received word that his cousin's army had finally arrived in the theatre. This put his men squarely between both Simons, which Montfort had been hoping for all along, so Edward and the Marchers conceived a bold plan. Since their intelligence reported that the relief force was camped out amid the comforts of the town instead of within the safety of the castle, they decided to strike there first. Riding thirty-four miles through the night, they reached Kenilworth at dawn on 1 August. There was no thought about whether to attack men in their sleep or not. They pounced on them, capturing many without a shred of clothing on. Some, including the younger Simon, managed to get away inside the castle, but several leading Montfortians were captured among the prisoners. One of the unfortunates was Stephen de Holwell, who was Simon's point man in his dispute with Gilbert over several properties. Found sheltering in a church, he was dragged out and beheaded on Gilbert's orders.

By the time Edward got back to Worcester, Montfort had forded the Severn and reached Kempsey Manor, which belonged to his good friend Walter de Cantilupe. He heard of the raid, but also that his son had regrouped. With Edward only a few miles away with a much larger force, he got his men moving on the night of 3 August in an attempt to give them the slip. He would march east to Evesham, then turn north to link up with his son.

He would have to move fast, because Evesham lies in a snare-shaped bend of the River Avon. If after they crossed the river the royalists appeared on Greenhill, they would be trapped. They reached the town before dawn on 4 August and intended to keep going despite the fatigue. Henry, however, insisted on having breakfast and attending Mass at the abbey before leaving and Simon obliged him. Around this time, the younger Simon had reached Alcester, about ten miles to the north, but he and his men too stopped to have breakfast.

Sometime that morning their banners appeared on Greenhill and jubilation broke out among the Montfortians. But something didn't seem quite right, so Simon's barber scampered up to the top of the bell tower and could see that it was in fact the royalist army. Edward had been shadowing them throughout the night. He sent his men and Gilbert's forward under the banners they captured at Kenilworth to lull the Montfortians into a false sense of security. That way Mortimer could swing his men around the rear to block any attempt to re-cross the river. The trap had still not sprung when Simon gathered his troops and addressed them for the final time:

> Fair lords, there are many among you who are not as yet tried and tested in the world, and who are young; you have wives and children, and for this reason look to how you might save yourselves and them; cross the bridge and you will escape from the great peril that is to come.

He was especially eager for Hugh Despenser to save himself, telling him there was nobody whose counsel was of greater value to the country. Ever the loyal Montfortian, Hugh replied, 'My lord, let it be. Today we shall all drink from one cup, just as we have in the past.'

None of them had any illusions about what was in store. 'Our bodies are theirs,' observed Simon, before adding a swipe at Gilbert. 'That red dog will eat us today.' He had similar unkind words for his sons, seeing their pride as the cause of the mess they were in, but in another account he exhorts young Henry to save himself. 'Rather you retire from this fearful contest lest you perish in the flower of youth.'

Bishop Cantilupe arrived and, just as he had done at Lewes, absolved the men, only this time they really needed it, and he preached so that 'they had less fear of death'. The final indication that the end was near was the blackness that covered the sky that morning. The grim clouds that rolled in with the royalist army brought very little rain, and this unnatural state of things only seemed to confirm their fate.

The Edward who had warned his uncle that he could have no peace unless he came to him with a halter around his neck didn't even offer him that much at Evesham. At his war council, he assembled a hit squad of sergeants-at-arms whose mission it was to find the Earl of Leicester and cut him down. The other men were instructed to forget about ransoms, there were to be no prisoners. Edward's intention was to carry out a bloodletting on the battlefield not seen in two hundred years. He not only wanted to cauterise the rebellion at the top, but also be in a good position to reward his followers with the lands of their dead opponents. As for the foot soldiers, they were to be massacred for pleasure.

Interestingly, Edward did not assign any particular party of men to find his father and ensure his safety. In fact, Henry almost didn't survive. The men who marched out of Evesham to do battle included the king, although he was wearing nothing to distinguish his rank. It surely wasn't Henry's choice to fight, but the decision was made that he would have to take his chances like the rest of them.

They were hardly good, since they were wholly outnumbered and had to advance uphill as the royalists had done at Lewes. But their initial impact made so much headway that Warin de Bassingbourne, one of the knights who had attempted to rescue Edward at Wallingford, denounced his men for their cowardice and rallied them. Soon their weight began to tell as the Montfortians were hemmed into an ever tighter circle. That's when the real killing began. The young knights were pulled off their horses and hacked to death. Peter de Montfort and Hugh Despenser were slain, as was Henry de Montfort. Legend credits Mortimer with thrusting the lance that killed Simon. Since he was moving up from the rear, it's probable that Montfort never saw it coming.

Henry was also pierced by a lance, despite crying out through the din of battle, 'I am Henry, the old king of England. Do not hit me. I am too old to fight.' Only lightly wounded, Leybourne somehow recognised him in the mayhem and led him to safety. It is hoped he was off the field when William Maltravers, the former Montfortian, felt obliged to prove he really was a royalist by committing a barbarous act for the ages. Taking an axe or sword, he began carving off the extremities of Simon's corpse. Mortimer then got in on it by cutting off the head and testicles for himself, eager to present them to his wife. After that it was a free-for-all on the torso. Whether savages by nature or not, their bloodlust was worked up, and besides, it was 'him'. It was Simon de Montfort, the man they had admired, respected, loathed and feared like no other. If striking a blow against his lifeless body went against the spiritual tenets they grew up with, and he was wearing a hair shirt at the time, then none deserved it better, for he had stirred up the kingdom for too long. Being a detestable alien probably made their work that much grislier.

Edward continued the charge into town, where he conducted a particularly gruesome slaughter, even outdoing his work at Lewes. Much like the Londoners the year before, the lightly armed Welshmen were the easy targets on this occasion. In the words of Robert of Gloucester, a contemporary witness, it wasn't war, only murder, with dead bodies strewn throughout the abbey courtyard and cemetery like butchered animals. So much blood accumulated on the high altar of the church that it ran down into the crypts below.

The monks charged with burying the dead had their work cut out for them. Edward is said to have stayed long enough to attend the interment of Henry de Montfort, his first playfellow, even openly weeping for him, but he showed no consideration for his uncle. If he had been upset at all by what happened to his body, it was probably because he would have to face Louis someday, maybe even his aunt, and account for the disgraceful act.

It was up to the monks to find what was left of Simon and bury him together with Despenser. But even then there were some who pressed to have the meagre bits dug up and disposed of elsewhere. Mortimer's wife Maud, a Braose whose father was the Marcher lord hanged by Llywelyn's grandfather, received her share of the remains in the middle of a church service and was reportedly spooked when she and the rest of the congregation saw Simon's hands clasped in a glow above the messenger's head.

None of the royalist lords lingered on the battlefield. The race was on to confiscate the properties of the dead and Gilbert was one of the first to despatch his men in search of new riches. Edward mainly concerned himself with reclaiming his lands in Cheshire. He probably never forgave Simon for trying to kick him out of the Marches, knowing as he did that the men of that region would always be his faithful companions and willing henchmen.

Their support had been vital in recovering his freedom, but in the end Gilbert's desertion and the younger Simon's lack of soldierly initiative played equally pivotal roles. No less telling were Montfort's own mistakes, his uncharacteristic slowness in comprehending the gravity of the situation and relying too much on the England east of the Severn to come to the rescue. The same energy and resourcefulness were there as usual, whether striking a deal with the Welsh or trying to cross at Newport, but in Edward he had finally met his match. Once he had him cornered, it was only a matter of time.

One of the many quotes attributed to Simon when he saw that the game was up has him admiringly watching the troop displacement that would spell his doom.

'By the arm of St James,' he declared, 'how well they advance. They did not learn that for themselves but from me.'

Simple pride aside, Montfort probably took some measure of contentment in knowing that he was going down to defeat at the hands of someone worthy of being king. He had lost all respect for Henry years ago and, reform or no reform, would always see him as a cynical accident of fate. A superb architect and wedding planner maybe, but no man to lead a nation. Edward was a different story. He was treacherous, cruel, a complete beast at heart, but Simon had seen a spark of justice and idealism in his eyes during their stance together against Henry in 1260. If those qualities asserted themselves, and were given the same vigour and dynamic spirit he applied to the less wholesome side of his character, then the nation would be as prosperous and formidable a land as any under his leadership.

For all his missteps as king, some of them more horrid than anything Henry ever did, Edward had seen the value of the community of the realm. He would adopt Simon's common enterprise as his own and ensure that a diverse Parliament always had a firm place in the monarchy. A contentious one to be sure, but as natural and justified as having a king at all.

Henry spent about a month recovering, first at Gloucester and then at Marlborough, where he showed that the brutal slaughter of his subjects did not faze his concern for the things that really mattered to him. Noticing that the picture behind the altar in the chapel needed renovating, he ordered it done together with repairs on certain amenities around the castle, like the fishponds. On 8

September, he summoned Parliament to Winchester, symbolic for being his birthplace, and declared that all lands that had been seized from the Montfortians would never be returned. Henceforth, they could consider themselves disinherited.

He was merely formalising what had been going on since the battle, with up to 300 families evicted from their ancestral homes. Mortimer has often been lambasted as the one greediest for the spoils, but Edward and seventy others gladly took their share. Cooler heads like Richard of Cornwall, Roger Bigod and Philip Basset protested, but from a safe distance. Richard's business acumen told him it would be a long road to economic recovery with greed as the guiding principle, but it had always been his and eventually he received lands himself worth nearly £700.

Before that, he was just happy to emerge from captivity with his life. When the garrison at Kenilworth learned of the treatment of Simon's body, their intent was to mete out the same fate to Richard. He was being held in chains by this time, the result of his son's collusion in the uprising. Simon had sent Henry of Almain to France on a diplomatic mission to Louis, presumably to try and get him to accept the Provisions as a *fait accompli*. Almain was still in France when Valence and Warenne landed with their forces, and Edward's subsequent escape with the help of the Clare brothers, who were his nephews, suggests he was in on it all along. He is next heard considering a proposal by the queen that he marry the daughter of Gaston de Bearn. His whereabouts around the time of Evesham are unknown, but marriage into the Bearn family alone was likely to break any remaining bonds of affection with his Montfort cousins.

The younger Simon wouldn't hear of any harm coming to his uncle, not least because he could still be useful. He released Richard from custody on 6 September and on the same day received letters from him promising to do everything in his power to help his mother and family. There was admittedly little he could do for any of them. After learning of the disaster at Evesham, and the deaths of her husband and oldest son, Eleanor withdrew into mourning for ten days. When she came out, she was wearing russet and refused all meat and fish, but was otherwise ready to take charge again.

While Despenser's widow immediately gave up the Tower and

fled to her father Philip Basset for protection, Eleanor held on firmly to Dover even as provisions waned. The most Henry would have to do with her was issue an order that neither she nor her family were to depart the kingdom without his permission. He was anxious to get his hands on whatever remnants there were of the Montfortian war chest. He found out how much when Amaury and Richard de Montfort escaped to France with nearly £7,000. Eleanor had outwitted him, but she knew her position was ultimately untenable. When Edward arrived with his forces, she negotiated a surrender that extended amnesty to the garrison and her household. Edward was mindful to be obliging, considering the shame of Evesham, and here he was as good as his word to his 'most dear aunt'. On 28 October, Eleanor left for France with her daughter, never to return.

Her departure coincided with the arrival of the queen, who disembarked at Dover the next day in the company of the new papal legate. Henry met them at Canterbury, where the year before the Montfortian army had been prepared to resist the queen's invasion. If now she was met by acclaim, as Wykes insists, it was surely a staged event. Henry was most happy to see her and had a couple of very special gifts waiting for her.

One of them came on 26 October when he officially invested their son Edmund with the earldom of Leicester. The title and land of their 'enemy' would go to compensate the young man who never got to be King of Sicily. The other gift was her share of the fine Henry slapped on London for its part in supporting Montfort. Of the £13,666 levied on every citizen, no matter whose side they were on, half would go to buy back his rights on the Continent that the queen had sold away to Louis. The other half was hers, and to sweeten their revenge, he gave her London Bridge as well.

The man who had saved her from that painful incident was not so fortunate. On 4 October, Mayor Thomas Fitz-Thomas led a group of forty citizens to offer their submission at Windsor. Despite having issued them safe-conduct passes, Edward threw the lot of them in the gaol. All but Fitz-Thomas were soon released. He languished for three years and even then had to pay a £500 fine to get out.

Other Londoners were evicted from their homes, some told not to come back on pain of death, and their property swallowed up by the Edwardians Warenne, Bassingbourne and Leybourne. A new member of their ranks to make out was an ex-Montfortian, Grimbald Pauncefoot. Like Gilbert de Clare, his treachery along the Severn proved most timely for Edward's campaign.

The royal family, reunited at last, spent Christmas court in Northampton, where the feudal host had been summoned to deal with Kenilworth. The choice of venue was also largely symbolic, since it was the scene of Henry's only victory against the Montfortians. He even had Northampton declared the official beginning of the armed struggle despite knowing that Simon and his men had not withdrawn their oaths of fealty until Lewes. In legal terms, this meant that they had waged rebellion and not war, and that gave Henry the justification for confiscating their lands outright.

In the end, it only mattered what he said. The survivors of Evesham were legally not rebels because they had fought under his banner, but their claims fell on deaf ears. With nothing to lose, hundreds of these disinherited subjects took to the woods and forests to survive through lawlessness and banditry. Their numbers included the younger Simon de Montfort, who did finally make it to the battlefield of Evesham that day, only to see his father's head being paraded off in true Marcher fashion. He eventually left Kenilworth after letting Richard go and joined other Montfortians still active in the Isle of Axholme. By Christmas, their situation had become hopeless and he asked for peace. He was escorted to Northampton by Edward, where Richard endeavoured to get him the most favourable terms possible. On 29 December, he was ordered to leave the realm, but he would receive £350 in place of his inheritance, conditioned on him not causing any more trouble. After that he was taken to London under guard and held at the Old Temple.

And so the grand Christmas celebrated by the Montforts in Kenilworth the year before had come to this. Simon and Henry de Montfort dead, Guy de Montfort recovering from his wounds at the prison in Windsor, Eleanor and the rest of the children exiled in France, and the family heir about to join them. The royalists were enjoying a complete restoration and enrichment at the expense of the vanquished, which could have only one possible outcome:

chaos throughout the land, worse than at any time when Simon was the guiding hand of state.

For the feast of St Edward that year, Henry wore his crown to remove the stain of his captivity and 'shine forth gloriously' in front of all those gathered. It had been almost a half century since he was crowned with a plain gold circlet during his first coronation. He was just a boy then and the country was torn by strife and poor kingship. Now he was an old man, beaming under an exquisitely crafted crown adorned with jewels and precious stones. Otherwise, little else had changed.

15

Aftermath
1266–1337

Perhaps knowing Henry and Edward too well, the younger Simon de Montfort did not believe they had any intentions of keeping their end of the bargain. He escaped his captors in London and fled to Winchelsea, whence he crossed to France in February 1266. He was soon joined by his brother Guy, who had been transferred from captivity in Windsor to Dover for no apparent reason other than allowing him to escape. Thus ended Simon's line of the Montfort family in England.

All the sons remained in France for the time being with the exception of Richard, who though still in his teens went to fight under Theobald II of Navarre in his Gascon campaign against Henry. He is last mentioned in the records of that year. Eleanor retired to the convent founded in Montargis by Simon's late sister Amicia, where she seems to have won the sympathy of Louis and his wife. They likely regretted not doing more to prevent all the bloodshed and misery and now worked to reconcile the two families. In 1267 Louis sent a trusted envoy to work out a deal. In order to save face, Henry pretended to go along and offered to give Simon his father's lands, but he had to be prepared to sell them to him or his heirs at any time and minus damages. This was no better than the first deal made back in England, so Louis pressed on and got Henry to allow Simon back into the kingdom, but the stipulation was he would have to answer for his crimes.

Nothing came of this, either, and not just because people like Gilbert and Mortimer were determined to keep England clear of the Montforts. Edmund was now the Earl of Leicester and nothing was going to change that. Simon suspected as much, and by 1268 he and Guy had already left to seek their fortunes elsewhere. This makes a total of three arbitrations that Louis and Margaret took up between Henry and the Montforts and all three ended in failure.

Louis certainly didn't get any encouragement from the pope, whose wrath over his treatment as legate still gnawed at him. In September 1266, he heard a rumour that the Montforts were planning an invasion and asked Louis to do everything in his power to keep them and Eleanor from recovering their lands. For more immediate revenge, he instructed his legate in England to eschew all other business until he had dealt with the bishops. The pope was furious they had lent their support to Montfort's revolutionary scheme and wanted them to answer for their conduct in person.

At the top of the list was Walter de Cantilupe, but he died in February 1266 while the legate was still making inquiries. Another four he suspended and ordered to appear in Rome. The weakest of the lot, John Gervais of Winchester, died in Viterbo in January 1268. The last one to receive a pardon was Stephen Berksted, the Bishop of Chichester and Simon's fellow triumvir. He had to wait until December 1272 before he could return to England, by which time both Clement and Henry were dead.

With that bit of business out of the way, the legate could try to somehow restore order in the kingdom. He was Ottobuono Fieschi, a nephew of Innocent IV and brother-in-law of Thomas of Savoy. He had played his part in the Sicilian business and so was already known to Henry when he arrived. That didn't seem to count much with the king, who insisted on pursuing his policy of vindictiveness. This hampered the legate in his other mission, to preach a crusade, hardly possible in a country still at war with itself. All he could do was beg and plead and hope the rebels would finally see the futility of further struggle.

He had some help from Edward, who scored several victories, mainly over the Channel ports, but there were too many pockets of resistance for him to be everywhere at once. His most legendary feat has him forcing a fearsome fellow named Adam Gurdon to submit after challenging him to hand-to-hand combat. He was praised for sparing Gurdon's life, packing him off instead to Windsor in chains, but that was better than what Gurdon's followers got. Edward had the lot of them strung up, leaving them to dangle after they stopped kicking and writhing. As with the carnage at Evesham, he wanted to make it clear that he was prepared to be merciful or cruel. It was their choice.

Better success was scored by his cousin Henry of Almain, who surprised Robert de Ferrers and other baronial rebels at Chesterfield in May 1266. Ferrers had been released from prison in December 1265, mainly on account of his Lusignan wife, but he again took to rampaging and spreading disorder everywhere. It would be three years before he was released from prison again, and only then after he agreed to pay a fine of £50,000 to recover his estates. Until he did so, his lands were to be given to Edmund. Ferrers accepted this monstrous swindle concocted by Edward and Almain only because he wanted to get out of prison. He had no hope of finding the money or having the agreement repudiated, and so the earldom of Derby, which had been in his family for generations, was now added to Leicester to make Edmund a major landowner and the first in the noble clan of Lancaster.

Of course, Edmund wasn't completely the master of his new domains, not with Kenilworth still holding out. All attempts to invest it ended in failure, and by August 1266, Parliament was summoned to Kenilworth to find a way out of the mess the royalists had created in their scramble for plunder. Led by the legate and Henry of Almain, an agreement called the Dictum of Kenilworth was drawn up offering the disinherited the chance to win their lands back through the payment of a fine to the new landlords. Depending on the degree of complicity, the fines were fixed between one year's income to seven, with ten years being the nominal value of land. Not all the rebels accepted the agreement, mostly because none of them had any cash to buy back their birthrights, and the garrison at Kenilworth only surrendered in December 1266 because they were starved out. There were also plenty of royalists not happy with having to disgorge their booty, and one of them was just not happy period.

Gilbert de Clare had found a lot to complain about following the victory at Evesham. He felt he had not been rewarded enough, even though, as with the Montfortians, he came over at the last possible minute. His other gripes included his mother's dower and having a bully like Mortimer as a neighbour. In the spring of 1267, Gilbert came to London with several knights and men-at-arms. Henry and Edward were away dealing with scattered uprisings in the north, but the legate, comfortably ensconced in the Tower of London, admitted Gilbert's little force as a prelude to talks about what was bothering him. Suddenly they were joined by insurgents under John d'Eyvill, and London was for all intents and purposes occupied for two months.

The siege of London that Henry had been planning after Evesham was beginning to look like it would happen after all. The legate was shut up in the Tower while the London commune ransacked what it could, although Gilbert forbade his men to take part and had four of them bound and tossed into the river for doing just that. Leybourne brought mercenaries over from Flanders to storm the city and was even prepared to burn it down by tossing chickens over the wall with fire lines tied to their feet.

This time moderates like the legate, Richard and Philip Basset won out, and the Dictum was modified to allow the disinherited to take possession of their lands now and pay off their fines through private agreements. In this way Gilbert became an unlikely champion of the surviving Montfortians. He wanted it to be known that he had not betrayed their cause, only Simon and his sons. Even if their disinheritance had been the direct result of that betrayal, most were happy to get whatever they could out of the new arrangement.

So eager was Henry to finally put an end to it all that he allowed d'Eyvill to remit the first-year payment of his five-year fine. Since the queen was the beneficiary of his fine, she was gingerly informed of the need to sacrifice so that there might be peace at last. Henry was not inclined to let Gilbert off so easily, not after he came back and found that his new palace in Westminster had been thoroughly trashed, but the legate got the king to accept £6,700 in pledges and surety from Gilbert for his good behaviour in the future.

With peace now a real likelihood, the legate could get on with preaching the crusade, and in June 1268 invited a legion of nobles gathered in Northampton to take the cross. The presence of John de Vescy among them was an indication of how far reconciliation had progressed. This Montfortian, another former Savoyard ward, had somehow salvaged one of Simon's severed feet and had it encased in silver upon returning to his lordship in the north. Disinherited like the others, he fought on even after the Dictum of Kenilworth until overwhelmed by Edward. Vescy's fine was fixed at a stiff £2,500, payable to the Flemish provider of Henry and the queen's foreign mercenaries, but he was evidently moved by Edward's mercy to shift his worship in an entirely new direction. No word on what became of Simon's foot, but he remained one of Edward's steadfast friends. He even married a Lusignan, thereby joining Ferrers and Warenne in the club of Savoyard-wards-cum-Lusignan-husbands.

For Edward, a crusade was what he needed for his restless spirit and warlike inclination. There was also the matter of giving thanks for the victory at Evesham, as well as atoning for the deliberate butchery. The problem was the economy was in no shape to support such a fatuous undertaking. In the years 1264 to 1268 revenue from the sheriffs totalled only £2,755 compared to £17,444 for the same period ten years earlier, and Henry was forced to do more pawning of the royal treasure. The papacy tried to help with a clerical tax that brought in upwards of £49,000, but £15,000 of that had to go to cover the queen's flurry of debts contracted abroad. Pope Clement threw in another £30,000 tax just for the crusade, but that barely covered a third of the total cost.

Edward's only hope was to ask Parliament for help. Henry had been denied a tax for the last thirty years because he refused to make concessions. Edward knew he would have to take a cue from Simon's parliaments instead and offer the knightly class something in return for their support. He might have thought they would be happy with the Statute of Marlborough passed in 1267, the codification of those provisions that had always had local appeal. Marlborough, however, did not address one problem that had oppressed the knights and gentry for as long as they could remember.

Henry's imbecilic taxation of the Jews had allowed magnates and members of the court, including the queen and Edward, to make a killing in the only money market in the country at the expense of the Jews and their Christian debtors. Now Edward and Henry of Almain drew up the Statute of Jewry, legislation designed to thwart this practice, and another infamous case of the crooks writing the law. The Jews stood to lose the most, which was all right to them because a crusade was meant to punish them as well. The knights nevertheless were sceptical, and it wasn't until Henry actually ordered the exchequer to enforce the legislation did Edward get his tax.

Meanwhile Henry started talking about fulfilling the crusading vow he made back in 1250. The reason was Louis' plans to go again, which would give him two crusades to Henry's zero. It was idle talk, of course, because everyone knew where Henry's heart really lay. After nearly a quarter of a century's construction, his new church at Westminster Abbey was finished enough for him to have the remains of his hero Edward the Confessor reburied inside. On 13 October 1269 he got his wish in a ceremony that saw him, Richard, Edward and Edmund carrying the coffin around the church themselves. The last time Henry looked so reverential was in 1247, when he accepted a vial of holy blood among his relics. Both that occasion and the blood were long forgotten, but there was no chance of that happening with his magnificent new church. He had spent £40,000 on it, but nobody ever begrudged him money for his artistic flourishes, or even the lavishness of his court and lifestyle. It was how he went about getting the money, and where much of it ended up, that had led to so much discord throughout the land.

Perhaps the greatest benefactor of the king's generosity did not live to see the ceremony. Peter of Savoy had died the previous year and showed what an ingrate he was by slipping in a codicil to his will only the week before his death. Instead of leaving everything to the queen as he had promised, he now bequeathed most of his English possessions to the sons of Thomas of Savoy. This created a delicate problem. It had nothing to do with importing a new generation of Savoyards, who were simply ignored with a buyout of £100 a year. Rather Edward, the queen and John of Brittany were all eager to get their hands on the honour of Richmond, that prime real estate that Henry had thoughtlessly given away to a nonentity. It took a lot of squabbling, but they were eventually able to work things out.

Edward's failure to nominate his mother as the guardian for his children and interests before his departure reflects neither wariness nor mistrust between these two congenitally greedy individuals. He had seen the indignation of the baronage and lower orders over the king's promotion of his alien relatives, how Montfort had reaped political capital off the unpopularity of the Savoyards and Lusignans. He didn't want to risk any needless exposure of the queen arousing these old passions while he was away and she was probably glad not to have it.

Peter's death left Roger Bigod the last surviving member of the seven confederates. He had taken no part at Lewes, but had cooperated with Simon's government to the end. Although quick to rejoin the royalists after Evesham, he and Henry fell out soon enough and rumours went about that the king was planning to give his earldom of Norfolk to a foreign supporter. Henry denied the report and Roger died with his estates intact in 1270. Brother Hugh had preceded him to the grave in 1266 and signalled his final disapproval of his former colleague Simon de Montfort by witnessing the charter that stripped the Montforts of the earldom of Leicester. Hugh's son succeeded the childless Roger as the Earl of Norfolk, but in 1302, burdened by debts and with no children of his own, he surrendered their family's earldom to Edward.

Even with the tax, the crusaders still didn't have enough money, and Edward had to turn to his uncle Louis for a loan of £17,000. He also asked him to settle a new dispute, now between him and the perennially disaffected Earl of Gloucester. Gilbert had taken the cross at the same ceremony in Northampton, but had come to see the entire expedition as one of Edward out to glorify himself. The jealousy and envy he felt for Montfort was now shifted to the man he helped raise to his exalted status. He may have disagreed with Simon's arrest of Ferrers, but that was nothing compared to Edward and his brother Edmund swiping Ferrers' earldom out from under him. And as everyone knew, the only reason why Edmund was going on crusade was because crusaders received special protection from legal action. Ferrers would not even be able to sue to get his land back until Edmund returned, whenever that was.

Convinced that Edward had it in for him, Gilbert even stayed away from the ceremony at Westminster Abbey. Louis agreed to intervene, but of course nothing came of it. In May 1270 Richard worked out a deal that allowed Gilbert to go on crusade separately from Edward, but would receive £5,000 if he agreed to become his man when he arrived. He was supposed to leave within one year, but a private war with Llywelyn kept him home. Like Henry and Leybourne, he died, in 1295, with his vow unfulfilled.

The last obstacle keeping the expedition from meeting the French deadline for departure was the death of Boniface. The archbishop had come back to England following the restoration, but he lacked the same vitality as before and was content to let the legate run the Church in England for him. Too ill to attend the ceremony at Westminster Abbey, which was nevertheless marred by clerical infighting, he left England shortly afterwards and died in his native Savoy in July 1270. Upon receiving word of it, Edward delayed his departure in an attempt to have his clerk Robert Burnell elected as the new archbishop. Burnell's penchant for the ladies and several bastard children made him quite unsuitable in the eyes of the monks and the choice eventually went to the pope.

The English contingent finally left in August, but found the French long gone. They could still easily catch them, because Louis had decided to launch his holy war in Tunis, nearly 2,400 km from Jerusalem. Apparently he had been talked into striking at the emir there by his brother Charles of Anjou, who had finally fulfilled the dreams of the papacy by defeating the Hohenstaufens. He killed Manfred in battle in 1266 and chopped the head off Frederick's other son in 1268. Now bearing the long sought-after title of King of Sicily, he wanted to build a Mediterranean Empire that included North Africa.

Why Louis succumbed to his younger brother's ambition is beyond comprehension and he was dead of dysentery before achieving a thing there. The disease grew into an epidemic and claimed a good part of his family and troops, but of course not Charles of Anjou. A storm then wrecked most of the French fleet in Sicily, and Charles and the new French king Philip III decided to go home. Edward pressed on to the Holy Land, where he accomplished nothing of note except to beat off an assassin in his tent.

A state of unease gripped England with so many knights and barons abroad. The younger Simon de Montfort was said to have slipped back into the country to pray at the tomb of his father and brother. The remains of both, together with Hugh Despenser's, had been moved to near the high altar of the church in Evesham. Henry was pressed into taking this action by Pope Clement, who put aside his rancour towards Montfort after Amaury went to Rome and assured him that his father had received absolution before his death. The king was miffed that the pope should even listen to Amaury, but he allowed the interment to take place.

It was just as well, because miracle stories had been spreading about cures to be had by visiting Simon's resting place in Evesham. Henry had included an article in the Dictum of Kenilworth making it a crime to talk about such things. Anyone who now wanted to pray to Simon for a miracle would have to do it in full view of the whispering church congregation. But he also had to contend with a spring that supposedly began to flow on the ground where Montfort fell. A popular story has a young girl fetching a pitcher of water from it for her sick mother. An officious servant thinks he's caught her in the act of carrying water from the reputed miracle well, but finds only beer in the pitcher instead. He lets her go, and by the time she administers it to her mother, it's water again and she's cured.

Forever a simple man, Henry might have contemplated sending his own servants to fetch him some of that water. He became seriously ill at least once while Edward was away and tried to goad him into returning. His brother was also showing the strain of years. Richard had made one more trip back to Germany in 1268, where he found the people had got along just fine without a king during his six years away, and there was little he could do or felt like doing to cope with the breakdown of law and order. His only significant act was to marry the beautiful Beatrice of Falkenburg as his third wife.

Back in England, he was mostly sidelined by Edward's juggernaut to control everything. For the marriage of his son Henry of Almain to Constance de Bearn, Richard was neither consulted nor asked. It was not until the crusaders were gone was he able to assert himself again in the affairs of government.

Henry of Almain never made it to the Holy Land. While in Sicily, Edward began to worry about the situation in Gascony, especially since Gaston de Bearn was showing no signs of coming along even though Louis had insisted that one-third of the loan he gave

Edward should go to meet Gaston's expenses. Edward knew he was the type of man to keep the money and stay home instead and cause trouble. He wanted Almain to go to Gascony and keep an eye on his new father-in-law.

Before that, he asked him to undertake a separate mission. Charles of Anjou and Philip III were heading to Viterbo, where the cardinals were gathered to elect a successor to Clement, who died in 1268. They had been at it for two years now, and Charles wanted to see if he might not induce them to wrap up the business with somebody to his liking. Charles would also use the occasion to meet his vicar-general for Tuscany, a young man who had rapidly risen through his ranks thanks to his impressive pedigree and fighting capability.

It was Guy de Montfort, the son of his old friend Simon. Guy and his brother Simon had found service under Charles through Philip de Montfort, the son of the Philip who had tried to promote their father as the governor of the Holy Land in 1241. At the Battle of Alba in 1268, Guy fought with legendary fury, even with his helmet twisted around at one point, and was rewarded by Charles with offices and land. He married Margherita Aldobrandesca, the daughter of the most powerful lord in the region. Edward was sufficiently impressed and, since Guy was sure to come to Viterbo to consult with Charles, he told Almain to seek out their cousin to suggest a possible reconciliation between their families.

Guy arrived with his brother, father-in-law and a large train of knights on 12 March 1272. The next day they found Henry of Almain hearing Mass in a little church, either having tracked him there or coming across him quite by accident.

'Henry of Almain!' Guy thundered from the doorway. 'You traitor! You shall not escape me now.'

Terrified, Almain dashed for the altar, but Guy's party pushed their way through the crowd. Guy dismissed his pleas for mercy with 'you had none for my father or brother'. The violence witnessed by the congregation must have been horrible, especially as one of the priests was killed and the other one wounded trying to defend Almain, and even then the cold-blooded attack wasn't over. Guy and his men dragged Almain's body out into the square and mutilated it in mock retribution for Evesham.

'I have had my revenge,' he declared as he and his troops got on their horses and fled north.

The crime shocked all of Europe. Charles and Philip quickly wrote letters to Edward and Richard expressing their sympathy and outrage, but in the end did nothing to bring the brothers to justice. There was an underlying feeling that somebody had it coming for the barbarity inflicted on Simon's body. Henry of Almain may or may not have been on the battlefield, but his defection and marital alliance with Gaston de Bearn were enough to seal his fate.

Of the fugitives, Guy's father-in-law managed to extricate himself from further scrutiny and the younger Simon died later that year in Siena. Guy remained on the run until Edward showed up on his way home from the crusade and demanded that the new pope take action. After he left, Guy threw himself at the mercy of the pope and received a sentence akin to house arrest. Within a decade he was back in favour again with Charles and the papacy. In 1288 he was captured by the Aragonese in a naval battle off Sicily. All attempts to ransom him failed, no doubt due to Edward's influence, and he ended up dying in prison in 1291, leaving behind two daughters.

Edward didn't take out his anger over the murder of Almain on the whole family. In fact, it might have heightened his sense of guilt over what had happened at Evesham. Passing through Paris on his way home in 1273, he loaned his aunt Eleanor £200 and wrote to his chancellor to say that he had admitted her to his 'grace and peace'. He even took steps to revive her dower payments after Philip III wrote him a disturbing letter. It seems that after Evesham, Louis had allowed Henry to take the £10,000 he was holding as security for settling Eleanor's dower. Since no settlement had been reached, Philip was worried that his father's soul was paying for this bit of chicanery in the afterlife. Eleanor had also found a firm friend in Margaret, and it was the Queen of France who urged Edward on her behalf to take pity on Amaury.

This Edward was unwilling to do. Amaury had been in Italy at the time of the murder, studying medicine in Padua, and although he had persuaded the authorities he had nothing to do with it, Edward suspected otherwise. Amaury's capacity as the family lawyer in

Rome further infuriated him when, speaking for his brother, he put the blame on Edward. Had he not disinherited them, they wouldn't be hanging around violent people.

In 1276 Amaury accompanied his sister Eleanor to Wales to be married to Llywelyn, an arrangement that had been worked out years before by Simon. With his trove of spies, Edward had ships waiting to intercept them near Bristol. Eleanor he treated kindly, but he locked Amaury away in Corfe. He remained inured to pleading by his cousin Eleanor, the archbishop, and the papacy to release him. Finally, after six years without any trial, he let him go with orders that he abjure the realm and never come back. Amaury promptly went to Paris, where he gave Edward more headaches by suing him, then returned to Italy to tutor Guy's daughters before dropping out of sight after 1292, some say after throwing off his priestly robes and becoming a knight.

Only after Llywelyn submitted to him in 1277 did Edward allow the marriage between him and young Eleanor to take place, which he even paid for and attended. She died giving birth to a daughter on 21 June 1282. By that time the Welsh were on the offensive again and Llywelyn was killed in a skirmish with the Marchers later that year. Edward had his head paraded around London before sticking it on a spike at the Tower of London for those who missed the first show. He placed their infant daughter Gwenllian in a nunnery in Lincolnshire with the strictest orders to preserve her chastity. Such a dangerous mixture of the royal Welsh and Montfort lines had to be allowed to die out. She died there in June 1337, perhaps never having learned of the tumultuous history of her ancestry.

The parents of these feuding cousins all died within a few years of each other. Richard had no sooner absorbed the blow of his son's murder when Edward's five-year-old son and heir John died while in his charge. He then suffered a stroke at the end of 1271 and died the following spring, age sixty-three. He was buried in Hailes Abbey, the magnificent Cistercian house he founded in Gloucestershire. He joined the bones of his son Henry before the high altar. In accordance with the practice of the time, Almain's heart had been removed and his body boiled free of other flesh, which was interred in Viterbo 'between two popes'.

His other son Edmund ensured plenty of traffic to their joint tomb by depositing a vial of holy blood in the abbey that he said he acquired in Germany. It far outstripped Henry's holy blood in popularity and survived until the sixteenth century, when scientists declared, in an age before there were microscopes, that the vial actually contained the blood of a duck. After that, they took the abbey apart as part of Henry VIII's Dissolution, the greatest wave of vandalism ever to afflict the British Isles.

Almain's heart was preserved in an urn at Westminster, which led Dante to describe it as the 'heart that still drips along the Thames' in his seventh circle of hell. Among the characters cast into this circle and its river of boiling blood is Guy de Montfort. Dante was five years old when Guy was the chieftain of Florence and it's quite possible he remembered seeing him on horseback during ceremonious occasions, a fine figure of a knight who combined the best and worst traits of the Montforts and Plantagenets. Among the companions Dante gave him in eternal damnation were Alexander the Great and Attila the Hun.

Whatever condolences Eleanor had for her brother in the wake of the tragedy between their children she left to prayers. She was about sixty when she died at Montargis on 13 April 1275, with only her daughter and Amaury by her side. She had continued to pursue the legal cases over her inheritance even while in seclusion, and in 1267 she won her suit against her nephew Hugh Lusignan. In 1286, eleven years after her death, Amaury and the other executors of her will secured Edward's help in forcing the Marshal heirs to pay Eleanor's outstanding debt to the convent of Saint-Antoine near Paris, where her heart was likely interred. Thus did the monumental dower issue finally come to an end after fifty-five years of contention. It's tempting to wonder whether there might have never been any revolution at all had Henry accepted the measure of the woman his sister was and settled their dispute before things got out of hand. But then again, with Henry things always got out of hand.

In November 1272, the king lay dying in Westminster. To his sadness, Edward was still abroad and the country plagued by disorder. He had only recently returned from Norwich, where he had to put down a particularly nasty uprising. Weak and ill upon his return to London, he could find no peace there, either. The courtyard around him was packed with demonstrations of support for the populist mayor of London. Even in his dying hour the spirit of Simon de Montfort was there to remind him that the kingdom belonged to more than just any one man.

Henry was probably glad it was over. All he ever wanted was to do great things and make people happy, and yet he only got grief in the end. At least he would have been pleased by his funeral in Westminster Abbey. He was crowned and dressed in full royal regalia before being laid to rest in the only true testament to his greatness. The people gazing at his tomb today probably don't realise that they owe the beauty of the church around them, as well as the onset of arts and crafts in modern-day England, to this simple little man whose tragedy was he thought he was cut out for more than just the finer things.

The contrast between the splendour of Henry's resting place and the lone slab of stone in Evesham marking Simon's final interment might suggest that the king got the last laugh in their epic struggle. In the beginning, however, it was Simon who dominated their combined legacy. The cult of worship that sprang up in Evesham almost immediately after the battle demonstrated Montfort's appeal across the land and all divisions of society. Nobles, clerics, landowners and peasants trekked from as far as East Anglia and Kent to walk over the hallowed ground where he fell. He had become a popular saint in every sense of the word, a martyr for those values they held dear. To call him a traitor, as the king's party did, was to call them all traitors. He had kept his oath, as the victors had not, and there was a higher authority than the king to which they would all have to answer on that score someday.

Plenty of other pilgrims were drawn to his shrine by the stories of miracles to be had at his grave and the famed Battlewell. Over two hundred testimonies have survived, including one from turncoat John Giffard. Even here Henry couldn't get a break. A knight who claimed his eyesight was restored while praying at Henry's tomb was believed by nobody except the queen mother. Her desire to develop a cult for Henry to rival the one thriving around Louis came to a bitter end in May 1290 when his body was moved to a permanent location near the high altar of Westminster Abbey and the occasion went practically unnoticed.

She herself died in relative obscurity a year later and was buried, not beside him as he had wished, but at the convent in Amesbury where she had retired. She had dedicated her life to seeing Edward on the throne, but while he honoured his father with a splendid effigy and his wife with the immortal Eleanor Crosses, he merely promised the nuns of Amesbury £100 if they celebrated his mother's life every day. That they did, but he went to his grave without paying a penny.

Like his father, Edward saw a mostly prosperous reign come to a bad end. He had been much more conscientious about governing through consent and adopted several of Simon's precedents during his rule, most famously the inclusion of burgesses in Parliament. His successful efforts to reabsorb the Montfortians included supporting Thomas de Cantilupe's election as Bishop of Hereford and making his peace with Stephen Berksted.

He was still the same old Edward, however, when it came to those he felt had broken faith or were otherwise troublemakers he could do without. A notorious spate of English political executions began under him, culminating in the gruesome public mutilations of his Scottish and Welsh opponents. The wars of his later years strained his relationship with the barons until they marched on him as they had done to his father, only in a much more muted style. He was forced to confirm Magna Carta, but then pulled a Henry by obtaining absolution from the pope.

Where he did mimic Henry to the good of the country was being a faithful and loving husband. He was heartbroken when his wife Eleanor of Castile, who spent most of her queenship accumulating land and properties, died in 1290. But whereas Henry had been a doting father on all five of his children, Edward was too stretched for the surviving nine of the sixteen he had with Eleanor. Their youngest, Edward, became heir after the four older boys died and he was only five when his mother was quite suddenly dead from a fever. His father by then was too consumed by wars abroad to take much interest in him. Bereft of close family ties, the boy turned to friends for trust and companionship, a development that would spell disaster in the next reign. Edward saw it coming, but was unable to sort it out before his death in 1307.

By that time Simon's cult had mostly disappeared, but in 1323 Edward II was entertained by peasant women in Yorkshire singing of Simon de Montfort. Being illiterate, they would not have been able to recite passages from the *Song of Lewes* or other laudatory works extolling the man and his cause, but even at the time of Evesham the peasants understood that a new sense of empowerment was here to stay. Immediately after the battle, a royalist party arrived in a village called Peatling Magna and found itself harangued by the crowd, who accused it plotting against the community of the realm.

It's unlikely that these peasant women sang about anything overtly connected to Montfortianism. The younger Edward had just put down a revolt by his cousin Thomas of Lancaster, Edmund's son and so the Earl of Leicester, and made him pay for it with his head. The king probably just wanted to learn more about this new folk hero who had captured the imagination of his adopted countrymen. He was no mythical, unreachable figure from the past like a King Arthur, but his story had equal elements of triumph and tragedy: a stranger steps ashore, wins the king's favour, marries his sister, topples him in revolution and falls in battle with the king's son. It was legend with all the makings of fact, and the most enduring and inspiring of these was his determination to achieve what he set out to do. But where Arthur had his holy grail, Simon had the Provisions, words etched on parchment that demanded the king be a good one. That they got as far as they did owed to his commitment to bringing them to wholesome effect, and that meant going with all, for all.

There would be other attempts at putting up a united front against the Crown, most notably the Peasants' Revolt in 1381 and the Pilgrimage of Grace in 1536, but not until the seventeenth century was the whole issue of power and privilege revisited with any intensity nearing that of the reform movement of the 1260s, only this time with the king losing his head. In the backlash against all this political rowdiness and extremism, Montfort's reputation went into a tailspin. He was seen as an interloper who cloaked harshness, aggrandisement, intemperance and violence in virtue and piety. Much of this severe reassessment owes to that aura of ambivalence that typically makes historical figures like him fascinating and controversial. Even in his own day, he was judged a great-hearted soul by some, a fomenter of discord by others. If the essence of Montfortianism is a common enterprise for a common goal, then reaching a consensus about the man himself goes completely against this grain. It is the final and perhaps most telling irony of all in his story.

Bibliography

Ambler, S., *The Montfortian Bishops and the Justification of Conciliar Government in 1264*, retrieved 6 January 2014 from Academia.eu: http://www.academia.edu/2532826/The_Montfortian_Bishops_and_the_Justification_of_Conciliar_Government_in_1264

Ashe, K., *Montfort: The Early Years* (Wake Robin Press, 2010)

Barker, J., *The Tournament in England 1100–1400* (Woodbridge: The Boydell Press, 1986)

Barlow, F., *Edward the Confessor* (Berkeley: University of California Press, 1985).

Bémont, C., *Simon de Montfort* (Oxford: Clarendon Press, 1930)

Blaauw, W. H., *The Barons' War* (London: Bell and Daldy, 1871)

Carpenter, D., 'A Noble in Politics: Roger Mortimer' in A. Duggan (ed.), *Nobles and Nobility* (Woodbridge: The Boydell Press, 2000)

Carpenter, D., 'Crucifixion and Conversion: King Henry III and the Jews in 1255', retrieved 8 October 2013 from Henry III Fine Rolls Project: http://www.finerollshenry3.org.uk/

Carpenter, D., *The Battles of Lewes and Evesham* (Keele, 1987)

Carpenter, D., 'The Meetings of Kings Henry III and Louis IX' in M. Prestwich, R. Britnell & R. Frame (eds), *Thirteenth Century England*, Volume X (Suffolk: Boydell & Brewer Ltd, 2005)

Carpenter, D., *The Reign of Henry III* (London: The Hambledon Press, 1996)

Carpenter, D., *The Struggle for Mastery, Britain 1066–1284* (London: Penguin Books, 2004)

Carpenter, D., 'Thomas Fitz-Thomas', retrieved 4 February 2014 from Oxford Dictionary of National Biography: http://www.oxforddnb.com/view/article/37419

Clanchy, M., *From Memory to Written Record: England 1066–1307* (Oxford: Blackwell Publishers, 1979)

Cohn, S. K., *Popular Protests in Late Medieval English Towns* (Cambridge: Cambridge University Press, 2013)

Costain, T. B., *The Magnificent Century* (Garden City: Doubleday & Company, 1951)

Davis, J. P., *The Gothic King: A Biography of Henry III* (London: Peter Owen Publishers, 2013)

D'Avray, D., *Medieval Christianity in Practice* (Princeton: Princeton University Press, 2009)

Denholm-Young, N., *Richard of Cornwall* (New York: William Salloch, 1947)

Douglas, D. C., Rothwel, H. (eds), *English Historical Documents: Volume 3 1189–1327* (2nd edn, New York: Routledge, 1995)

Goering, F. M., *The Letters of Robert Grosseteste, Bishop of Lincoln* (Toronto: University of Toronto Press, 2010)

Gransden, A., *Historical Writing in England* (Abingdon: Routledge, 1996)

Hamilton, J., *The Plantagenets: History of a Dynasty* (London: Continuum UK, 2010)

Harris, O. D., 'Jewish Community of Leicester', retrieved 17 February 2014 from Jewish Communities and Records: http://www.jewishgen.org/jcr-uk/Community/leices-gen/jews-medieval-leices.htm

Hershey, A., 'Success or Failure? Hugh Bigod and Judicial Reform during the Baronial Movement' in Peter R. Coss, S. D. Lloyd (eds), *Thirteenth Century England V* (Woodbridge: The Boydell Press, 1995)

Hoskin, P., 'Cantilupe's Crusade?', retrieved 21 November 2013 from Academia.edu: http://www.academia.edu/2281601/Cantilupes_Crusade_Walter_de_Cantilupe_Bishop_of_Worcester_and_the_baronial_rebellion

Howell, M., *Eleanor of Provence* (Oxford: Blackwell Publishers Ltd, 2001)

Hume, D., *The History of England, Volume II* (Oxford: 1876)

Hutton, W. H., *Simon de Montfort and His Cause, 1251–1266* (London: David Nutt, 1907)

Kushner, T., *The Jewish Heritage in British History: Englishness and Jewishness* (Abingdon: Frank Cass & Company, 1992)

Labarge, M. W., *Simon de Montfort* (London: Eyre & Spottiswoode, 1962)

Laborderie, O. D., Carpenter, D. A., Maddicott, J. R., 'The Last Hours of Simon de Montfort: A New Account', *English Historical Review 15* (2000)

Lloyd, T. H., *The English Wool Trade in the Middle Ages* (Cambridge: Cambridge University Press, 1977)

Luard, H. R. (ed.), *Annales Monastici: The Annals of Tewkesbury* (London, 1864)

Luard, H. R. (ed.), *Annales Monastici: The Annals of Dunstable* (London, 1866)

Luard, H. R. (ed.), *Annales Monastici: The Chronicle of Thomas Wykes* (London, 1869)

Maddicott, J., 'Politics and the People' in Janet E. Burton, Phillipp R. Schofield, Björn Weile (eds), *Thirteenth Century England XIV* (Woodbridge: The Boydell Press, 2013)

Maddicott, J., *Simon de Montfort* (Cambridge: Cambridge University Press, 1994).

Maddicott, J., 'The Battle of Lewes Conference April 2012', retrieved 17 January 2014 from the Sussex Archaeological Society: http://sussexpast.co.uk/wp-content/uploads/2012/05/Simon-de-Montfort-the-Battle-of-Lewes-and-the-development-of-Parliament.pdf

Maddicott, J., 'The Crusade Taxation of 1268–1270' in Peter R. Coss, Simon D. Lloyd (eds), *Thirteenth Century England II: Proceedings of the Newcastle Upon Tyne Conference* (Woodbridge: The Boydell Press, 1988)

Giles, J. A., *Matthew Paris's English History from 1235 to 1273, Vol. I, II, III* (London: Henry G. Bohn, 1854)

Morris, M., *A Great and Terrible King* (London: Windmill Books, 2009)

Morris, M., *The Bigod Earls of Norfolk* (Woodbridge: The Boydell Press, 2005)

Mundill, R. R., *The King's Jews: Money, Massacre and Exodus in Medieval England* (London: Continuum, 2010)

Oldenbourg, Z., *Massacre at Montségur* (London: Phoenix Press, 1961)

Oman, C., *The Art of War in the Middle Ages* (Methuen, 1898)

O'Shea, S., *The Perfect Heresy* (London: Profile Books, 2000)

Park, D., Griffith-Park R., *The Temple Church in London: History, Architecture, Art* (Woodbridge: The Boydell Press, 2010)

Perry, F., *Saint Louis* (New York: G. P. Putnam's Sons, 1900)

Powicke, M., *King Henry III and the Lord Edward Vols I, II* (Oxford: Clarendon Press, 1947)

Powicke, M., *The Thirteenth Century* (Oxford: Oxford University Press, 1962).

Powicke, M., *Ways of Medieval Life and Thought: Essays and Addresses* (New York: Biblo & Tannen, 1951).

Prestwich, M., *Edward I* (Berkeley: University of California Press, 1988)

Prestwich, M., *Plantagenet England* (Oxford: Oxford University Press, 2005)

Prothero, G. W., *The Life of Simon de Montfort* (London: Longmans, Green and Co., 1877)

Ray, M., 'Three Alien Royal Stewards' in M. Prestwich, R. H. Britnell, R. Fram (eds), *Thirteenth Century England X: Proceedings of the Durham Conference 2003* (Woodbridge: The Boydell Press, 2005)

Ridgeway, H., 'Henry III and the "Aliens", 1236–1272' in P. R. Coss, S. D. Lloyd (eds), *Thirteenth Century England II: Proceedings of the Newcastle Upon Tyne Conference 1987* (Woodbridge: The Boydell Press, 1988)

Rigg, A. G., *A History of Anglo-Latin Literature, 1066–1422* (Cambridge: Cambridge University Press, 1992).

Riley, H. R. (ed.), *The Chronicles of the Mayors and Sheriffs of London, 1188–1274* (London, 1863)

Shirley, W. W. (ed.), *Royal Letters* (London, 1866)

Strickland, A., *Lives of the Queens of England* (London: Henry Colburn, 1840)

Treharne, R., *The Baronial Plan of Reform* (Manchester: Manchester University Press, 1932).

Treharne, R., *Documents of the Baronial Movement of Reform and Rebellion* (Oxford: Clarendon Press, 1973)

Turner, E. T., *Manners and Household Expenses of England in the Thirteenth and Fifteenth Centuries* (London, 1841)

Valente, C., 'Simon the Montfort, Earl of Leicester, and the Utility of Sanctity in Thirteenth-Century England', *Journal of Medieval History 21* (1995)

Westerhof, D., *Death and the Noble Body in Medieval England* (Woodbridge: The Boydell Press, 2008)

Wild, B., 'A Captive King: Henry III Between the Battles of Lewes and Evesham' in J. Burton, F. Lachaud, P. Schofield, K. Stöber, B. Weiler (eds), *Thirteenth Century England XIII: Proceedings of the Paris Conference 2009* (Woodbridge: The Boydell Press, 2011)

Wilkinson, L. J., *Eleanor de Montfort: A Rebel Countess in Medieval England* (London: Continuum Books, 2012)

Wilkinson, L. J., 'Joan, Wife of Llywelyn the Great' in M. Prestwich, R. H. Britnell, R. Fram (eds), *Thirteenth Century England X: Proceedings of the Durham Conference 2003* (Woodbridge: The Boydell Press, 2005)

Wilkinson, L. J., 'Women in Thirteenth-Century Lincolnshire', *Royal Historical Society* (2007)

Wright, W. A. (ed.), *The Metrical Chronicle of Robert of Gloucester* (London, 1887).

Wright, T. (ed.), *The Political Songs of England* (London, 1839)

Notes and Commentary

Introduction: All the Thunder and Lightning in the World
It happened to belong to: Powicke, King Henry III, p. 253.
The thunder and lightning I fear beyond measure: Paris III, pp. 294–295.

1 Steel and Wax, 1208–1231
Upon this I returned without finding grace: Bémont, *Montfort*, p. 5. All references are to the second edition, published in 1930.
They would have the chance: Labarge, *Montfort*, pp. 37–38.
He had enough and ordered an army of Christian soldiers: The material here for Catharism and the Albigensian Crusade depend heavily on Zoé Oldenbourg's *Massacre at Montségur*, 1961, and Stephen O'Shea's *The Perfect Heresy*, 2000.
His chief regret was he didn't have the chance: Oldenbourg, p. 73.
He seemed to be everywhere at once: O'Shea, pp. 108–109.
The Spaniards were routed: Oldenbourg, pp. 166–168.
Another jotted down a rumour: *Dunstable*, p. 338.
It won't be the last we hear of this little county: Labarge, *Montfort*, pp. 21–22.
The other, Petronilla, would become an abbess: Powicke, *King Henry III*, p. 201; Maddicott, *Montfort*, pp. 5–6.
Lacking all other evidence: Bémont, *Montfort*, pp. 1–2; Maddicott, *Montfort*, p. 4.
He did not know English when he first stepped ashore: Labarge, *Montfort*, pp. 22–23. An idea of the English language of Simon's day might be gleaned from the beginning of the Lord's Prayer as

spoken in the Midlands around a hundred years after his death: 'Oure fadir, þat art in heuenys, halewid be þi name. þi kyngdom come to. Be þi wile don ase in heune and in erþe ...'

His 'pleasant and courteous way' of speaking: Prothero, *Life*, p. 380.

Henry Plantagenet was born: Much about Henry's early life and reign is taken from David Carpenter's *The Reign of Henry III*, Maurice Powicke's *King Henry III and the Lord Edward* and Thomas B. Costain's *The Magnificent Century*.

So he hired renowned craftsman: Powicke, *King Henry III*, p. 459.

Henry was not adverse: Maddicott, *Montfort*, pp. 8–9.

Simon was, moreover, family too: Maddicott, *Montfort*, p. 9. Ranulf's mother Bertrade was the sister of Montfort's grandfather, Simon II.

The following year my lord the king: Bémont, *Montfort*, pp. 4–5.

Henry received them in August 1231: Wilkinson, *Joan, Wife of Llywelyn the Great*, pp. 91–94. The execution of William de Braose had as much to do with Llywelyn's revenge against the Braose family as it did to finding young William in bed with his wife Joan, who was an illegitimate daughter of King John and so Henry's half-sister.

He had already made his own brother: Denholm-Young, *Richard of Cornwall*, pp. 20–22.

The other earls would take it amiss: Labarge, *Montfort*, pp. 31.

They consisted of twelve estates: Maddicott, p. 46.

As its Latin roots indicate, feudalism was a hierarchy of tenancies: Carpenter provides an excellent discussion of feudalism and the economy of England in the thirteenth century in *The Struggle for Mastery*, pp. 32–46, 84–86, 410–411.

The richest earldoms at this time: Maddicott, *Montfort*, p. 8–9, 55.

Some like him had been a part of Ranulf's affinity: Maddicott, *Montfort*, 59–74.

Both were in evidence in what was his first official act: In his study *Englishness and Medieval Anglo-Jewry*, Colin Richmond uses the word *Judenrein* to describe Simon's action in Leicester, perhaps not so much to insinuate a connection between Angevin England and Nazi Germany, rather because there is no decent English equivalent of the German 'Jew-free'. His mistaken reference to Simon as the founder of Parliament, however, brims with sarcasm.

He wouldn't take it all in one swoop: Carpenter, *The Struggle for Mastery*, pp. 41–42, 251–252.

This was a vital service in a cash-starved economy: Douglas, D. C., Rothwel, H. (eds), *English Historical Documents: Volume 3 1189-1327* (2nd edn: New York: Routledge, 1995)

Where he learned Hebrew is anybody's guess: Mundill, *The King's Jews*, pp. 132–133.

Whether she sympathised with the Jews: Maddicott, *Montfort*, pp. 15–16; Bémont, *Montfort*, pp. 27–28.

He hurled missives from the Bible: Mantello and Goering, *The Letters of Robert Grosseteste*, pp. 65–69.

2 More of the Great Bounty, 1232–1238

After William Marshal I died in 1219: Powicke, *The Thirteenth Century*, pp. 23–25.

Wearing a silky white suit and gloves, Henry arrived in Portsmouth: Denholm-Young, *Richard of Cornwall*, pp. 16–17.

The Archbishop of Canterbury: Carpenter, *The Struggle for Mastery*, p. 315.

He not only dismissed Roches and his circle: Powicke, *King Henry III*, pp. 144–145.

However he managed it, he was in a perfect position: Powicke, *King Henry III*, pp. 126–137. Maddicott, *Montfort*, p. 14.

The complicated business of giving and receiving: Labarge, *Montfort*, p. 33. Paris I, p. 238.

It didn't, and Henry was forced to pay Frederick £20,000: Howell, *Eleanor of Provence*, pp. 10, 13.

Rich widows were expected to remarry: Denholm-Young, *Richard of Cornwall*, pp. 18–19.

Everyone was distraught: Wilkinson, *Eleanor de Montfort*, pp. 36–37. William Marshal I had got into a nasty scrape with an Irish bishop over property and the bishop excommmunicated him, but William and his heirs remained unmoved, so he cursed the family with early extinction.

Faced with his first armed revolt: Denholm-Young, *Richard of Cornwall*, pp. 10–13.

So deeply aggrieved did he feel by this wanton act: Paris I, p. 34; Denholm-Young, *Richard of Cornwall*, pp. 28–29.

He and Joan had already been married by proxy: Powicke, *King Henry III*, pp. 159–60.

A well-travelled yarn has her writing a poem about a knight: Howell, *Eleanor of Provence*, p. 7.

The count and his wife, both poets incidentally: Paris I, pp. 7–10; Howell, *Eleanor of Provence*, p. 12–14.

Her coronation in London was a lavish affair, but only for him: Strickland, *Lives of the Queens*, p. 46.

Eleanor of Provence was described as *venustissima*: Howell, *Eleanor of Provence*, p. 5.

The removal of the queen's bed made it clear: Howell, *Eleanor of Provence*, pp. 15–20.

Simon held firm and so held the basin for Henry: Paris I, pp. 8–10.

He started using the title of earl: Paris I, p. 68. The other two were John de Lacy, the Earl of Lincoln, and Geoffrey the Templar. Paris says the nobility hated them because, unlike the Savoyards, they were from the same kingdom, which indicates that Simon by this time had been fully assimilated in his adopted country.

He only consulted them when he wanted money: Maddicott, *Montfort*, pp. 18–20.

If she had suffered any embarrassment through his attentions: Labarge, *Montfort*, pp. 45–47; Maddicott, *Montfort*, pp. 17–18.

The ten manors he eventually settled on her as a marriage portion: Wilkinson, *Eleanor de Montfort*, p. 26.

When she became seasick during the voyage: Wilkinson, *Eleanor de Montfort*, p. 30.

Magna Carta stipulated a settlement period of forty days: Labarge, *Montfort*, pp. 41–42.

She became a nun: Paris II, p. 442. Her governess, Cecilia de Sandford, became so enamoured of her own ring that she was determined to wear it to her grave. As she lay dying, a friar thought it unbecoming for her to be ornamented on her deathbed and told the servants to remove it. Aroused by the intrusion, she managed to clench her ring with strength worthy of rigor mortis before expiring.

Becoming a bride of Christ, however, was clearly a political move: Wilkinson, *Eleanor de Montfort*, pp. 44–47.

At some point in her widowhood: Paris II, p. 442.

Simon was grateful to receive her, it was said: Labarge, *Montfort*, pp. 47–48. This is Paris' estimation of Simon's feelings, and Labarge adds 'as well he might'.

No one could miss the irony that these were the same issues: Maddicott, *Montfort*, p. 22.

Richard, characteristically, withdrew his opposition at the last minute: Denholm-Young, *Richard of Cornwall*, p. 36.

At least £300 of it came from an alderman in Leicester: Mantello and Goering, *The Letters of Robert Grosseteste*, pp. 171–172; Paris I, p. 124. Paris supports the charge of extortion and decries the marriage as 'unlawful'.

Montfort then betook himself back to Frederick: Paris I, p. 129.

An apocryphal story has him later fleeing the country: Paris I, pp. 126–129. Labarge, *Montfort*, p. 48. There was at least a bit of Schadenfreude to be had for the archbishop in the terror inflicted on his archenemy, Otto, during his absence. The legate, who had been ordered by the pope to come out in favour of Simon's marriage, was in Oxford when his brother got into a fight with an Irish chaplain and ended up tossing a cauldron of boiling water into his face. The brother was killed in the ensuing student riot, and Otto sank his spurs into his horse and kept them there until he reached the safety of Henry's chambers. The ringleaders were later caught and carted off to London, where they were made to walk several miles barefoot as penance before studies were allowed to resume.

He gave his consent for the child to be named after him: Wilkinson, *Eleanor de Montfort*, p. 69.

The rite itself was performed by the bishop of Lichfield: Bémont, *Montfort*, p. 58.

3 *The Churching, 1239–1243*

It was Henry himself who explained the nature of kingship: Carpenter, *The Struggle for Mastery*, p. 340.

The £50 'relief' for taking possession of his half of Leicester: Labarge, *Montfort*, p. 69.

Henry had advanced him £1,565 for his trip to Rome: Maddicott, *Montfort*, p. 25.

His gift to Eleanor that Christmas included a robe and surcoat: Wilkinson, *Eleanor de Montfort*, p. 56.

The timing was opportune, for Simon was chosen among the noblemen: Paris I, p. 172.

His uncle Richard could scoff at his island subjects: Carpenter, *The Struggle for Mastery*, p.

It would be hoped that the new Edward looked nothing like his namesake: Barlow, Edward the Confessor, p. 71.

The story goes back, as most seem to during this period: Powicke, *Ways of Medieval Life and Thought*, pp. 38–58.

And so the birth of this healthy boy with the English name: Paris I, p. 172.

You seduced my sister before marriage: Paris I, p. 194.

In a modern novel, seduction is also the reason given: Ashe, *Montfort, The Early Years*, pp. 148–153. The archbishop was probably even then still fuming that Otto had pulled rank and performed the baptism of Edward, with Montfort, one of the men instrumental in bringing the legate into the country, by his side.

The King of England honoured me by giving me his sister: Bémont, *Montfort*, pp. 60–61.

He was poisoned in Viterbo that autumn: Paris I, p. 241.

Henry was justifiably nervous: Paris I, p. 236.

When Ranulf's estate was settled: Bémont, *Montfort*, pp. 60–61; Carpenter, *The Struggle for Mastery*, p. 316; Paris I, p. 172.

He had already taken steps to recover it by suing: Maddicott, *Montfort*, p. 24.

Then, the same day that he had invited us to the queen's churching: Bémont, *Montfort*, p. 61.

Simon poured his heart out in a letter to Grosseteste: Mantello and Goering, *Letters of Robert Grosseteste*, pp. 264–265.

At that time the king sent orders to his proctors in Rome: Maddicott, *Montfort*, p. 29.

Two others were also dismissed: Paris I, pp. 245–246.

The charges against Simon paled in comparison: Paris I, p. 238.

Even though Marshal was grieving for his sister: Paris I, pp. 239, 256.

By then he had missed the crusade, and he was killed: Denholm-Young, *Richard of Cornwall*, p. 40.

Henry was sufficiently frightened to plead with the pope: Paris I, p. 266.

Already fifty years old at the time: Paris I, pp. 314–315.

It would be the last time the Montfort brothers: Bémont, *Montfort*, p. 65.

Somewhere around the time Amaury died: Turner, *Manners and Household Expenses*, pp. xix–xx.

Philip was part of the efforts by a local faction: Maddicott, *Montfort*, p. 30.

He probably had to go in that direction: Denholm-Young, *Richard of Cornwall*, p. 45. Denholm-Young calls the project 'scatterbrained'.

When she died in March 1238: Wilkinson, *Eleanor de Montfort*, pp. 14–15.

Their pride wounded, Hugh and Isabella began putting together: Perry, *Saint Louis*, pp. 107–108.

In order to get the money, Henry had to call a parliament: Paris I, p. 397.

He was forced to fill his barrels with money: Denholm-Young, *Richard of Cornwall*, pp. 45–46.

He did, but told the king he was not inclined: Bémont, *Montfort*, p. 65.

He turned on Hugh, demanding that the man he called 'father': Denholm-Young, *Richard of Cornwall*, p. 47.

A fierce rearguard action in the vineyards: Powicke, *King Henry III*, p. 215; Labarge, *Montfort*, p. 62. John Mansel and Roger Bigod, the Earl of Norfolk, also got honourable mentions.

Hugh had secretly gone over to the King of France: Paris I, pp. 424–425.

He then alienated Richard in a fiasco typical: Denholm-Young, *Richard of Cornwall*, p. 49.

Other barons also began going home: Paris I, p. 436. Paris notes that the remaining nobles got lazy and slept most of their time away, something difficult to imagine in Montfort.

As a boy, James had been betrothed to Simon's sister: Oldenbourg, *Massacre at Montségur*, p. 146; Bémont, *Montfort*, p. 67.

He concluded another five-year truce with Louis and left: Powicke, *The Thirteenth Century*, pp. 103–104.

The wedding took place at Westminster in November 1243: Paris I, p. 459.

Henry promised to give the Montforts £333 annually as a marriage: Maddicott, *Montfort*, p. 33.

An even grander display of affection was granting them custody: Labarge, *Montfort*, p. 70.

4 On the Margins of Favour, 1244–1248

Amaury was born sometime in 1242/1243: Maddicott, *Montfort*, pp. 43–44. Maddicott's research reverses the traditional order that had Guy as the third son.

Henry, as the eldest and heir: Wilkinson, *Eleanor de Montfort*, p. 89.

He warned her about reports: Wilkinson, *Eleanor de Montfort*, pp. 12–13. Labarge, *Montfort*, pp. 42–43, 78. In the words of another woman, Margaret Labarge, Eleanor was 'shrill and nagging'.

Eleanor was as devotional as he was: Maddicott, *Montfort*, pp. 40, 86.

A nice vignette of a medieval family: Labarge, *Montfort*, p. 79.

Henry helped here and there with gifts: Maddicott, *Montfort*, p. 54. Gilbert de Umfraville came into his inheritance at the height of the conflict. At first adhering to Simon's side, he joined other northern lords in their allegiance to the Crown before the end.

Wardships were lucrative forms of patronage: Paris II, p. 114; Denholm-Young, *Richard of Cornwall*, p. 46.

At least three dozen Savoyards, total strangers to the realm: Ridgeway, *Henry III and the 'Aliens'*; Maddicott, *Montfort*, p. 51; Denholm-Young, *Richard of Cornwall*, p. 46.

Things then got worse when Walter Marshal died: Park and Griffith-Jones, *The Temple Church in London*, pp. 82–83; Paris II, pp. 119–123.

Henry probably quashed it out of fear: Maddicott, *Montfort*, pp. 130–131. Henry's reluctance to go forward with a decision has found sympathy among biographers like Maddicott.

They wanted to restore the offices of justiciar: Carpenter, *The Reign of Henry III*, pp. 61–62.

Henry had only been a boy then: Paris II, pp. 7–13.

Unwilling to yield even a little to parliamentary control: Powicke, *The Thirteenth Century*, pp. 32–33.

Royal revenue at this time was about £36,500: Carpenter, *The Struggle for Mastery*, pp. 348–349.

That wasn't the case for minor barons and clerics: Carpenter, *The Struggle for Mastery*, pp. 350–351.

As part of rehabilitating himself in the eyes of his brother-in-law: Maddicott, *Montfort*, p. 36.

He had moved closer to the spiritual world: Labarge, *Montfort*, p. 77; Maddicott, *Montfort*, p. 79. Much has been made of the similarities between these two men, the bishop and the earl, who were separated in age by a generation. John Maddicott finds both men to be uncompromising zealots, although Grosseteste for him was the kinder and more humane of the two. Margaret Labarge also sees neither willing to compromise, least of all on their rights, but describes both as head and shoulders above their contemporaries and attributing their canonisation in the popular eye to their unyielding firmness and faith. One thing for certain is that once aroused they gave it their all, something hard to imagine in a dilettante like Henry.

When his leg was crushed during the Poitou campaign: Rigg, *History of Anglo-Latin Literature*, p. 198.

Henry tried to justify himself by saying: Paris I, pp. 374–375.

The monks next tried to install William Raleigh, the Bishop of Norwich: Paris I, pp. 136, 277. Although a leading jurist in the country, Raleigh dismissed the plea of the Jews to have their case heard by the king's court with the reasoning that circumcision was a Church matter.

It took papal intervention to reconcile them: Carpenter, *The Struggle for Mastery*, p. 349.

He was an incredibly odd choice: Powicke, *King Henry III*, p. 361.

The issue, of course, was money: Paris III, pp. 7–8.

Any prelate bearing less than £20 was turned out: Paris I, pp. 332–333, 479. Otto finally left England after more than three years.

The barons had enough of the unpleasant little clerk: Paris II, pp. 56–57.

At the next parliament, held in July: Denholm-Young, *Richard of Cornwall*, pp. 56–57.

In 1247 he undertook a secret mission to France: Maddicott, *Montfort*, p. 36.

He had acquired a crystal vial of holy blood: Labarge, *Montfort*, pp. 83–84.

By all accounts, the Lusignan siblings were an ill-bred: Paris I, p. 322; Paris II, p. 234.

She even twisted the knife by turning sixteen castles: Paris II, p. 130.

To top it off, Beatrice's brother Boniface: Paris II, pp. 133–134, 230.

Simon and Eleanor may have been motivated: Maddicott, *Montfort*, pp. 106–107.

5 The Trial, 1249–1253

This last sliver of the old Angevin empire: Carpenter, *The Struggle for Mastery*, p. 345.

One of these was Gaston de Bearn: Paris I, p. 431.

First and foremost was his fame as a warrior: Maddicott, *Montfort*, p. 110.

His terms were stiff, but that was no problem: Strickland, *Lives of the Queens*, p. 58.

The regional metropolis Bordeaux was ruled at that time: Bémont, *Montfort*, p. 77.

When he returned to England for Christmas: Paris II, p. 312.

Act energetically and unremittingly: Bémont, *Montfort*, p. 84–85.

Sir, I have heard for certain that some knights of Gascony: Shirley, *Royal Letters*, pp. 52–53.

Finding himself completely without resources: Paris II, pp. 420–421.

The king gave him another £2,000: Paris II, p. 465; Labarge, *Montfort*, p. 114.

While there, they found: Howell, *Eleanor of Provence*, p. 63.

The Montforts and the queen also shared: Bémont, *Montfort*, pp. 42–43.

In another missive, Marsh rhetorically asks: Hutton, *Montfort and His Cause*, pp. 19–20.

Simon was being accused of extorting all kinds of wealth: Paris II, pp. 476–477.

The king, beside himself with anger: Labarge, *Montfort*, p. 119.

It opened on 9 May 1252 in the refectory of Westminster Abbey: Bémont, *Montfort*, p. 106.

Since the king obviously had no more faith in him: Paris II, pp. 487–488.

The queen wanted the province sufficiently tamed for Edward: Howell, *Eleanor of Provence*, pp. 64–65.

Another baron Simon could depend on for support: Bémont, *Montfort*, p. 48.

Henry was forced to accept the verdict of his council: Paris II, pp. 507.

Her anxiety over her husband's ordeal: Wilkinson, *Eleanor de Montfort*, pp. 82, 92.

Part of the queen's sympathy: Howell, *Eleanor of Provence*, pp. 65–66.

After years of struggle, Henry had forced the monks: Paris II, p. 396, 519.

Boniface was something of a bully himself: Paris II, pp. 346–347.

Henry was more furious at the queen: Howell, *Eleanor of Provence*, pp. 67–69.

Simon didn't even wait for his followers: Paris II, pp. 509, 527. Simon's father was legendary for refusing to leave his men in the lurch.

But the Gascons were relentless: Bémont, *Montfort*, p. 115.

The commissioners came ready to relieve him of his command: Paris II, p. 530.

It was a generous settlement that Henry insisted: Maddicott, *Montfort*, p. 121. This accusation has found sympathy among modern biographers.

It was a surprising turn of events: Labarge, *Montfort*, pp. 131–134.

While that may not have surprised him: Paris III, pp. 23–26.

Landing on 20 August 1253, he immediately launched a war: Maddicott, *Montfort*, pp. 120–121; Bémont, *Montfort*, p. 119.

At that point his only notable loss was old Hugh Lusignan: Perry, *Saint Louis*, p. 169.

Another notorious member of the expedition: Perry, *Saint Louis*, p. 193.

His mother Blanche of Castile had to deal with the calamity: Paris II, pp. 451–452, 455–456.

They asked him to be their seneschal: Paris III, pp. 16–17, 21–22, 56–57.

To compensate Montfort for his losses and expenses: Maddicott, *Montfort*, pp. 122–123.

It was costing him a fortune to quell a mutinous province: Carpenter, *The Struggle for Mastery*, p. 345. While nearly all contemporaries sympathised with Montfort in his dispute with the king, modern historians generally see his rule there as a failure, simply because 'he was not the right man' for the job, says Powicke. Despite having courage, resolution and energy, 'he lacked in every other quality necessary for success' (*King Henry III*, p. 219). Carpenter similarly sees a man who 'carried all before him' and therefore was 'demanding and dangerous' (*The Struggle for Mastery*, p. 341). Maddicott attributes his greatest moral failing to a ruthless, overbearing harshness. Interestingly, he goes further in turning the tables on a long-cherished Montfortian tradition. In 1252 Grosseteste sent Simon the tract of a speech he wrote condemning the tyrannical practices of Boniface. It was long presumed that by this act the Bishop of Lincoln was deliberately firing Simon's imagination in the service of justice. Maddicott, seconded by Prestwich, now suggests that what Grosseteste really wanted was for Simon to read his own administration in his warnings about tyranny (*Montfort*, p. 99; *Plantangenet England*, p. 108). All these findings of a severe, high-handed administrator rather reflects the combined need of modern historians to see him the way Paris did, as following in his father's footsteps. While the elder Montfort was still highly regarded in the thirteenth century, outside the region that came under his yoke anyway, today's glorification of the Cathars and Occitania makes demonising him the current trend. What is often overlooked about father and son is that neither wanted the thankless jobs they got stuck with, both of which inevitably required a hard hand, as all wars do, and much of the enmity they incurred was due to the fact that they did their jobs so thoroughly. Conceivably, there would have been less to squawk about if others on either side had risen to the occasion as well.

6 *Shifting Alliances, 1254–1255*

The magnates and clergy no doubt guessed: Powicke, *King Henry III*, p. 234.

Then Simon showed up from the Continent: Denholm-Young, *Richard of Cornwall*, pp. 78–79.

Henry had sent for his children because the diplomatic efforts: Paris III, p. 83; Howell, *Eleanor of Provence*, p. 124.

The knighting of the heir to the throne: Prestwich, *Edward I*, pp. 9–10.

There was one last technicality that Henry needed to wrap up: D'Avray, *Medieval Christianity in Practice*, pp. 44–45.

Eleanor was just thirteen when she miscarried the first time: Morris, *A Great and Terrible King*, p. 22.

He created quite a bit of grumbling the last time he returned: Matthew Paris I, pp. 455–456.

Louis was wary of the new alliance between England and Castile: Powicke, *King Henry III*, p. 239.

The first stop for Henry's retinue, described as a small army: Paris III, p. 104.

The royal parties met in Orleans: Carpenter, *Meetings of Kings Henry III and Louis IX*, pp. 5–6; Howell, *Eleanor of Provence*, pp. 136–137.

Grateful though he was to Louis for his hospitality: Labarge, *Montfort*, p. 147.

Knowing Richard of Cornwall had 'an unquenchable thirst: Denholm-Young, *Richard of Cornwall*, pp. 81–82.

With a singularly bad conscience: Paris III, p. 101.

Frederick swore to invade to show who was going to depose whom: Denholm-Young, *Richard of Cornwall*, pp. 52–53.

They were successful in so far as Innocent: Powicke, *King Henry III*, p. 358.

By the time he made the offer to Henry: Paris III, pp. 89–91. Henry's ambitions for Sicily have gained him a surprising number of modern apologists. The revisionist view looks squarely at the geopolitical considerations and concludes that Henry was definitely on to something. Sicily was rich, cultured, the key to a Mediterranean empire that would glorify England and lock France out. The new consensus suggests it might have worked had the cost not been so prohibitively high, at least twice as much as he could hope to raise from the English clergy (Howell, *Eleanor of Provence*, p. 132; Powicke, *The Thirteenth Century*, p. 121). This despite experience suggesting that any happy ending to the affair was bound to be elusive, and not just because Henry had fumbled his first two grand adventures abroad. Back in 415 BC, Athens had enough money for its own Sicilian business and watched helplessly as it swallowed up two armies and the remnants of its empire. The man who did eventually win the island, Charles of Anjou, was also forced to watch it slip from his grasp later on.

His friendship with Louis and standing at the French court: Maddicott, *Montfort*, p. 140.

In fact, fifteen-year-old Margaret was miserable in her barren castle: Howell, *Eleanor of Provence*, p. 102.

The citizens of London made a gift to him of £100: Paris III, p. 113; Powicke, *King Henry III*, pp. 308–309, 312.

It is no wonder that I covet money: Paris III, pp. 114–115.

Although still anxious to convert the Jews: Powicke, *King Henry III*, p. 313.

She claimed he was playing with some Jewish boys: Paris III, pp. 138–140.

That it was all about blood money can be inferred from the work: Carpenter, *Henry III Fine Rolls Project*.

Undoubtedly joining Henry at the table of this feast: Paris III, pp. 137–138.

Rostand, however, had Henry's full support: Paris III, p. 152.

His authority included the clause *non obstante*: Powicke, *King Henry III*, pp. 324–325.

Pope Innocent was naturally furious that anybody should question: Paris III, pp. 35–38, 66–68.

He was in fact resentful of the way his nobles and bishops: Paris III, p. 125.

He had convinced Henry to give him the seals: Paris III, p. 133.

Taking the lead was the Bishop of London: Paris III, p. 147.

The prelate who should have led the opposition: Howell, *Eleanor of Provence*, p. 143.

At this same Parliament he railed against the man: Paris III, p. 150.

Normally easy-going about the money his barons owed him: Carpenter, *The Reign of Henry III*, p. 96.

The merchants turned to their new lord: Prestwich, *Edward I*, p. 15.

Gathering up a large retinue of horsemen: Paris III, p. 157. Paris put the number at an improbably high two hundred.

7 *Famine Before Revolution, 1256–1257*

His desperation can be seen in his order: Davis, *The Gothic King*, p. 21.

Henry's poverty also forced him to scrounge: Paris III, pp. 130–131, 169–170, 196.

One convenient source of revenue was the distraint of knighthood: Labarge, *Montfort*, p. 125.

Henry's anxious state of mind can be seen: Paris III, pp. 174–175, 197.

The poor sheriff; he never had it easy under any king: Powicke, *King Henry III*, pp. 97–99.

The incentives he offered them were the authority of the title: Carpenter, *The Reign of Henry III*, pp. 172–174.

The last general eyre before the 1250s: Carpenter, *The Struggle for Mastery*, p. 350.

Henry's constant extortion of the Jews forced them: Maddicott, *Montfort*, p. 126; Maddicott, *The Crusade Taxation*, p. 101.

Henry always insisted that these men were as much obliged: Carpenter, *The Struggle for Mastery*, p. 351.

These oppressive landlords included not only the magnates: Howell, *Eleanor of Provence*, p. 140; Maddicott, *Montfort*, pp. 174–176.

The king had also done nothing to find: Maddicott, *Montfort*, pp. 145–146, 149.

Margaret de Lacy, the widow of Walter Marshal: Wilkinson, *Women in Thirteenth-Century Lincolnshire*, pp. 54–56.

Henry's almost perverse preference for his half-brothers: Bémont, *Montfort*, pp. 130–131.

It began at the end of January 1256 when William of Holland: Paris III, pp. 166–167.

Richard, however, was covetous of any crown: Denholm-Young, *Richard of Cornwall*, p. 89.

He fumed about Henry robbing the wine merchants: Paris III, pp. 194–195.

All the shady dealings didn't stop a German delegation: Paris III, pp. 207–209.

The English silver penny had been filed and clipped: Denholm-Young, *Richard of Cornwall*, pp. 63–64; Paris III, p. 230.

It was basically up to the pope to decide: Powicke, *King Henry III*, pp. 245–246.

Even though Alfonso sneered that Richard was only pretending: Denholm-Young, *Richard of Cornwall*, pp. 95–96.

Louis waxed on about how the two kings had married: Howell, *Eleanor of Provence*, p. 137.

Henry was glad to play on those fears: Paris III, pp. 132, 164–166.

As in every other scheme of Henry's: Paris III, pp. 254–255.

The second advantage would have Louis compensate Henry: Powicke, *King Henry III*, pp. 251–252.

Since there was no telling Henry that: Prestwich, *Edward I*, pp. 15–16. The guests at Mansel's feast, where as many as seven hundred dishes were served, included the King of Scotland.

Richard was just then doling out money left and right: Paris III, pp. 200–201.

Geoffrey Langley had won the queen's favour: Howell, *Eleanor of Provence*, p. 116; Morris, *A Great and Terrible King*, p. 29.

Matthew Paris recalls how Edward and his riders would trash or steal: Paris III, pp. 205, 217–218.

Indeed he was, for he had planned a surprise performance: Howell, *Eleanor of Provence*, pp. 138–139; Powicke, *King Henry III*, pp. 375–376.

Peace was possible, and here Simon was playing an ever more active role: Maddicott, *Montfort*, p. 143; Labarge, *Montfort*, p. 148.

One of his raids included the Leicester estates: Paris III, pp. 205, 234–235, 242. Henry didn't always turn a blind eye to the troubles his brothers brought on themselves. Shortly after this confrontation, one of William's squires went on a rampage in London before being beaten and stabbed to death. William complained about the actions of the Londoners to Henry, who upon learning of the facts, told him, 'The offender only received what he deserved.'

In May 1257 the death of his four-year-old daughter Katherine: Davis, *The Gothic King*, p. 190.

While he teetered on collapse, the Welsh put aside their differences: Paris III, p. 243.

The rains and blight that ruined herds and harvests alike: Paris III, pp. 255–256.

Through all the madness of the Sicilian business: Denholm-Young, *Richard of Cornwall*, p. 64.

8 1258

That same threat had been carried out against his father: Carpenter, *The Struggle for Mastery*, p. 286.

When the pope threatened, he listened: Carpenter, *The Reign of Henry III*, p. 185.

It started, inevitably, with one of the Lusignans: Howell, *Eleanor of Provence*, pp. 148–149.

In 1247 he was twenty-five and recently knighted: Barker, *The Tournament in England*, pp. 48–49.

Branded a traitor, he was further drawn into their orbit: Paris III, pp. 14–15. This Hugh Lusignan perished during the final rout of Louis' army in Egypt, nine months after his father was killed on the beachhead. He was succeeded as the Count of La Marche by his son Hugh, who would die during Louis' second crusade.

The arrangement was the occasion for one of Paris' highly colourful rants. Henry wished 'the nobles of his kingdom to degenerate' and 'mix their blood with the scum of foreigners' while Clare revealed 'a vile, avaricious disposition' that made him 'defile his offspring with this poisonous source'.

The queen was disturbed by the proximity of this powerful baron: Howell, *Eleanor of Provence*, p. 142.

Clare's break with the Lusignans came out into the open: Labarge, *Montfort*, p. 154; Paris III, p. 279.

He too had a personal quarrel with the Lusignans: Carpenter, *The Reign of Henry III*, p. 192.

While he didn't have Simon's oratory or Clare's ranking: Morris, *The Bigod Earls of Norfolk*, p. 57.

Three days later Henry submitted and agreed to work out the

details: Powicke, *King Henry III*, p. 384. Powicke notes that Geoffrey Lusignan might also have been on the committee as the barons claimed. The clerk who enrolled the writ had mistakenly included Richard de Clare instead.

Either he didn't pay any regard to Bigod's opening line: Howell, *Eleanor of Provence*, p. 154.

As far back as 1237, four years before Peter arrived on the scene: *Ibid.*, p. 21.

Henry might have been peeved by the Savoyards: Paris III, p. 269.

Famine had claimed thousands of poor people in London alone: Paris III, pp. 266, 291.

Feeding the poor had always been a pet project of Henry's: Carpenter, *The Meetings of Kings Henry III and Louis IX*, pp. 17–18. It wasn't just another case of Henry's famed generosity but, as Carpenter writes, 'he clearly believed it dignified his royal state and secured the more certain promise of divine aid, prayers being all the more powerful if issuing from many lips'.

He was handed a list of grievances: Hutton, pp. 75–91. The actual Provisions appear to be the paperwork of the committee and were never officially published.

When it came time for everyone to swear an oath: Paris III, p. 287.

Evidently they took his threat seriously: Powicke, *King Henry III*, pp. 384–385.

But even there they found no peace: Howell, *Eleanor of Provence*, p. 158.

A pair of chroniclers reported that even Simon himself: Maddicott, *Montfort*, pp. 161–162.

During the Albigensian Crusade, his father had been merciless: O'Shea, *The Perfect Heresy*, pp. 130–131.

He refused to take the oath on his own: Paris III, p. 287.

The same was true of John de Warenne: Morris, *The Bigod Earls of Norfolk*, p. 20; Powicke, *King Henry III*, pp. 584–85. Warenne would be best remembered for his later response to the request that he produce the warrant to his land. 'This is my warrant,' he declared, showing a sword that was supposedly used by his ancestor in helping William I conquer England. This was after he presumably used another sword to mortally injure one of the king's faithful administrators during a dispute before the justices at Westminster Hall. Ever loyal to Edward, he got off with a fine, much of which went unpaid.

The Provisions that arose out of her desire: Powicke, *King Henry III*, p. 402. Queen's gold was her 10 per cent cut of royal fines, tacked on exclusive of the amount due. If the offender owed the king £20, he gave her £2 as well.

She already got a taste of what the future might hold: Howell, *Eleanor of Provence*, pp. 155–156.

Boniface had certainly played his part: Howell, *Eleanor of Provence*, pp. 139, 158–159.

Nowhere, apparently, was this self-interest more evident: Maddicott, *Montfort*, p. 154.

If Simon's principal motivation was something other than personal gain: Maddicott, *Montfort*, p. 149. As Maddicott writes, 'It was hardly economic decline that drove him to reform.'

The other confederates were just as busy that summer: Prestwich, *Edward I*, pp. 26–27.

Alexander glumly replied that since Henry had not: Carpenter, *The Reign of Henry III*, p. 186.

Beneath the gloss he vented his frustration by sabotaging: Bémont, *Montfort*, pp. 162–168.

There was little in his early career: Hoskin, *Cantilupe's Crusade*.

Boniface's name, followed by those of Walter and Simon: Powicke, *King Henry III*, p. 400.

The importance of this document cannot be underestimated: Bémont, *Montfort*, pp. 168–169.

As expected, he found himself besieged by plaintiffs: Denholm-Young, *Richard of Cornwall*, p. 29; *Dunstable*, p. 135. This happened in Cornwall in 1233. It was the first eyre there in over thirty years and Richard was promised all the profits.

Not all the complaints were about the sheriffs: Hershey, *Success or Failure?*

Pulling what might aptly be called 'a Henry': Paris III, pp. 280, 301.

He had been the leading magnate when he left the country: Denholm-Young, *Richard of Cornwall*, p. 98.

9 *For and Against the Common Enterprise, 1259–1260*

It was a nervous group of barons that met Richard: Denholm-Young, *Richard of Cornwall*, pp. 98–99.

Simon de Montfort was lingering on the Continent: Paris III, p. 316.

His role in drafting his father's will reflects: Clanchy, *From Memory to Written Record*, p. 232. Reading and writing were separate skills in those days, the latter more akin to art than speech and requiring countless hours to master the use of parchment and quill. Young Henry had evidently been an excellent student, for his father's will, written in French, easily passed for the work of a professional scribe.

He wanted his family to be freed of all the debts: Maddicott, *Montfort*, pp. 174–177.

Such complaints might somehow infringe his rights: Powicke, *King Henry III*, p. 397; Powicke, *The Thirteenth Century*, p. 148.

I do not care to live with people so deceitful: Paris III, pp. 326–327.

In March of that year, he entered into a formal alliance with Edward: Prestwich, *Edward I*, pp. 27–28; Powicke, *King Henry III*, p. 405.

Edward had a big problem with the treaty: Prestwich, *Edward I*, p. 29.

It was an unexpected impasse: Wilkinson, *Eleanor de Montfort*, pp. 96–97.

Henry's weak justification was that other members of the royal family: Nowhere have Simon and Eleanor come in for such a beating than in this episode. Matthew Paris mentioned it without comment in one of his last entries before his death in June 1259, but the royalist chronicler Thomas Wykes was scathing, even suggesting that what the Montforts were really after was Normandy itself, and after that the English Crown. This doesn't say much for his credentials, since Wykes had to know there were five male heirs between Henry III and Henry de Montfort.

But modern historians have also been withering. Words like 'blackmail', 'machinations' and 'dubious' all crop up in descriptions of the Montforts' actions against a king who might as well be called Poor Henry. One curious line of logic even asserts that Edward's concerns for his own interests in the treaty were sincere, whereas the Montforts were just being cynical

(Morris, *A Great and Terrible King*, p. 43). In general, their holdout is viewed as the clearest proof that Simon and Eleanor were more interested in what benefited them personally than in what was good for the realm.

The treaty, however, was never the issue, rather Henry's shabby treatment of his sister. It all started when she was in his power. Now, twenty-five years later, he was in her power and she was not going to let him off the hook just because a group of supremely important men were snarling at her audacity (as might well be the case today). Henry, the Marshals, the Archbishop of Canterbury, they all pushed her around when she was in a vulnerable state. Now she had a man with more courage and ability than heavies like Clare and Valence, who was ready to stand his ground next to her. She didn't care what grief she caused Henry, he was going to make good her claims once and for all.

Henry had done as much for their half-brother William: Maddicott, *Montfort*, p. 136.

When Henry later accused him of violating his oath in this manner: Maddicott, *Montfort*, pp. 189–191.

Often nothing ever came of it because the arbitrators: Labarge, *Montfort*, p. 190.

The Montforts were claiming arrears of £24,000: Carpenter, *The Struggle for Mastery*, p. 372; Maddicott, *Montfort*, p. 53.

Of the 170 Savoyards who came to England: Ridgeway, *Henry III and the 'Aliens'*, pp. 81–82.

He was to receive enough money to maintain a force: Powicke, *King Henry III*, p. 414.

If he never got around to using these knights: Bémont, *Montfort*, p. 179.

Another reason why the arbitration was doomed: Maddicott, *Montfort*, pp. 186–187.

Upon learning of it, Simon hit back: Maddicott, *Montfort*, pp. 187–188.

He berated Simon in a quarrel so violent that the French: Paris III, p. 327.

The background for this shift was the parliament of October 1259: Maddicott, *Montfort*, pp. 184–185.

Two days after the October parliament opened, Edward ditched him for good: Carpenter, *The Reign of Henry III*, pp. 241–251. As with Clare, Edward swore an oath to Simon, in this case not to make war on anyone associated with the baronial enterprise unless that person refuses to accept the award of the king's court. Carpenter suggests that the award in question was the arbitration on Eleanor's dower. Inasmuch as Simon expected trouble from barons like Clare and Bigod over a possible repartition of the Marshal estate, he wanted Edward's help in wrenching any gains out of them. Simon was also eager not to be seen as pursuing his own interests, so he made sure the wording of the oath was deliberately vague. Here, says Carpenter, we see four facets typical of Montfort's career: 'His commitment to the enterprise of the barons; his cultivation of his private interests; his concern for his public reputation; and his confidence in the use of force.' Whether or not this was the case, his recruitment of Edward into the reform movement underscores his keen perception of men. Edward had little concern for his own public reputation and his militancy offset the faintheartedness Montfort could now sense in other baronial leaders. And of course, both of them had their reasons for blocking the treaty with France.

They offered redress for even the lowest rungs of feudal society: Howell, *Eleanor of Provence*, p. 164. The Provisions of Oxford generally refer to all the enanctments of the reform period, including these Provisions of Westminster.

The King of France made sure there was nothing unbecoming: Labarge, *Montfort*, p. 161.

Eager to show Louis that the reforms had not impinged on his dignity: Carpenter, *The Meetings of Kings Henry III and Louis IX*, pp. 16–21.

The problem of the match for Henry was that the Duke of Brittany: Howell, *Eleanor of Provence*, pp. 161–162.

After hearing 268 complaints in one year: Carpenter, *The Struggle for Mastery*, p. 370; Hershey, *Success or Failure?*, pp. 79–81;

Montfort wasn't having any of it: Howell, *Eleanor of Provence*, p. 164.

Reform seemed good to Roger Bigod when there were less: Morris, *The Bigod Earls of Norfolk*, p. 80.

When he lost his position on the council as a result: Howell, *Eleanor of Provence*, pp. 162–164.

He could afford to act tough from his proximity to Marcher country: Morris, *A Great and Terrible King*, p. 43.

He wasn't just out to assert his independence: Maddicott, *Montfort*, p. 194.

He told Edward how greatly pleased and rejoiced he was: Treharne, *Documents of the Baronial Movement*, p. 177.

He snitched this information back to Henry: Morris, *A Great and Terrible King*, p. 44.

Louis nudged him along by giving him nearly £6,000: Carpenter, *The Meetings of Kings Henry III and Louis IX*, p. 22.

By this you can clearly deduce for yourself: Treharne, *Documents of the Baronial Movement*, p. 189.

Henry had summoned parliament in the meantime: Denholm-Young, *Richard of Cornwall*, pp. 102–103.

He was finally admitted to a gathering at St Paul's: Morris, *A Great and Terrible King*, p. 45.

He decided to put him on trial again: Howell, *Eleanor of Provence*, p. 171. Maddicott, *Montfort*, p. 197–199.

He either denied the charges outright: Bémont, *Montfort*, p. 188. The *Flores Historium* chronicler considered the charges so incredible that he refused to copy them down so as to avoid spreading falsehoods.

The king says that he was forced to return to England: Treharne, *Documents of the Baronial Movement*, pp. 207–209. The inclusion of so many mediocre charges all point to what Henry was really after, destroying Montfort's public reputation. By pulling him down off his high horse, as it were, revealing him to be motivated by greed and self-interest, that would diminish any moral authority he was bringing into the fight. Let the French see who the real Simon de Montfort was, let the rest of the realm know that he was protecting his interests behind the glamour of the Provisions. If anything though, churchmen like Cantilupe and Rigaud became even greater adherents, and the lesser men were willing to rally around anyone committed to upholding the Provisions, whatever his private interests may be. Henry would have to wait centuries for his public relations campaign to succeed, starting with David Hume in the eighteenth century and his estimation that Simon's 'violence, ingratitude, tyranny, rapacity, and treachery' all give a 'bad idea of his moral character' (*The History of England II*, p. 215–216). While even generally laudatory works felt the need to apologise for what they deemed were shortcomings of his character, it was the starker studies of the twentieth century that became almost obsessed with his grievances, and tended to rely on them as the barometer of his true intentions towards reform. In a way, we have the long paper trail of arbitration and complaints to thank for that. The undoubted magnetic hold he enjoyed over a wide swath of people, from kings and bishops down to the humblest peasants and street urchins, is hard to make out in the endless itemisation of numbers and gripes etched into parchment.

Given the geographical remoteness: Maddicott, *Montfort*, pp. 196, 199–200.

He even implicated the king by saying he had begged him: Treharne, *Documents of the Baronial Movement*, p. 205.

It was further postponed in July when the Welsh overran: Powicke, *King Henry III*, p. 417.

Simon would either be victorious in the field or prefer death to defeat: Labarge, *Montfort*, p. 188.

Dying around the time of the muster for Wales: Above, pp.

The king and queen saw his death as an opportunity: Howell, *Eleanor of Provence*, pp. 172–174.

Montfort was there too, with his two older sons: Labarge, *Montfort*, pp. 188–189.

Montfort probably closed his eyes to this watery version: Maddicott, *Montfort*, pp. 201–203; Denholm-Young, *Richard of Cornwall*, p. 106. Richard was the only one of the three, and the only baron period, to use the new escape clause that allowed landlords to decide what redress they would give their tenants.

The first step called for Edward and his entourage: Howell, Eleanor of Provence, p. 175.

In 1259 the pope had sent one of his chaplains to England: Treharne, *The Baronial Plan of Reform*, p. 143.

Undaunted, the pope officially consecrated Aymer: Bémont, *Montfort*, pp. 167–168.

10 Royalist Resurgence, 1261–1262

In what had to be a masterful performance: Treharne, *Documents of the Baronial Movement*, pp. 219–239; *The Baronial Plan of Reform*, pp. 253–255.

Instead he reverted to form and let petulance and immaturity: Labarge, *Montfort*, pp. 194–195.

Still, he had shrewdly avoided attacking the whole concept: Maddicott, *Montfort*, p. 208.

Simon turned to Louis because the families of the two Frenchmen: Maddicott, *Montfort*, pp. 205–206.

Simon and Eleanor had asked the French royal couple: Labarge, *Montfort*, pp. 192–193. Labarge probably had it wrong to think she instigated the suit to 'belabour them with a stick', and right if what she and Simon were hoping for was to increase their holdings in France in case the situation in England became intolerable.

This particular case would drag on for ten years: Wilkinson, *Eleanor de Montfort*, p. 132.

It was a sign of Henry's confidence that he was able to invite him: Treharne, *The Baronial Plan of Reform*, pp. 256–257.

But first, the queen laid down the condition: Howell, *Eleanor of Provence*, p. 180.

He was also there to secure the passage: Powicke, *The Thirteenth Century*, p. 165.

One of his first acts: Treharne, *The Baronial Plan of Reform*, pp. 261–262.

The one conspicuous absentee: Prestwich, *Edward I*, pp. 35–37. One chronicler unconvincingly states that Edward stood ready to support the barons.

He had spent enormous sums of money: Howell, *Eleanor of Provence*, pp. 180–181.

Louis thought that war could be averted: Maddicott, *Montfort*, pp. 209–210.

Henry knew he was poking a hornet's nest: Treharne, *The Baronial Plan of Reform*, pp. 263–265.

Among the barons tossed out: Powicke, *The Thirteenth Century*, p. 165. Powicke calls Hugh Bigod a 'conscientious waverer'.

There, Henry's man was Mathias Bezill: Ray, *Three Alien Royal Stewards*, p. 53.

The division in the country came to a head: Labarge, *Montfort*, pp. 197–198.

The Earl of Gloucester's second bout of treachery: Howell, *Eleanor of Provence*, p. 184.

The summoning of the knightly class to Parliament: Treharne, *The Baronial Plan of Reform*, 1932, p. 271.

He scorned any thought of life under such an unfettered king: Labarge, *Montfort*, p. 198.

Louis, moreover, had instituted his own reforms: Maddicott, *Montfort*, p. 168.

The main issue was the appointment of sheriffs: Denholm-Young, *Richard of Cornwall*, pp. 112–113. Richard had returned from Germany, just in time perhaps to see his ailing wife Sanchia again. Perhaps, because he was doing business in London when she died on 9 November, and then he missed her funeral at Hailes Abbey six days later, although her Savoyard uncles Boniface and Peter were in attendance.

Henry did have one setback: Treharne, *The Baronial Plan of Reform*, pp. 275–278.

At a tilting in 1252, Leybourne killed the same knight: Barker, *The Tournament in England*, p. 48.

As Edward's steward, he repulsed a raid: Treharne, *The Baronial Plan of Reform*, p. 193.

Edward's accounts were audited: Prestwich, *Edward I*, p. 37.

He claimed he was being framed: Treharne, *The Baronial Plan of Reform*, p. 286.

They probably wouldn't have felt any better knowing: Howell, *Eleanor of Provence*, pp. 186–189.

He had been summoned to attend *parlement*: Carpenter, *The Meetings of Kings Henry III and Louis IX*, pp. 25–26.

Henry's feisty mood grew nasty: Bémont, *Montfort*, p. 197.

Simon's replies merely showed that there were two sides: Labarge, *Montfort*, p. 200. Oddly, Simon is the one who usually comes off badly here in the hands of biographers like Bémont and Labarge. They charge him with ingratitude and having little of the same affection for Henry that the king once showed him. This, however, neglects his early years in England, when he stood by Henry in the face of growing opposition from the other barons. Eight years it lasted, and they might have enjoyed plenty more together had it not been for the infamous churching of 1239, when Henry gave in to court intrigue and forced him and Eleanor into exile, seemingly unconcerned if they ever came back. Mention of Henry's manipulation and ingratitude is nowhere to be found, nor is any condemnation of the unseemly way he used the seemingly impartial arbitration of Queen Margaret to settle a personal score instead of making one last effort at reconciling with at least his sister.

How ill can be seen in an arrangement made: Howell, *Eleanor of Provence*, pp. 189–190.

Henry survived, but the epidemic claimed more than sixty members: Treharne, *The Baronial Plan of Reform*, p. 289.

Just days later Simon did in fact show up: Maddicott, *Montfort*, p. 219. Here again is another episode in the life of Simon de Montfort that has historians pondering what his true intentions were. As John Maddicott explains in his biography, Montfort was in possession of the papal bull at the time he initiated the arbitration in January 1262, but did not publish it until ten months later, after all hopes of settling his claims had vanished. It's reasonable in this context to ask if the bull was just one more piece of extortion Simon was hanging over Henry's head to get him to pay up. The Montforts, however, were never impoverished during the whole course of the reform period. On the contrary, they steadily faced disinheritance on account of his defiance. The only other answer then to their *modus operandi* would have to be out of principle. The king owed them, and if they had to start a revolution to get what was coming to them, then so be it. If that were truly the case here, then one of the pivotal moments in English history was the work of a very small soul indeed. This interpretation of the timing of the bull also fails to take into account one of Montfort's primary gifts: savvy. Henry had already swept the barons aside when Simon came into possession of the bull. To have employed it at the turn of 1261–62, while they were at their weakest, would have been a mark of desperation. On this occasion, with the king in France and his Savoyard court decimated by illness, the bull could be used to light a fuse under the English clergy and baronage while they were assembled for Parliament.

Peter of Savoy was identified as the culprit: Labarge, *Montfort*, p. 204.

He suspected that the elder Clare had used his ascendancy: Treharne, *The Baronial Plan of Reform*, pp. 284–286.

Mortimer was trapped and surrendered when invited to: Treharne, *The Baronial Plan of Reform*, p. 291.

The situation became dire enough for Henry to reproach his son: Powicke, *The Thirteenth Century*, p. 171.

The uprising marked a disastrous end: Labarge, *Montfort*, p. 205.

11 The Return of the Alien, 1263

They ended up waiting four days: Hutton, *Simon de Montfort and His Cause*, pp. 111–113. The Savoyard knight was Imbert de Montferrand, plucked from the entourage of Peter d'Aigueblanche to serve as one of Henry's marshals.

The years of strife had turned Montfort's property claims: Maddicott, *Montfort*, p. 222. The grievances and claims by this point seem to have been on Henry's side. His new proposal was concerned with retrieving the demesne manors he felt the Montforts had extorted from him in 1259 but at the same time he was anxious to recover the £10,000 Louis was holding until the settlement was made.

Henry next tried to assure Simon and the other malcontents: Labarge, *Montfort*, p. 206.

He had with him a company of foreign knights: Maddicott, *Montfort*, p. 223.

It was said that, having been frustrated in his attempts: Denholm-Young, *Richard of Cornwall*, p. 119.

Rumours that the king had in fact expired: Carpenter, *The Reign of Henry III*, pp. 253–254·

The previous year John Mansel was in Sussex: Maddicott, *Politics and the People*, p. 11.

This mobilisation of peasants and freeholders under a charismatic leader: Carpenter, *The Reign of Henry III*, p. 219.

Writing years later, the chronicler Thomas Wykes was unimpressed: Wykes, p. 134; Blaauw, *The Barons' War*, p. 99.

Even if the letter was only meant to justify the ensuing violence: Maddicott, *Montfort*, p. 226.

His role in the Sicilian fiasco had made him roundly detested: Labarge, *Montfort*, p. 208.

Henry's response was to appoint captains: Maddicott, *Montfort*, pp. 228–229.

On 24 June a delegation of leading citizens: Carpenter, *The Reign of Henry III*, pp. 267–268.

The queen committed several foreign ladies to Mansel for safekeeping: Howell, *Eleanor of Provence*, p. 195.

Finding the place locked up: *Dunstable*, p. 222; Park, *The Temple Church in London*, p. 9.

There they proceeded to raid the countryside: Prestwich, *Edward I*, p. 39.

As the boat neared the bridge, the crowd began shouting 'whore': Howell, *Eleanor of Provence*, p. 196.

In the meantime, his next move had been to slip away to Bristol: Labarge, *Montfort*, p. 213.

In response, the Montfortians marched on Windsor: Howell, *Eleanor of Provence*, p. 198, 205. Howell calls the prospect of the king having to confront Edward in this fashion 'inhumane humiliation', but Henry had been prepared to teach his son a similar lesson when Edward defied him in 1260.

Richard's son had taken off after John Mansel: Howell, *Eleanor of Provence*, p. 195.

Henry betrayed his brother's vague sympathies: Denholm-Young, *Richard of Cornwall*, p. 122.

The council resurrected to rule the land: Treharne, *The Baronial Plan of Reform*, pp. 314–315.

Simon was virtually the prime minister: Maddicott, *Montfort*, pp. 239–240.

Henry's entire reign had always been marked by anti-alien feelings: Carpenter, *The Reign of Henry III*, pp. 270–272.

The proposed banishment of all aliens: Carpenter, *The Reign of Henry III*, p. 273.

There was no better example than Boniface: Ridgeway, *Henry III and the 'Aliens'*, p. 87.

Although he had to be accepted because he was the archbishop: Maddicott, *Montfort*, p. 254.

Like Montfort, he had been in England for three decades and

had an English wife: Ray, *Three Alien Royal Stewards*, p. 59. Bezill was looking for an heiress to marry, so when Beatrice de Bassingham became a widow, she was told by Henry in words to the effect that she could remarry again to anyone she wanted as long as it was Mathias Bezill.

The Montfortians were in fact keen to keep Henry's sheriffs: Treharne, *The Baronial Plan of Reform*, pp. 315–317.

Together they contrived to have Louis summon Henry to France: Maddicott, *Montfort*, pp. 242–243.

He even admonished him in a letter: Labarge, *Montfort*, p. 215.

He obliged insofar as the conference he set up included many leading French nobles: Treharne, *The Baronial Plan of Reform*, pp. 321–322.

Although Henry returned to England in time: Howell, *Eleanor of Provence*, p. 202.

They had been given a fair shake under Simon: Maddicott, *Montfort*, p. 244.

Since their grievances with Edward and the queen were as raw as ever: Prestwich, *Edward I*, p. 41.

As the bickering intensified, Edward announced that he wanted to be excused: Treharne, *The Baronial Plan of Reform*, pp. 322–323.

Bribed by Edward and pardoned by Henry: Blaauw, *The Barons' War*, p. 183.

He went to Simon and explained: Hutton, *Simon de Montfort and His Cause*, p. 114.

The young man had not only let him down: Prothero, *Montfort*, p. 257.

As Almain indicated, his father Richard of Cornwall had preceded him: Denholm-Young, *Richard of Cornwall*, p. 123.

That drew an angry response from the king: Treharne, *The Baronial Plan of Reform*, pp. 332–333.

A group of oligarchs went one step further by barring the gates: *Dunstable*, p. 226.

And so Henry sank to the diabolical depths of his father: Carpenter, *A Noble in Politics: Roger Mortimer*, p. 200.

If age had been a factor: Powicke, *King Henry III*, pp. 434–435.

When Edward fell short of cash, he sold the wardship: Howell, *Eleanor of Provence*, p. 147.

The bits of propaganda being disseminated at this time: Treharne, *The Baronial Plan of Reform*, pp. 334–335.

The one about aliens alludes to his bringing in mercenaries: Shirley, *Royal Letters*, p. 245.

As for Mansel's lands, Simon committed them to the care of his second son: Maddicott, *Montfort*, p. 256; Labarge, *Montfort*, p. 219.

Together they wrote to the pope asking him to assist Henry: Powicke, *King Henry III*, pp. 453–454.

The two queens meanwhile were busy on another front: Treharne, *The Baronial Plan of Reform*, p. 238.

Just two days after Henry's attempt to ensnare Simon: Maddicott, *Montfort*, pp. 257–258.

12 *Lewes and the Days of May, 1264/I*

He was 'unmindful of his own honour': *Dunstable*, p. 227; *Tewkesbury*, p. 177.

His point-blank dismissal of the constitutional crisis: Treharne, *Documents of the Baronial Movement*, pp. 280–291.

In the letters empowering him to act: Maddicott, *Montfort*, pp. 258–262.

Cantilupe's brief, while overly long and inclined to nitpicking: Treharne, *Documents of the Baronial Movement*, pp. 259, 287–289.

Even the royalist chronicler Wykes felt that Louis had acted: *Wykes*, p. 139.

Henry found that out when he returned to England: Labarge, *Montfort*, p. 227.

They were understandably aggrieved to see him and his Marcher accomplices: Howell, *Eleanor of Provence*, pp. 207–208.

Montfort, still laid up at Kenilworth with a broken leg: *Dunstable*, p. 227.

Edward had raced back ahead of his father: Maddicott, *Montfort*, p. 263.

All these raids and counter-raids finally came to a head: *Dunstable*, p. 228.

Once again Edward asked Walter de Cantilupe to intercede for him: Labarge, *Montfort*, pp. 226–227.

The English bishops were much influenced by Grosseteste: Ambler, *The Montfortian Bishops*, pp. 3–4.

In truth, he didn't think there was much to negotiate: Maddicott, *Montfort*, p. 262.

Henry's response was profound irritation: Blaauw, *The Barons' War*, p. 124.

Meanwhile in London, the bells of St Paul's provided the signal: Blaauw, *The Barons' War*, p. 120.

With his red dragon banner flapping in the wind: Powicke, *King Henry III*, p. 460.

Henry was outraged when he learned that the haul of prisoners: Blaauw, *The Barons' War*, p. 129.

With the Montfortian Midlands now at the king's mercy: Labarge, *Montfort*, p. 230.

The revolution had unleashed an urban frenzy: Cohn, *Popular Protests in Late Medieval English Towns*, p. 277.

It suggests that some warning was in the air: *Chronicles of the Mayors and Sheriffs*, p.66.

The Dunstable annalist says it was Simon himself who instigated the attack: *Dunstable*, p. 230.

None of those claims are mentioned by Wykes: *Wykes*, pp. 141–143.

As for his culpability, the leader of any popular movement: Morris, *A Great and Terrible King*, p. 126. In his biography of Edward, Morris calls Simon a 'well-known fanatic' with a 'virulent hatred' of the Jews, but the only example he offers, the Leicester expulsion of more than three decades earlier, hardly justifies these assertions.

The Montfortians held London and Dover: *Wykes*, p. 140.

Gilbert was at his castle in Tonbridge at the time: *Dunstable*, p. 230.

Rochester stood firm: Carpenter, *The Battles of Lewes and Evesham*, pp. 22–34. Carpenter says the assault was a 'mixture of stratagem and daring which were his hallmark'.

The men left behind by Montfort to maintain the semblance of a siege: Blaauw, *The Barons' War*, p. 133.

Gaston de Bearn himself had volunteered to come to the king's aid: Howell, *Eleanor of Provence*, pp. 208–209.

The path to the sea took a toll: Hamilton, *The Plantagenets: History of a Dynasty*, p. 43. Hamilton suggests Henry learned of such uses in terror from Montfort's time in Gascony, but beyond the general complaints of the Gascons, there is no record of Simon ordering any mutilations or executions, much less on the scale carried out by the royalists in the campaign leading up to Lewes.

There was only one way to find out if a similar fate awaited the Montfortians: Carpenter, *The Battles of Lewes and Evesham*.

Sometime later the bishops arrived in Lewes: Blaauw, *The Barons' War*, p. 159.

This episode too recalls Muret a half-century earlier: Oldenbourg, *Massacre at Montségur*, pp. 165–166.

With his offer rejected, Montfort inched his army closer to Lewes: Blaauw, *The Barons' War*, pp. 160–162.

Since many of the young nobles had yet to be knighted: Prothero, *Life*, pp. 275–276.

A quick council of war decided that Henry would lead the royalist left wing: Carpenter, *The Battles of Lewes and Evesham*.

Edward started things off with a smashing charge: Blaauw, *The Barons' War*, pp. 194–196.

Montfort had kept a fourth division in reserve: Oman, *The Art of War in the Middle Ages*.

By this time Edward and his men had returned to the battlefield: Blaauw, *The Barons' War*, pp. 197–199. Warenne would take flight again thirty-three years later after William Wallace thrashed his forces at Stirling Bridge.

The king and his son had to be coaxed out: Maddicott, *Montfort*, pp. 272–275.

Edward also got something, the release of his Marcher friends: Labarge, *Montfort*, p. 218. Modern historians agree that the only way to achieve a complete victory was by offering compromises. It's a point worth noting here, because many of these same historians find the ability to compromise so much lacking in Simon's character.

Their jeering led to the composition of a song: Wright, *Political Songs*, pp. 69–71.

Another poem, much longer and more serious: Wright, *Political Songs*, pp. 72–121.

Simon's cause may have been doomed: Powicke, *The Thirteenth Century*, p. 188.

13 The Rise of the Montfortian State, 1264/II

It was the Victorian era that ushered in and nurtured the legend: These same Victorians erected a statue at the Houses of Parliament, not to Simon de Montfort but to Richard the Lionheart. The choice reflects the fieriness of his nickname, meant no doubt to glorify the apex of the mighty British Empire, but is wholly absurd given Richard's well-known exploitation of and contempt for the English people.

The feudal system implanted by the Normans: Maddicott, *The Battle of Lewes Conference*.

He was taken on a circuitous route to London: Powicke, *King Henry III*, pp. 472–473.

This was implicit recognition that Parliament was the forum: Maddicott, *The Battle of Lewes Conference*, pp. 3–6.

The major point of issue was the endorsement of a new constitution: Maddicott, *Montfort*, p. 287.

Indeed, Henry's first letter to Louis after Lewes: Powicke, *The Thirteenth Century*, p. 191.

The ball was in France's court: Powicke, *King Henry III*, p. 473.

The queen and the exiles heard of the royalist defeat: Howell, *Eleanor of Provence*, pp. 213–216.

Men gathered along the coast from all around to defend what they saw as a great cause: Maddicott, *Montfort*, p. 291; Howell, *Eleanor of Provence*, p. 217. Howell writes, 'Simon de Montfort's style of charismatic leadership and his acute discernment of popular psychology enabled him to play on such deep instinctive loyalties.'

Mortimer turned over one of his sons as a hostage: Powicke, *King Henry III*, pp. 476–477.

A more immediate threat came in the form of the papal legate: Maddicott, *Montfort*, pp. 292–293.

The legate was astounded by the ingratitude of the English: Powicke, *King Henry III*, pp. 479–480.

He had already written to him to protest: Howell, *Eleanor of Provence*, pp. 213, 219.

It reiterated the rule of the Three and the Nine: Maddicott, *Montfort*, pp. 293–295.

By now the bishops were feeling the strain: Maddicott, *Montfort*, pp. 296–297. The inclusion of Eleanor's dower in the negotiations was a sign, suggests Maddicott, that Montfort was worried about being swept out of power in the final arrangement and so wanted to make sure he received the personal satisfaction he felt was due him.

The intimidation proved too much for the Bishop of Winchester: Howell, *Eleanor of Provence*, p. 220.

When the bishops returned to England, they were searched and dispossessed: *Wykes*, p. 156. The chronicler suggests they had asked to be searched.

On 11 October, the legate got his answer when an English knight approached: Maddicott, *Montfort*, pp. 299–302.

As Clement IV, he never forgave Simon for the failure to reach an agreement: Bémont, *Montfort*, p. 226. When Clement was later approached by Henry of Navarre for permission to marry, he authorised him to choose anyone he wanted with the exception of 'the daughters of Simon de Montfort and his adherents'.

He would write to the new legate appointed in his place: Powicke, *The Thirteenth Century*, p. 199.

Apparently it had been of such size and ferocity: Howell, *Eleanor of Provence*, p. 217.

Stymied on the invasion front, the queen turned to the royalist insurgents: Labarge, *Montfort*, p. 241.

They were ordered to turn their lands over for temporary custody: Prestwich, *Edward I*, p. 47.

It was hardly a fair exchange: Maddicott, *Montfort*, p. 312.

His own voice comes through in some of his letters: Powicke, *King Henry III*, p. 474.

The general policy was to project an image of business as usual: Wild, *A Captive King*, pp. 44–48.

Eleanor de Montfort saw to it that her brothers dined in the regal fashion: Denholm-Young, *Richard of Cornwall*, p. 130.

The poor had been especially affected, losing everything: Hutton, *Simon de Montfort and His Cause*, p. 135.

The exchequer was closed for most of the year: Maddicott, *Montfort*, p. 283.

Local trade was disrupted by bandits lurking about: Gransden, *Historical Writing in England*, p. 468; Lloyd, *The English Wool Trade in the Middle Ages*, pp. 25–26.

Since Montfort's government was striving to restore normal commercial relations: Powicke, *King Henry III*, p. 515.

Re-establishing the Jewish communities in peace was admittedly a more arduous task: Powicke, *King Henry III*, pp. 516–517.

Pardoning the debts owed by their Christian borrowers: Maddicott, *Montfort*, pp. 315–316.

Since holding him in custody was neither practical nor acceptable: Maddicott, *Montfort*, pp. 317–318.

The holiday for the Montfort family at Kenilworth was a magnificent occasion: Labarge, *Montfort*, p. 243.

And just as the tutor is accustomed to lead his pupil: *Wykes*, pp. 153–154.

14 Darkness at Evesham, 1265

The knights from two counties held by the Marchers failed to show: Powicke, *King Henry III*, p. 488.

Gilbert staked a claim to his step-grandfather Richard of Cornwall: Hutton, *Simon de Montfort and His Cause*, p. 143.

This inexplicable action, combined with Giffard falling into enemy hands: Blaauw, *The Barons' War*, pp. 200–201.

The only way to settle their differences like real knights: Bémont, *Montfort*, p. 237.

Gilbert was incensed and let slip that he thought it was: Hutton, *Simon de Montfort and His Cause*, p. 143.

Even Boniface was being wooed to come back and resume his post: Powicke, *King Henry III*, p. 491.

Still, he was as keen as ever to set them up: Prestwich, *Plantagenet England*, pp. 119–120. Prestwich writes he would have had 'no respect from his contemporaries had he not pursued his private concerns'.

Both older sons, Henry and Simon, were made constables: *Chronicles of the Mayors and Sheriffs of London,* pp. 77–78. The royalist writer here says that Simon and his sons condoned the practice of drowning merchant crews and taking one-third of the plunder, but admits the charge is hearsay.

Wykes even disparaged Henry de Montfort as the 'wool merchant': *Wykes*, pp. 158–159; Lloyd, *The English Wool Trade in the Middle Ages*, p. 26.

Montfort also had to reprimand his son Simon on one occasion: Labarge, *Montfort*, p. 248.

His namesake son received even more notoriety: Maddicott, *Montfort*, pp. 325–326.

Henry was furious and wanted him arrested: Maddicott, *Montfort*, p. 322–323. This transfer also bequeathed to Simon the feud over Bristol between the Clares and Edward. Simon was to hold Bristol and five royal castles to ensure Edward's good behaviour after his release.

On 11 March 1265, Westminster Hall was the scene of an elaborate ceremony: Powicke, *King Henry III*, pp. 488–489.

The mayor of London, Thomas Fitz-Thomas, was probably speaking for many: Maddicott, *Montfort*, p. 311.

He and Eleanor had stayed in regular contact in the time they were apart: Wilkinson, *Eleanor de Montfort*, p. 111; Turner, *Manners*, p. xlv.

Gilbert never did show up for the tournament: *Wykes*, pp. 161–162.

For this he brought the whole court with him: Maddicott, *Montfort*, p. 311.

One who came and left was Thomas de Cantilupe: Powicke, *King Henry III*, p. 492.

He was looking for information about the 'rights and liberties': Labarge, *Montfort*, pp. 24–25.

He tried to convince himself that everything would still end peacefully: Powicke, *King Henry III*, pp. 495–496. The lack of any summons for the boroughs seems an indication that his experimental parliament in January would not be repeated, but it's more likely he was merely observing the provision for Parliament to meet and was in no position at that time to work out the particulars.

Incredibly, Montfort continued to make concessions: *Wykes*, pp. 163–164; Prothero, *Life*, pp. 330–331. The story of Edward's escape was naturally embellished to give it a more romantic flavour. He first asked to try all the horses to deliberately wind each of them except the ones he and Thomas used for their escape.

Some veteran defenders of the Provisions like William de Tracy and John de Burgh: Maddicott, *Montfort*, p. 337.

Suddenly finding himself cut off in hostile territory: Powicke, *King Henry III*, pp. 498–501. In return for recognition of his conquests, Llywelyn was obliged to pay £20,000 in instalments plus provide military support against the Marchers. The treaty contains a proviso about a 'successor' for Henry should he happen to be deposed for failing to comply with the ordinance.

Finally gathering up a force, he detoured south to sack Winchester: Powicke, *King Henry III*, p. 708. The younger Simon went to London to recruit and also tend matters involving Isabella de Forz, the richest widow in the land whose marriage rights his father had acquired for him for £350. Isabella was sympathetic to the Montfortian cause, but wanted nothing to do with the young man and fled his advances.

One of the unfortunates was Stephen de Holwell: Maddicott, *Montfort*, pp. 339–340; Blaauw, *The Barons' War*, p. 264.

Around this time, the younger Simon had reached Alcester: *Robert of Gloucester*, p. 561.

The trap had still not sprung when Simon gathered his troops: Laborderie, Maddicott, Carpenter, *The Last Hours of Simon de Montfort*.

None of them had any illusions about what was in store: Maddicott, *Montfort*, p. 341; Blaauw, *The Barons' War*, pp. 274–275.

At his war council, he assembled a hit squad of sergeants-at-arms: Laborderie, Maddicott, Carpenter, *The Last Hours of Simon de Montfort*; Maddicott, *Montfort*, p. 342.

The men who marched out of Evesham to do battle included the king: Prothero, *Life*, p. 343.

Henry was also pierced by a lance, despite crying out through the din of battle: Hutton, *Simon de Montfort and His Cause*, pp. 146–151; *Wykes*, pp. 172–175. Another chronicler attributes the deathblow to a certain knight who later drowned while at the court of Edward's sister Queen Margaret of Scotland. It was said that the crabs were already making a meal of him by the time his body was retrieved.

Edward continued the charge into town: *Robert of Gloucester,* p. 560; Laborderie, Maddicott, Carpenter, *The Last Hours of Simon de Montfort.*

It was up to the monks to find what was left of Simon: Blaauw, *The Barons' War,* p. 287–288. Carpenter, *A Noble in Politics: Roger Mortimer,* p. 201. Carpenter suggests that Maud despised Montfort because his sons had abused her when they took Wigmore at the beginning of the civil war. In that case, she might have preferred the head of Henry de Montfort instead.

The race was on to confiscate the properties of the dead: Bémont, *Montfort,* p. 245.

Noticing that the picture behind the altar in the chapel needed renovating: Powicke, *King Henry III,* p. 503.

He was merely formalising what had been going on: Morris, *A Great and Terrible King,* p. 72.

Richard's business acumen told him it would be a long road: Denholm-Young, *Richard of Cornwall,* p. 135.

He was being held in chains by this time: Howell, *Eleanor of Provence,* p. 229.

After learning of the disaster at Evesham: Wilkinson, *Eleanor de Montfort,* p. 123. *Wykes,* p. 179. Here even the family detractor Wykes sympathises with her grief.

He was anxious to get his hands on whatever remnants there were: Labarge, *Montfort,* pp. 262–263.

Henry met them at Canterbury: Howell, *Eleanor of Provence,* p. 234.

If now she was met by acclaim, as Wykes insists: *Wykes,* pp. 178–179.

The other gift was her share of the fine Henry slapped on London: Howell, *Eleanor of Provence,* p. 197.

All but Fitz-Thomas were soon released: Carpenter, *Thomas Fitz-Thomas.*

A new member of their ranks to make out was an ex-Montfortian: Prestwich, *Edward I,* p. 54.

He even had Northampton declared the official beginning of the armed struggle: Powicke, *King Henry III,* p. 518.

He was escorted to Northampton by Edward: Denholm-Young, *Richard of Cornwall,* p. 137.

For the feast of St Edward that year, Henry wore his crown: Powicke, *King Henry III*, pp. 517–518.

15 Aftermath, 1266–1337

All the sons remained in France for the time being: Wilkinson, *Eleanor de Montfort*, pp. 130–133.

This was no better than the first deal: Powicke, *King Henry III*, pp. 535–536.

In September 1266, he heard a rumour that the Montforts were planning: Wilkinson, *Eleanor de Montfort*, pp. 128–129.

Another four he suspended and ordered to appear in Rome: Powicke, *King Henry III*, p. 529.

He had played his part in the Sicilian business: Powicke, *King Henry III*, p. 526.

He was praised for sparing Gurdon's life: Howell, *Eleanor of Provence*, p. 235.

It would be three years before he was released from prison: Prestwich, *Edward I*, p. 61; Morris, *A Great and Terrible King*, p. 89.

Depending on the degree of complicity: Powicke, *King Henry III*, pp. 536–537.

His other gripes included his mother's dower and having a bully like Mortimer: Morris, *A Great and Terrible King*, p. 79. The two were fighting for control of the lands of Humphrey de Bohun, who had been mortally wounded at Evesham.

The legate was shut up in the Tower while the London commune ransacked: Prestwich, *Edward I*, p. 58. Powicke, *King Henry III*, p. 544.

So eager was Henry to finally put an end to it all: Howell, *Eleanor of Provence*, p. 241.

This Montfortian, another former Savoyard: Howell, *Eleanor of Provence*, p. 236; Powicke, *King Henry III*, p. 698.

The problem was the economy was in no shape to support such a fatuous undertaking: Powicke, *King Henry III*, p. 506.

Henry's imbecilic taxation of the Jews had allowed magnates: Maddicott, *The Crusade Taxation*, pp. 93–115; Morris, *A Great and Terrible King*, pp. 88–92.

He had spent £40,000 on it, but nobody ever begrudged him money for his artistic flourishes: Carpenter, *The Struggle for Mastery*, p. 382; Powicke, *King Henry III*, p. 575.

Instead of leaving everything to the queen as he had promised: Howell, *Eleanor of Provence*, pp. 242–243, 250.

Although quick to rejoin the royalists after Evesham: Morris, *The Bigod Earls of Norfolk*, pp. 94–95.

Hugh's son succeeded the childless Roger as the Earl of Norfolk: Morris, *A Great and Terrible King*, p. 351.

Even with the tax, the crusaders still didn't have enough money: Morris, *A Great and Terrible King*, p. 89.

And as everyone knew, the only reason why Edmund was going on crusade: Prestwich, *Edward I*, pp. 70–71.

Convinced that Edward had it in for him: Powicke, *King Henry III*, p. 579.

The archbishop had come back to England following the restoration: Powicke, *King Henry III*, p. 576.

Burnell's penchant for the ladies and several bastard children: Morris, *A Great and Terrible King*, p. 117.

Apparently he had been talked into striking at the emir there: Morris, *A Great and Terrible King*, pp. 93–94.

The king was miffed that the pope should even listen to Amaury: Labarge, *Montfort*, p. 267.

A popular story has a young girl fetching a pitcher of water: Prothero, *Life*, p. 372.

For the marriage of his son Henry of Almain to Constance de Bearn: Denholm-Young, *Richard of Cornwall*, pp. 139–141, 144.

Henry of Almain never made it to the Holy Land: Prestwich, *Edward I*, p. 72.

They had been at it for two years now: Blaauw, *The Barons' War*, p. 340.

At the Battle of Alba in 1268, Guy fought with legendary fury: Powicke, *Ways of Medieval Life and Thought*, pp. 79–81.

The violence witnessed by the congregation must have been horrible: Blaauw, *The Barons' War*, pp. 341–343.

Guy remained on the run until Edward showed up: Bémont, *Montfort*, pp. 270–271.

Passing through Paris on his way home in 1273: Wilkinson, *Eleanor de Montfort*, pp. 134–135.

Amaury's capacity as the family lawyer in Rome further infuriated him: Blaauw, *The Barons' War*, p. 346.

With his trove of spies, Edward had ships waiting to intercept them: Bémont, *Montfort*, pp. 260–263, 266–267.

He placed their infant daughter Gwenllian in a nunnery: Maddicott, *Montfort*, p. 371.

Richard had no sooner absorbed the blow of his son's murder: Denholm-Young, *Richard of Cornwall*, p. 76. It was dedicated in 1252 by Walter de Cantilupe and thirteen other bishops.

He joined the bones of his son Henry before the high altar: Denholm-Young, *Richard of Cornwall*, p. 174.

Almain's heart was preserved in an urn at Westminster: Westerhof, *Death and the Noble Body in Medieval England*, p. 58.

She had continued to pursue the legal cases: Wilkinson, *Eleanor de Montfort*, p. 132.

In 1286, eleven years after her death: Labarge, *Montfort*, p. 271; Wilkinson, *Eleanor de Montfort*, p. 1.

The courtyard around him was packed with demonstrations of support: Powicke, *King Henry III*, p. 588.

The cult of worship that sprang up in Evesham almost immediately: Valente, *Simon the Montfort and the utility of sanctity in thirteenth-century England*.

She had dedicated her life to seeing Edward on the throne: Howell, *Eleanor of Provence*, pp. 306–311.

Immediately after the Battle of Evesham, a royalist party arrived in a village called Peatling Magna: Powicke, *King Henry III*, p. 509–510.

Even in his own day, he was judged: The opinions of Adam Marsh and Henry III, respectively.

List of Illustrations

26. Map by Thomas Bohm, User design
27. British Library Royal 20 A II f. 9
28. Author's collection
29. Author's collection
30. British Library Royal 20 C VII f. 1v
31. Author's collection
32. British Library Royal 10 E VI f. 49v
33. Royal British Library 14 B VI Membrane 6
34. Wandering Soles
35. Author's collection
36. Better than Bacon @ Flickr
37. Eleanor Parker

Index